T0279602

AGREEING TO DISAGREE

OTHER BOOKS IN THE SERIES:

Not a Suicide Pact
The Constitution in a Time of
National Emergency
Richard A. Posner

Out of Range
Why the Constitution Can't End the
Battle over Guns
Mark V. Tushnet

Unfinished Business
Racial Equality in American History
Michael J. Klarman

Supreme Neglect
How to Revive Constitutional Protection
for Private Property
Richard A. Epstein

Is There a Right to Remain Silent?
Coercive Interrogation and the Fifth
Amendment After 9/11
Alan M. Dershowitz

The Invisible Constitution
Laurence H. Tribe

Uninhibited, Robust, and Wide-Open
A Free Press for a New Century
Lee C. Bollinger

From Disgust to Humanity
Sexual Orientation and
Constitutional Law
Martha C. Nussbaum

The Living Constitution
David A. Strauss

Keeping Faith with the Constitution
Goodwin Liu, Pamela S. Karlan,
Christopher H. Schroeder

Cosmic Constitutional Theory
Why Americans Are Losing Their
Inalienable Right to Self-Governance
J. Harvie Wilkinson III

More Essential Than Ever
The Fourth Amendment in the Twenty First
Century
Stephen J. Schulhofer

On Constitutional Disobedience
Louis Michael Seidman

The Twilight of Human Rights Law
Eric A. Posner

Constitutional Personae
Heroes, Soldiers, Minimalists, and Mutes
Cass R. Sunstein

The Future of Foreign Intelligence
Privacy and Surveillance in a Digital Age
Laura K. Donohue

HATE
Why We Should Resist it With Free Speech,
Not Censorship
Nadine Strossen

Democracy and Equality
The Enduring Constitutional Vision of the
Warren Court
Geoffrey R. Stone and David A. Strauss

Beyond Belief, Beyond Conscience
The Radical Significance of the Free
Exercise of Religion
Jack N. Rakove

The Religion Clauses
The Case for Separating Church and State
Erwin Chemerinsky and
Howard Gillman

Liars
Falsehoods and Free Speech in an Age of
Deception
Cass R. Sunstein

Saving the News
Why the Constitution Calls for Government
Action to Preserve Freedom of Speech
Martha Minow

The Collapse of Constitutional Remedies
Aziz Z. Huq

Agreeing to Disagree: How the
Establishment Clause Protects Religious
Diversity and Freedom of Conscience
Nathan S. Chapman and
Michael W. McConnell

David A. Strauss
GERALD RATNER DISTINGUISHED SERVICE
PROFESSOR OF LAW
UNIVERSITY OF CHICAGO LAW SCHOOL

Kathleen M. Sullivan
STANLEY MORRISON PROFESSOR OF LAW
STANFORD LAW SCHOOL

Cass R. Sunstein
ROBERT WALMSLEY UNIVERSITY
PROFESSOR
HARVARD LAW SCHOOL

Laurence H. Tribe
CARL M. LOEB UNIVERSITY
PROFESSOR OF LAW
HARVARD LAW SCHOOL

Mark V. Tushnet
WILLIAM NELSON CROMWELL
PROFESSOR OF LAW
HARVARD LAW SCHOOL

J. Harvie Wilkinson III
JUDGE
U.S. COURT OF APPEALS FOR THE
FOURTH CIRCUIT

Kenji Yoshino
CHIEF JUSTICE EARL WARREN PROFESSOR
OF CONSTITUTIONAL LAW
NEW YORK UNIVERSITY SCHOOL
OF LAW

GEOFFREY STONE AND OXFORD UNIVERSITY PRESS GRATEFULLY ACKNOWLEDGE THE INTEREST
AND SUPPORT OF THE FOLLOWING ORGANIZATIONS IN THE INALIENABLE RIGHTS SERIES:
THE ALA; THE CHICAGO HUMANITIES FESTIVAL; THE AMERICAN BAR ASSOCIATION;
THE NATIONAL CONSTITUTION CENTER; THE NATIONAL ARCHIVES

AGREEING TO DISAGREE

*How the Establishment Clause
Protects Religious Diversity and
Freedom of Conscience*

Nathan S. Chapman and Michael W. McConnell

OXFORD
UNIVERSITY PRESS

OXFORD
UNIVERSITY PRESS

Oxford University Press is a department of the University of Oxford. It furthers
the University's objective of excellence in research, scholarship, and education
by publishing worldwide. Oxford is a registered trade mark of Oxford University
Press in the UK and certain other countries.

Published in the United States of America by Oxford University Press
198 Madison Avenue, New York, NY 10016, United States of America.

CIP data is on file at the Library of Congress

ISBN 978–0–19–530466–4

DOI: 10.1093/oso/9780195304664.001.0001

Printed by Sheridan Books, Inc., United States of America

"We sponsor an attitude on the part of government that shows no partiality to any one group and that lets each flourish according to the zeal of its adherents and the appeal of its dogma."

Zorach v. Clauson, 343 U.S. 306, 313 (1952)

"The church must be reminded that it is not the master or the servant of the state, but rather the conscience of the state. It must be the guide and the critic of the state, and never its tool."

Martin Luther King Jr.
A Knock at Midnight, in STRENGTH TO LOVE 57 (1964)

Contents

. . .

Introduction   1

PART I: HISTORY

1. Establishment at the Founding   9
2. Framing the First Amendment   33
3. Disestablishment in the States   42
4. Application of the Establishment Clause to the States   75

PART II: MODERN CONTROVERSIES

5. The Rise and Fall of the *Lemon* Test   87
6. Accommodation of Religious Exercise   94
7. No-Aid Separation, Neutrality, and Religious Schools   117
8. Prayer, Bible Reading, and Coercion   144
9. Conflicts Over Symbols   157
10. Church Autonomy   173
11. Conclusion: Neutrality Beyond the
    Establishment Clause   186

Notes   193
Index   215

Introduction

THE ESTABLISHMENT CLAUSE of the First Amendment may be the most contentious and misunderstood provision of the entire Constitution. It reads: "Congress shall make no law respecting an establishment of religion." It lies at the heart of America's culture wars. But what, exactly, *is* an "establishment of religion"? And what is a law "respecting" it?

When those words were added to the Constitution, every American lawyer and probably every citizen knew what they meant. As British subjects, Americans had long lived under the "church by law established," with some colonists embracing it and others dissenting from it. Two of the thirteen original colonies never had establishments of religion, two had intermittent and largely notional establishments, and several others scuttled their establishments at Independence. When the First Amendment was adopted in 1791, however, roughly half the states still maintained some form of establishment of religion. There were lively debates in the early decades in almost every state over whether to retain, dismantle, or resurrect a religious establishment. Whether for or against establishments, everyone knew what they were.

The national government never had a religious establishment—the First Amendment saw to that—and the last state establishment of religion, in Massachusetts, was formally dismantled in 1833. The term "establishment of religion" thus passed from usage; today it has no reference outside of constitutional law. Some of the legal practices that constituted an establishment have contemporary analogs, but some of them do not—and in any case the legal attributes of a "church by law established" have been lost to history.

To make matters worse, the Supreme Court has offered conflicting, changing, and ambiguous interpretations. After near–radio silence on the provision for more than a century, the Court decided in *Everson v. Board of Education* (1947) that the Clause applies against the states and turned to history to interpret its meaning. The justices zeroed in on a narrow range of evidence, interpreting the Clause to erect what Thomas Jefferson called "a wall of separation between church and state." So confused were the Court's cases that the distinguished legal historian Leonard Levy commented that "the Supreme Court would not recognize an establishment of religion if it took life and bit the Justices." In *Lemon v. Kurtzman* (1971), the Court triumphally announced a "test" to implement this separationist vision of the Clause. The aptly named "*Lemon* test" was unfortunately vague, misleading, and ungrounded in history or principle. Since then, the Court has gradually abandoned the *Lemon* test, but it has not substituted a new one, leaving Establishment Clause cases to be governed by a collection of context-specific rules—many of them the virtual opposite of the prior understandings under *Lemon*. No other constitutional provision has experienced such interpretive tergiversation.[1]

But that is not all. The First Amendment contains *two* provisions about religion, yoked together in a single grammatical unit: "Congress shall make no law respecting an establishment of religion, or prohibiting the free exercise thereof." This is the only part of the Constitution that comprises two rules with two different verbs ("respecting" and "prohibiting") and two different objects ("establishment" and "free exercise"), but a single topic ("religion"). What is the relation between these two provisions?

The simplest and most sensible possibility is that they are mutually reinforcing. The Free Exercise Clause protects the right to practice religion according to conscience and conviction, and the Establishment Clause prevents the government from coercing or using governmental power to induce religious beliefs and practice. Thus, no one may be punished, penalized, or prevented from engaging in religious practice, and no one "shall be compelled to frequent or support any religious worship, place or ministry whatsoever" (in the words of Thomas Jefferson's Bill for Establishing Religious Freedom, adopted in Virginia in 1786).[2] Under this view, which we defend in this book, the Religion Clauses work together to prohibit the government from using sticks *or* carrots to induce uniformity of religious belief and practice.

But many think that free exercise and nonestablishment point in opposite directions; indeed, the modern Supreme Court has repeatedly said that the two provisions are "in tension."[3] The tension arises from the widespread idea that the point of the Establishment Clause is to protect a secular public sphere from the dangerously divisive and irrational impulses of religion. The purpose of the Establishment Clause, in this view, is to reduce the influence of religion in the public sphere and consign it to the private realm of individual, family, and church. (Throughout this book, we abide by the legal convention of using the term "church" to include the organizational forms of all religious faiths—synagogues, mosques, temples, kiva societies, etc.)

Many of the most difficult and recurring controversies over the Religion Clauses hinge on which of these understandings to follow. May the government exempt religious believers from compliance with legal obligations applicable to others, such as military conscription or drug laws? May the government include religious schools or other service providers in spending programs open to their nonreligious counterparts? May religious speakers offer prayers at public events where nonreligious speakers would be free to choose their messages? In all these cases, the first view would lead to an affirmative answer and the second to a negative. Taken to its logical extreme, the second view even suggests that the two Religion Clauses contradict each other. If the government is forbidden to give benefits or support to religion, as the Court's Establishment Clause cases sometimes say, is the Free Exercise Clause itself unconstitutional? Special constitutional protection for the exercise of religion (and not other belief systems) sounds like a benefit and a preference. And if the government is forbidden to deny benefits to an entity solely on the basis of its religious status, as the Court's Free Exercise cases sometimes say, doesn't that render many of the Court's Establishment Clause cases, such as those forbidding aid to religious schools, unconstitutional?

A third possible relation between the two Religion Clauses is that they address different types of questions. The Free Exercise Clause is a classic protection for a specific liberty, not unlike freedom of speech or property. The government may not "prohibit" the exercise of religion, meaning that it may not penalize or prevent it. But the Establishment Clause is a structural provision, akin to the enumeration of powers, declaring that Congress (meaning the federal government) has no authority over ("respecting") the specific subject area of religious establishments. It is difficult to understand, under this theory, how the Establishment Clause could logically have been applied to the states as one of the individual rights provisions "incorporated" under the Fourteenth Amendment.

Even more than other provisions of the Constitution, then, the correct interpretation of the Establishment Clause is a matter of deep uncertainty and continuing controversy. And these uncertainties and controversies *matter*. The proper interpretation of the Establishment Clause tells us much about the character of the American republic and our political culture. Does, or should, religion have a privileged place in that culture? Or does the First Amendment, properly understood, require exclusion of religion from the public sphere? In other words: Does secularism have a privileged place? Or is the Constitution agnostic—"neutral"—on the question, leaving the degree of religious influence on the public order to be decided by the people themselves through decentralized and deregulated institutions?

This book will address these questions in two stages. We will first explore the history of establishment and disestablishment in the United States. Virtually all of the justices of the Supreme Court—even those not ordinarily regarded as "originalists"—have maintained that in deciphering the Religion Clauses, "the line we must draw between the permissible and the impermissible is one which accords with history and faithfully reflects the understanding of the Founding Fathers" (quoting Justice William J. Brennan Jr.).[4] Starting with the original meaning of a constitutional provision always makes good sense, but especially when that provision refers to legal arrangements that have gone the way of the dodo. Imagine applying Congress's power to "grant letters of Marque and Reprisal" without understanding the law of maritime warfare circa 1789. The trouble is that the history of religious establishment relied on by the Court has been radically incomplete and often misleading.[5] For a more complete understanding, we must examine the scope of the British, colonial, and early state establishments; attend to the debates over the Establishment Clause in the First Congress; and trace the process of disestablishment in the states. We then turn to the most significant areas of modern disputation: education (both religious exercises in public schools and the legal status of private religious schools), public funding of religiously related public services, free exercise accommodations (including exceptions from general laws to respect religious conscience), regulation of the internal decisions of religious organizations, and public religious symbols. In each case, we explore how the historic principles of disestablishment should apply to the circumstances of our day. The fundamental point that emerges is that the Establishment Clause is not a thumb on the scale for secularism in public matters (let alone the opposite) but a constitutional commitment for Americans to agree to disagree about matters of religion—to refrain from using the power of government to coerce or induce uniformity of belief, whether that belief is Christian or non-Christian, secular or religious. All faiths are free to flourish, or not, according to the zeal of their adherents and the appeal of their dogma—not according to the will of the majority, the power of elites, or the authority of the state.

Unlike most treatments of the issue, this book will focus on the establishment of religion as *law*. We will not attempt to contribute to the vast literature on Locke, Hobbes, Spinoza, Rousseau, Bayle, Mill, and other philosophers and their views on the relation of religion to government. Instead, we will look at changes in enacted laws and constitutions, and at the arguments for and against those changes in legislative debates, courts, petitions, newspaper essays, and speeches. These debates may not be as profound as the philosophers, but they tell us what disestablishment was really about.

PART I

. . .

History

CHAPTER I

. . .

Establishment at the Founding

MANY OF THE words of the United States Constitution sound like ordinary English of the twenty-first century. We are familiar with the words "speech," "property," "law," and "search." "Establishment of religion" is different. It has been so long—190 years—since any state in the Union has had an establishment of religion that we have almost forgotten what one is. When the words "Congress shall make no law respecting an establishment of religion" were added to the Constitution, though, virtually every American knew from experience what those words meant. They would continue to debate some of the details for generations, but the basic contours of an establishment of religion were well understood. The Church of England was established by law in the mother country, nine of the thirteen colonies had established churches on the eve of the Revolution, and about half of the states continued to have some form of official religious establishment when the First Amendment was adopted. The pros and cons of religious establishment were hotly debated from Georgia to Maine.[1]

Unsurprisingly, when the Supreme Court in the 1940s began to decide cases about an establishment of religion, it turned to founding-era history. As Justice William Brennan, ordinarily skeptical of interpretation based on history, suggested two decades later, the question is what are "those substantive evils the fear of which called forth the Establishment Clause of the First Amendment?"[2] Unfortunately, though, the Court made no serious attempt to canvass the history of establishment—whether in Britain, the American colonies, or the early American states—or to distinguish between the First Amendment and various conflicts over establishment at the state level. Instead, the justices focused on one event in one state: the rejection of Patrick Henry's Assessment Bill in Virginia in 1785 in favor of Thomas Jefferson's alternative Bill for the Establishment of Religious Freedom. Without surveying the legal institutions of establishment, the arguments advanced for them, or the broader history of disestablishment, the Court asserted that "the provisions of the First Amendment . . . had the same objective and were intended to provide the same protection against governmental intrusion on religious liberty as the Virginia statute."[3]

Based on this truncated history, the Court declared the animating principle of the Establishment Clause to be the "separation of church and state," an overly simplistic notion that proved far more judicially pliable, and far more hostile to religion, than anyone in the founding generation could have imagined. The true evil of religious establishment contemplated at the adoption of the First Amendment was the use of government power to foster or compel uniformity of religious thought and practice.

Though the details differed by jurisdiction, establishments all relied on an array of legal devices designed to bring about religious uniformity and discourage religious dissent. These included laws restricting public office to members of certain religious groups; laws requiring church membership, attendance, or financial support; and prohibitions on dissenting forms of worship. It is no coincidence that the statutory centerpiece of the British establishment was entitled the "Uniformity Act." At the founding, a majority of the states had these sorts of laws and Americans understood them to be the essence of religious establishment.

We must also examine why so many Americans *defended* religious establishments. In the Supreme Court's version of the story, a "large proportion of the early settlers of this country came here from Europe to escape the bondage of laws that compelled them to support and attend government favored churches." The transplantation of established churches to these shores "became so commonplace as to shock the freedom-loving colonials into a feeling of abhorrence," leading directly to the First Amendment. One would never know from the justices' careless description of history that no small number of the "freedom-loving colonials" considered official sanction for religion natural and essential, that the movement toward disestablishment was hotly contested by many patriotic and republican leaders, and that there were serious arguments—not mere "feelings of abhorrence"—on both sides of the issue. The justices never analyzed any of the books, essays, sermons, speeches, or judicial opinions that set forth the philosophical and political arguments *in favor* of an establishment of religion, and relied on only one of the hundreds of arguments made *against* establishment.[4]

A broader base of understanding is essential for recognizing what "establishment of religion" was and why Americans ultimately abandoned it.

ESTABLISHMENTS IN THE COLONIAL PERIOD

Before Independence, the Church of England—now known in the United States as the Episcopal or Anglican Church—was the "church by law established" in the mother country, in the five southern colonies (Maryland through Georgia), and in four counties of metropolitan New York. This Anglican establishment was top-down, hierarchical, and governed by the Crown, Parliament, royal governors, and local landowners. New England, outside of Rhode Island, had a different kind of establishment. The settlers of Massachusetts, Connecticut, New Hampshire, and Vermont were mostly Puritans (later called Congregationalists), members of a branch of Reformed Protestantism based on the teachings of John Calvin. The establishment of religion consisted of a complex web of statutes and executive pronouncements, which varied in their details even among the Anglican establishments and even more so between those establishments and the Puritan establishments of New England. Despite their differences, though, there were many common elements. Americans understood those elements to be an "establishment of religion."

Establishment in England. The established Church of England had deep roots. When Henry VIII broke from Rome in 1533, his intent was simply to replace the Pope with the monarch as head of the English church, largely preserving Catholic religious practice. The Pope was stripped of authority to name bishops in England, to control its liturgy or articles of faith, and to receive revenue from religious taxes. All these powers devolved on the King. The 1534 Act of Supremacy made the king the supreme head of the Church of England and gave him "authority to reform and redress all errors, heresies, and abuses."[5] During the reign of Henry's son Edward VI, Parliament assumed a larger role, and the Church of England shifted toward Protestantism.

In subsequent decades, convocations of churchmen composed and Parliament enacted the Thirty-nine Articles of Faith, which set forth the doctrinal tenets of the church, and the Book of Common Prayer, which determined the liturgy for religious worship (later prescribing use of the Authorized or "King James" translation of the Bible). The Acts of Uniformity of 1549, 1559, and 1662 required all ministers to conform to these requirements, making the Church of England the sole institution for lawful public worship. Their purpose, as stated in the preamble to the 1662 version, was to effect a "universal agreement in the public worship of Almighty God."[6] When an early draft of the First Amendment forbade Congress from enacting "articles of faith or modes of worship," the framers had the Thirty-nine Articles and Acts of Uniformity in mind.

The English establishment was largely unconcerned with people's internal consciences and beliefs. Few were prosecuted for heresy after Elizabeth acceded to the throne; there was no inquisition to ferret out nonconforming opinions. Dissenters from the Church of England (mostly Catholics, radical Protestants, and Quakers) could usually employ their priests or ministers and take their sacraments in private "chapels" so long as these were not open to the general public. This is likely one reason the framers of the First Amendment chose to protect the "free exercise" of religion rather than mere freedom of conscience: The establishmentarian tradition from which they broke prohibited religious exercise outside of the state church and left private conscience largely uncoerced.

The Toleration Act of 1688 suspended the penalties for violation of the Uniformity Acts for trinitarian Protestants (Presbyterians, Independents [the English term for Congregationalists], Lutherans, and Baptists). It was not until the mid-nineteenth century that Catholics, Jews, Unitarians, and others gained the freedom of public worship.

Two other sets of statutes, the Test and Corporation Acts, limited civil, military, ecclesiastical, and academic offices to participating members of the church. This had two—maybe three—effects. First, it ensured that the government, the military, the courts, and the universities would be run by people who shared the governing assumptions of the realm—most particularly, the supremacy of the king in England and the lack of authority of the Pope in Rome. This was an obstacle to the efforts of James II, a Catholic, to protect his position by naming Catholics to high positions in the army and the administration, and to any effort by radical Protestants to bring about a reprise of the Commonwealth. Second, the Test and Corporation Acts provided an incentive for ambitious members of the ruling class to conform to the established church, at least outwardly, and bring up their children accordingly. This was probably a more effective instrument of conformity than outright coercion. But the primary effect of the Acts was likely to foster hypocrisy. The Test Act made no attempt to determine a person's genuine beliefs. It simply required taking communion in the Church of England within the preceding six months and an oath abjuring belief in transubstantiation. This excluded dissenters of integrity from holding office; it did nothing to exclude those willing to pretend. When Jefferson complained that established religion tended to "beget habits of hypocrisy," this is what he was talking about.[7]

There were also specific "Penal Acts" suppressing the practice of faiths whose tenets were thought to be inimical to the regime. The Act Against Papists and the Conventicle Act prohibited unlicensed religious meetings; various other statutes punished dissenters for engaging in prohibited religious worship. At first, Catholics, Puritans, and Quakers were the particular targets, because they appeared to threaten the political legitimacy of the state. Presbyterians took on this unwelcome role from the 1660s to the 1680s, especially in Scotland. The flavor of these laws is indicated by their titles: "An Act to prevent and avoid dangers which may grow by Popish Recusants," or "An act to retain the queen's subjects in obedience."[8]

The United States Constitution explicitly forbade all of these types of laws. Whatever else it might mean, the Establishment

Clause bans any American version of the Act of Supremacy or the Uniformity Acts; the Test Clause of Article VI bans the equivalent of the Test and Corporation Acts; and the Free Exercise Clause prevents any American version of the Penal Acts.

Establishment in the American Colonies. Established religion came to America's shores with the earliest colonists. It assumed two principal forms: an exclusive Anglican establishment in the southern states and a localized Puritan establishment in the New England states other than Rhode Island. Although equally coercive, the Anglican and Puritan establishments were profoundly different in spirit: The New England establishments were based on the intense religious convictions of Protestant dissenters, often in opposition to English authorities, whereas the Anglican establishments enjoyed the support of the Crown and were designed in part to foster loyalty and submission to royal governance. These two forms persisted throughout the colonial period, and the New England form endured several generations after adoption of the First Amendment. Despite their differences, the two types of establishment had many legal elements in common.

In England, the Church of England was governed by bishops beholden to the Crown for their position. The Bishop of London's jurisdiction extended to the American colonies. Since there were no bishops on the ground in America, day-to-day authority over local Anglican churches was effectively exercised by a committee of laypersons, called the vestry, elected by freeholders of the parish to control the local purse strings. The vestry was almost always composed of leading landowners. Thus, church structure was effectively oligarchic—in contrast to the monarchical character of the Church in England and the more republican character of New England churches. When the Independence movement gained momentum after 1774, patriot vestries frequently came into conflict with Tory clergymen, who had taken oaths of allegiance to the king. Such ministers were often ousted, sometimes were violently assaulted, and frequently fled.[9]

The most elaborate set of laws comprising an establishment of religion in colonial America was Virginia's. Before Independence, Thomas Jefferson counted at least twenty-three applicable English statutes (dating to the reign of Edward VI) and seventeen Virginia statutes (dating to 1661).[10] Virginia's Diocesan Canons of 1661 are especially informative; they catalog the legal provisions necessary to sustain an establishment.[11] The Canons:

- required the people of the parish to erect churches at public expense and to set aside profit-making land for the financial support of the ministry (called "glebe lands");
- set forth rules for the selection, powers, and duties of the vestries;
- prescribed that ministers would be inducted only if they demonstrated ordination by a bishop, approval by the colonial governor, and selection by the local vestry;
- set the minister's salary and gave him a cause of action if the parish failed to pay;
- prescribed liturgy, sacraments, and catechism to be performed only in accordance with the Church of England;
- mandated observance of the sabbath and various holy days (including a day of fasting in honor of martyred King Charles I), as well as weekly sermons and biannual celebration of the Lord's Supper;
- authorized vestrymen to bring misdemeanor charges against persons caught swearing, sabbath breaking, skipping church, slandering, "backbiting," or committing the "foule and abominable sins of drunkennesse fornication and adultery";
- required local churches to maintain official registers of births, burials, and marriages;

- limited lawful marriage to ceremonies performed by ministers of the Church of England; and
- set aside public land for a college and free school "for the advance of learning, education of youth, supply of the ministry, and promotion of piety."

Subsequent legislation addressed such matters as the effect of baptism on slave status (none); the punishment of "such ministers as shall become notoriously scandalous by drunkingnesse, swearing, fornication or other haynous and crying sins"; and prohibition of unlawful disturbances of divine service. Of particular note were laws fining "scismaticall persons" who refused to have their children baptized, prohibiting the immigration of Quakers, and outlawing Quaker religious assemblies. A similar model of establishment prevailed throughout the South, though in the Carolinas and Georgia there was much greater toleration of dissenters.

The Puritan establishment in New England had a different structure, decentralized and more democratic. Based on their reading of the New Testament Book of Acts, most New England Puritans believed that church authority is vested in the people of the local congregation, who elect lay elders to govern the church and hire ministers. There are no bishops or the equivalent; indeed, there are no higher church authorities at all. This control by the local congregation gives the denomination its modern name, Congregationalism. As in the South, the elected elders were generally the leading men of the community, but in less oligarchic New England, the church had a more republican hue. Consider our first two Vice Presidents. John Adams went home to Braintree during the recess of the Senate and plowed his own farm. Thomas Jefferson returned to elegant Monticello, served by hundreds of enslaved persons. The vestries of Virginia and elder boards of Massachusetts reflected a similar sociocultural difference.

Because the New England Puritans were at religious odds with the authorities in London, who had power to veto acts of the colonial legislatures, these colonies could not easily establish their religion by law. In theory, the system would allow a town majority to choose a minister of non-Puritan persuasion, but this rarely happened. Colonial authorities sought to preserve Puritan orthodoxy first by giving power to choose ministers to members of the congregation rather than the entire town, subject to disapproval by the latter, and later by submitting disputes to the clergy of neighboring churches, which could almost always be counted on to be orthodox Reformed Protestants. Eventually, London forced New England to tolerate a wider range of religious choices—especially Anglicans—and to allow non-Puritans to govern churches when they composed a majority in the town.

Elements of an Establishment. An establishment is the promotion and inculcation of a common set of beliefs through governmental authority. An establishment may be narrow (focused on a particular set of beliefs) or broad (encompassing a range of opinion). It may be more or less coercive, and it may be tolerant or intolerant of other views. During the period between initial settlement and ultimate disestablishment, American religious establishments moved from being narrow, coercive, and intolerant to being broad, relatively noncoercive, and tolerant. Although the laws constituting the establishment were ad hoc and unsystematic, they can be summarized in six categories: (1) control over doctrine, governance, and personnel of the church; (2) compulsory church attendance; (3) financial support; (4) prohibitions on worship in dissenting churches; (5) use of church institutions for public functions; and (6) restriction of political participation to members of the established church. By the mid-nineteenth century, many Americans also perceived that laws prohibiting blasphemy and enforcing sabbath observance had been components of a religious establishment.

(1) Governmental Control. Modern constitutional doctrine stresses the "advancement of religion" as the key element of establishment, but in the Anglican establishments of America, the central feature was control rather than advancement. The two principal means of control were laws governing doctrine and the power to appoint and discipline clergy. Parliament's Uniformity Acts did not apply of their own force in the colonies, so power over liturgy and doctrine fell to the colonial legislatures. The Virginia Assembly enacted a local version of the Uniformity Acts, requiring erection of churches and regular attendance at worship services, and decreeing "a uniformity in our church as neere as may be to the canons in England."[12]

Anglican ministers in the colonies had to be ordained, in person, by an English bishop; take an oath of allegiance to the Crown; and swear to conform to the established liturgy. In Virginia and some other southern colonies, they also had to be approved by the governor and were invested for one-year terms by the local vestry, which was typically dominated by the local gentry. This structure was calculated to produce a ministry subservient to the Crown and the local oligarchy. Because ministers in the Anglican colonies were often poorly paid and regarded as low-status, priests were often poorly educated and sometimes in disgrace.[13] In the North, where the Church of England was not established (except in metropolitan New York), clergy were often supported by a missionary society called the Society for the Propagation of the Gospel in Foreign Parts. They were thus often better paid and largely independent of their parishioners, with the result that many Anglican ministers in the North were leading intellectual voices for the Tory side in the debates over Independence.

Unlike the southern Anglican churchmen, the Puritan clergy of New England were typically educated at Harvard or Yale, were esteemed members of the community, and were chosen by vote of the congregation rather than either a hierarchy or an oligarchy. In efforts to combat populist itinerant preachers during the Great Awakening of the mid-eighteenth century, New England legislatures imposed educational qualifications for serving as a minister and limited preaching to "settled" ministers called by a congregation. One of the earliest arguments for the separation of church and state, Elisha Williams's brilliant sermon, *On the Essential Rights and Liberties of Protestants*, criticized these laws on the ground that the government had no right to decide who could preach. Significantly, this attack on the establishment came from within the church as a protest against government control of religion, rather than from outsiders protesting government support.[14]

Even after churches lost any public financial support in Virginia, Maryland, and South Carolina, the state legislatures continued to exercise authority over them, including legislation addressing articles of faith. In Massachusetts, the leader of the Baptist opposition to establishment charged that the authorities were "assuming a power to govern religion instead of being governed by it."[15]

(2) Compulsory Attendance. English law subjected those who "absent[ed] themselves from the divine worship in the established church" to a fine of one shilling for a single absence and twenty pounds for a month's absence.[16] Anglican and Puritan colonies enacted similar laws. Until 1833, the Massachusetts Constitution provided:

> [The] people of this commonwealth have also a right to, and do, invest their legislature with authority to enjoin upon all the subjects an attendance upon the instructions of the public teachers [of piety, religion, and morality], at stated times and seasons, if there be any on whose instructions they can conscientiously and conveniently attend.[17]

These laws were not just symbolic. In a study of grand jury presentments in Virginia between 1720 and 1750, missing church was the most commonly indicted offense in five of the eleven counties surveyed; it was the second or third most common offense in six others.[18] Defenders of these laws did not consider them to be a violation of freedom of conscience, because they did not apply to persons who could not "conscientiously attend" services. They were directed against laziness or disinterest, not (in theory) sincere dissent. In New England, however, Baptists were regularly prosecuted not only for failure to baptize their children but also for failing to attend worship at Congregationalist churches; many of them refused to file certificates of attendance at their own churches, thinking this was no business of the state.[19]

(3) Public Financial Support. Churches cost money: for paying the minister, maintaining the building, and supporting the mission. In England, the principal source of revenue for the church was income from land holdings, most of them dating to before the Reformation. The church also derived income from mandatory tithes and, in very small amounts, from general tax revenue.

In the colonies, the established churches relied on essentially the same sources of revenue—land grants and compulsory tithes. In America, however, tithes were understood as taxes; the government could reduce or eliminate them without affecting the minister's property rights. After the early settlement period, colonial governments generally did not appropriate public money for churches, though they did for church-related educational or charitable institutions such as colleges or orphanages.

Land grants were among the most important privileges of the colonial established churches. In New England, governments granted public lands to churches for meeting houses, parsonages, day schools, and orphanages. In the Anglican colonies, counties were required to construct a house of worship and a parsonage. In New York, both Trinity Church (Anglican) and the Dutch Reformed Church received extensive land grants accompanying their charters. Throughout the South, lands—including profit-making glebe lands—were set aside for churches and the support of ministers.

All of the American colonies with established churches also compelled taxpayers to pay tithes to support churches and ministers. New England governments typically allowed each town to negotiate a salary with the minister and to impose the taxes necessary to comply with the contract. The Virginia assembly fixed the salary of the parish minister at sixteen thousand pounds of tobacco per year, plus the profits from glebe lands and fees. The parish vestry was also responsible for church maintenance, poor relief, and other civil functions. The Anglican establishments of the South retained their exclusive right to public subvention until the Revolution, but the New England colonies, under royal pressure, moved gradually to what we may call a "multiple establishment," under which taxpayers could designate their tithes to whatever church they attended.

Unsurprisingly, upon declaring independence, the states stopped requiring tithes to support the Church of England, which advocated royal supremacy and was dominated by Tory clergy. By contrast, the Congregationalist establishment of New England—heirs of a long theological lineage of resistance to royal tyranny—emerged from the Revolution with renewed prestige. John Adams commented that "we might as soon expect a change in the solar system, as to expect [that Massachusetts] would give up their establishment." Even the states that abandoned the Anglican establishment debated—and some adopted—compelled tithes along the New England "multiple establishment" model. Many Americans continued to maintain, as the Continental Congress declared in 1778, that "true religion and good morals are the only solid foundations of public liberty and happiness."[20]

(4) Prohibition of Worship by Other Denominations. Most of the colonies had restrictions on public worship outside of the approved denomination, though many colonies tacitly tolerated it. Some welcomed dissenters, either formally or de facto, as a means of promoting economic development or because of their founders' commitment to religious toleration.

Quakers were persecuted in both Anglican and Puritan colonies, and in a few instances exiled or executed for their faith. Only in Pennsylvania, officially, and the Carolinas, unofficially, were they welcomed. Baptists were also widely despised. But Catholics were the most common target of religious intolerance. Because Catholics, at least in theory, regarded the authority of the Pope in Rome as superior to that of the British monarch, they were not trusted to be faithful subjects of the Crown. Moreover, the Catholic Church was aligned with France and Spain, who were a perpetual threat to the British colonies in the North Atlantic. Most of New England, South Carolina, and Georgia maintained laws forbidding Catholic churches.[21] There was no Catholic church in mainland British America south of Maryland until the 1790s. As late as 1777, a movement in New York led by future Chief Justice John Jay unsuccessfully sought to deny "professors of the religion of the Church of Rome" the right to own real property or exercise civil rights in the state.[22]

In the decades after the First Great Awakening, Baptist ministers faced widespread persecution in Virginia. Although the Toleration Act of 1688 allowed Trinitarian Protestant ministers to preach, it was interpreted to apply only to ministers ordained to a specific congregation. Baptist ministers were often itinerant. As a matter of principle, Baptist ministers also refused to apply to the proper authorities for a license to preach, believing that God alone was the governor of the church. Their egalitarianism also tended to subvert the social hierarchy—in many places they accepted slaves as brothers in

Christ and women as preachers. According to one Baptist source, about thirty Baptist ministers were imprisoned in Virginia between 1768 and 1775. Seeing Baptist ministers in jail inspired the young James Madison, recently graduated from the (Presbyterian) College of New Jersey (now Princeton), to write his first impassioned encomium to religious liberty in a letter to his college friend William Bradford:

> That diabolical, hell-conceived principle of persecution rages among some. . . . There are at this time in the adjacent county not less than five or six well-meaning men in close [jail], for publishing their religious sentiments, which in the main are very orthodox. . . . I have squabbled and scolded, abused and ridiculed so long about it, that I am without common patience. So I must beg you to pity me, and pray for liberty of conscience to all.[23]

Baptists were also targeted in New England, especially Massachusetts, for refusal to pay religious taxes. The law permitted them to direct their religious taxes to their own church. But many Baptists still refused, on the grounds that contributions were a matter of voluntary obligation, and the state had no authority either to compel contributions or to stipulate which church a believer must subscribe to.

(5) Use of the State Church for Civil Functions. In the early colonies, social welfare was rudimentary at best. The New England colonies typically tasked town and county courts with supporting the poor.[24] The established church played this role in the Anglican colonies. Virginia vestries were charged by law with "caring for the poor, the aged and infirm, the sick and insane, and for orphans and other homeless children."[25] These expenses were financed through a combination of taxation on the general population and private contributions.

Another important civic function of the Anglican church was to perform marriages and keep public records of births, burials, and marriages. The principal purpose of these records was to ascertain the number of taxable units, or "titheables," in the parish and in the county. In both England and the Anglican colonies marriages could be lawfully performed only by ministers of the Church of England, and the law declared the offspring of marriages performed by ministers outside the established church illegitimate. Church officials in some Anglican colonies, including Virginia, also made biennial presentments to the county court for misdemeanor offenses such as swearing, profanity, sabbath breaking, absence from church, drunkenness, fornication, adultery, and slander. The presentments were perhaps the most "governmental" of all duties of church officials in Virginia.

Churches, religious groups, and ministers also provided almost all of the primary and secondary education in the colonial and early republican period. Outside of New England, education was almost entirely privately funded. Over time, governments, especially in the Northeast, also contributed to denominational schools for the needy.

(6) Limitation of Political Participation to Members of the State Church. A central feature of the establishment in England—not repealed until 1828—was the limitation of public office to members of the Church of England. The Test and Corporation Acts required that, in order to hold civil, military, academic, or municipal office, an aspirant had to have taken communion in the established church within a certain period and to swear an oath against belief in transubstantiation, the Catholic doctrine that the bread and wine of communion are transformed into the body and blood of Christ.[26] The right to vote for members of Parliament was limited to those who would take an oath forswearing the "ecclesiastical or spiritual" authority of any foreign prince or prelate, the belief in transubstantiation, and the veneration of Mary or the saints.[27]

Restrictions on office holding were also common in America. Consider South Carolina. Many who settled in South Carolina in the seventeenth century, including most of the colonial governors, had been religious dissenters. But in 1704, the assembly enacted a law akin to the Test Acts, barring from the legislature any person who could not swear an oath that he took communion in the Church of England, or that he conformed to Anglican doctrine and had not taken communion in a different church for the past year. This act was said to be necessary "to quell all factions which so much disturb'd the peace of the Government."[28]

Until 1662, Massachusetts limited full citizenship to those who supplied proof of a genuine conversion experience. Unlike the Test and Corporation Acts, which were concerned only with outward conformity, these requirements targeted inward religious sincerity. The requirement did not outlast the seventeenth century; later generations' religious commitment was less intense, and the Crown pressured the colony to be more tolerant, especially of Anglicans.

Religion-based office-holding restrictions survived Independence in every state except Virginia. Although the Test Clause of Article VI prohibited religious tests for office at the federal level, states continued to impose and enforce such limitations into the nineteenth century. Massachusetts removed its religious test for office through constitutional amendment in 1821. Only in 1961 did the Supreme Court hold state religious tests unconstitutional.[29]

Many colonies categorically excluded ordained clergy from serving in an elected civil office. Some states maintained this disability well past Independence. The Supreme Court has held such provisions unconstitutional for interfering with the office holder's free exercise of religion. The Court seemed to think that such disabilities were a vestige of disestablishment—an attempt to separate church and state. The reality is more complicated. This was closest to the case for the Puritan colonies, which sought to separate the functions of secular and religious leadership. But it was not at all the case in the Anglican colonies, where the disability on serving in legislatures was a vestige of establishment. The theory was that the Church of England was fully represented in Parliament through the bishops' seats in the House of Lords. Prohibiting other members of the clergy from serving in Parliament therefore served to keep the church from double-dipping, and, as jurist William Blackstone said, to ensure that clergy would "attend the more closely to the service of almighty God." The residue of this tradition is apparent in some of the first state constitutions. The South Carolina Constitution of 1778, which was perhaps the most establishmentarian of the early constitutions, barred clergy from service in the legislature, while the Georgia Constitution of 1798, which ended establishment, *removed* the clergy disqualification provision from the Constitution of 1777. It was not until the nineteenth century that prohibitions on clergy holding office were believed to be an incident of separation of church and state rather than an incident of establishment. The Supreme Court held the exclusion of clergy from public office to violate the Free Exercise Clause in 1978.[30]

Most colonies also imposed religious restrictions on the right to vote.[31] Sometimes these were affirmative, such as extending the franchise only to members of the Protestant religion, the Church of England, or some other defined denomination. Sometimes they were negative, such as denying the franchise to Catholics, Jews, Quakers, or others. Catholics were the most frequently excluded group.

THEORIES OF ESTABLISHMENT

To understand the basis for religious establishment in political theory, we must distinguish between two different, almost antithetical rationales, which we may call the *theological* and the *political.*

Establishment, under the theological rationale, aimed to glorify God, to save souls, and to ensure God's providence for the nation. Under the political rationale, the purpose of an establishment was to use the authority of religion to help shape public opinion and character in a way favorable to the principles of the regime. One was based on the primacy of religion, the other on the utility of religion to the state. Although logically antithetical, the two rationales sometimes coexisted in practice.

The political rationale treated religion as a means for promoting the civic purposes of the state. It rested on the social utility rather than the truth of religion. Machiavelli, who called religion "the instrument necessary above all others for the maintenance of a civilized state," urged rulers to "foster and encourage" religion "even though they be convinced that it is quite fallacious."[32] Truth and social utility may, but need not, coincide. A liberal state may aspire to be neutral among competing understandings of the good, but many hard-nosed thinkers have taught the contrary: that a wise ruler will attempt to shape the habits, inclinations, and character of the people rather than depend on punishments and rewards. As Edmund Burke argued, "It is the Right of government to attend much to opinions, because, as opinions soon combine with passions, even when they do not produce them, they have much influence on actions."[33] In this respect, establishment of religion resembles government control of the press, of education, and of other aspects of public culture.

Although it was not devoid of political elements, the Puritan establishment of New England was primarily theological in nature, at least in its first century. The Puritans and Pilgrims who came to New England at the beginning of the seventeenth century wished to establish a "City upon a Hill," the first community in the history of the world to be governed by Christian precepts, properly understood (by Puritan lights). In the harsh wilderness of New England, the early settlers hoped to form a homogeneous community where fellow citizens and fellow believers were one and the same. As time wore on, the justification for the New England establishment shifted toward the political: to the inculcation of the public virtue needed in good republican citizens. Isaac Backus, a Baptist minister and leading advocate of disestablishment in Massachusetts, mocked the change in justification: "A little while ago," he said, the establishment was "for religion," but now it is said to be "for the good of *civil society*."[34]

In England, the monarch was the supreme head of the church; Parliament controlled the liturgy and articles of faith; the Crown, meaning the Prime Minister, appointed bishops; and government offices were confined to members of the church. This arrangement may fairly be called a union between church and state. But it was not a theocracy. Quite the contrary: The church did not control the government; the government controlled the church. The technical term for governmental control over the church in the English tradition is *Erastianism*, after the sixteenth-century Swiss-German theologian Thomas Erastus.[35]

Establishmentarian theory in the eighteenth century shifted from pure Erastianism to the idea of "alliance" between church and state—the title of a celebrated essay by William Warburton, the Bishop of Gloucester and the leading eighteenth-century defender of establishment. Warburton argued that church and state were distinct and mutually independent, but allied in a joint enterprise of the governing of society. The state needed the aid of the church to reinforce obedience to the laws and the performance of moral duties; the church needed the aid of the state for protection and financial support, in return for which it ceded its independence. Warburton's arguments were often borrowed by supporters of establishment in colonial America.[36]

MONARCHICAL AND REPUBLICAN ESTABLISHMENT

Tocqueville observed that "every religion has some political opinion linked to it by affinity."[37] Thus, establishments of religion take their tone from the character of the regime. The Anglican establishment was monarchical in nature; the Puritan colonial establishments and all of the state establishments after Independence were republican. The shift was not from establishmentarianism to disestablishmentarianism, nor from religiosity to secularism, but from a church that preached the importance of submission to royal authority to one that preached the importance of the common good.

The Church of England, the "church by law established" in both Britain and the southern colonies, emphasized obedience to the government as both a religious and a civic obligation. The Thirty-nine Articles declared that monarchs are given "in holy Scriptures by God himself" the prerogative to "rule all estates and degrees committed to their charge by God, whether they be ecclesiastical or temporal."[38] The first provision of the 1603 Canons of the Church of England, applicable to the Anglican colonies, required ministers at least four times each year to deliver sermons teaching that the king "is the highest power under God." This was to be done "purely and sincerely (without any colour or dissimulation)."[39]

True to this heritage, Anglican ministers, especially in the middle and northern colonies, were the most prominent public advocates against the American Revolution. A Connecticut minister claimed that while there had been "most rebellious outrages committed, on account of the Stamp Act" in some parts of the colony, "those towns where the Church [of England] has got footing, have calmly submitted to the civil authority." Samuel Seabury, later to become the first Episcopal bishop in America, proclaimed, "Our Duty to obey our Rulers and Governors arises from our Duty to obey God." An Anglican minister in 1774 urged his countrymen to be loyal to the mother country on the ground that "the principles of submission and obedience to all lawful authority are as inseparable from a sound, genuine member of the Church of England, as any religious principle whatsoever."[40]

In post-Independence America, the arguments for establishment took a republican cast. Reformed Protestants were natural republicans. As early as 1604, James I himself recognized the subversive implications of these churches' nonhierarchical structure: "No bishop," he said, "no king." George III blamed the Revolution on America's Puritan clergy, whom he purportedly called "the Black Regiment" (because of the austere black robes they wore). Edmund Burke pointed to the religious sensibility of America as a leading explanation for the Revolution:

> The people are Protestants, and of that kind which is the most adverse to all implicit submission of mind and opinion. This is a persuasion not only favorable to liberty, but built upon it. . . . All Protestantism, even the most cold and passive, is a sort of dissent. But the religion most prevalent in our northern colonies is a refinement on the principle of resistance: it is the dissidence of dissent, and the protestantism of the Protestant religion.[41]

Moreover, the Reformed Protestant emphasis on rectitude, sobriety, thrift, and virtue marched hand in hand with the civic republican virtue to which the new nation aspired.

To be sure, Madison expressed doubts that religious scruples would be adequate to restrain public vice and advocated constitutional devices such as the extended union and checks and balances. Jefferson went further. He regarded traditional religion as inimical to republican government and hoped that disestablishment would destroy it. Moreover, as we will see in Chapter 3, many—maybe most—of those founding-era Americans who regarded religion and morality as essential to republican virtue also believed that establishment of religion, with its attendant government control, was counterproductive to the cause of vital and genuine religion. But by the 1780s the argument for established religion rested almost entirely on the thesis that public virtue was necessary for republicanism, that religion was the most effectual means for promoting public virtue, and that a liberal form of multiple establishment was the most reliable means for fostering religion.

Thus, the official justification for governmental support for religion, by the 1780s, had ceased to have any real theological component. It was entirely political and republican in nature. There was little mention of the need to glorify or worship God or to promote the salvation of the citizenry. There was only the civic justification that belief in religion would preserve the peace and good order of society by improving men's morals and restraining their vices. As Virginia Presbyterians declared in a position statement favoring the general assessment bill in that state: "Religion as a spiritual system is not to be considered as an object of human legislation, but may in a civil view, as preserving the existence and promoting the happiness of society."[42]

CHAPTER 2

Framing the First Amendment

THE MEMBERS OF the First Congress debated the terms of the First Amendment against the backdrop of a well-known political, legal, and religious landscape of religious establishment. James Madison, who shepherded the provision to ratification, had been at the forefront of disestablishment in Virginia and had already produced some of the most wide-ranging arguments in favor of disestablishment of anyone before or since. The members were also sensitive to the fact that many states had not yet shelved their religious establishments, and some were eager to keep them in place. The result was a provision that at once forbade the federal government from establishing a national religion and guaranteed that it had no power to interfere with a state establishment.

Religion was scarcely mentioned at the Constitutional Convention in 1787, though the Jews of Philadelphia, led by the redoubtable Jonas Philips, did submit a petition through Benjamin Franklin asking that all religions be placed "on an equal footing"—a demand for equality, not separation.[1] Near the end of the Convention, the Committee of Style added a provision that "no religious test or qualification shall ever be annexed to any oath of office under the authority of the U.S.," thus barring any equivalent to the British Test and Corporation Acts. In the waning days of the Convention, George Mason, author of the Virginia Declaration of Rights, suggested that the new Constitution be "prefaced with a Bill of Rights," but the motion was defeated almost unanimously, probably because the delegates were impatient to get home. This was the framers' biggest political miscalculation. The absence of a Bill of Rights became the most potent argument of the Anti-Federalists, the opponents of the Constitution. Along with freedom of the press and the civil jury trial, freedom of religion was the focus of greatest concern. The Baptist General Committee, for example, announced opposition to the proposed Constitution on the ground that it had not "made sufficient provision for the secure enjoyment of religious liberty."[2]

The supporters of the Constitution defended the lack of explicit protection for such rights on the ground that the new federal government had been given no power to regulate religion (or the press) to begin with. "There is not a shadow of right in the general government to intermeddle with religion," Madison told the Virginia ratifying convention.[3] This argument was not quite convincing. Although Congress had been given no enumerated power over religion, it had been given power to enact laws "necessary and proper" for carrying out the other enumerated powers, laws that might incidentally affect religious exercise. Congress could raise and supply armies; would it provide chaplains and build places of worship on military installations? Would it draft Quakers or other religious pacifists into the armed forces? Congress had power to grant copyrights; could it grant a monopoly over religious texts like Bibles or hymnals? It could impose import taxes; would it tax the importation of religious objects? It could spend money; would it subsidize churches?

Desperate to ratify the Constitution, Federalists in key states promised to support the addition of a Bill of Rights under the procedures of Article V. Seven states drafted proposals for amendments, and five of them (plus a minority report in Pennsylvania) proposed religious freedom guarantees. Once the Constitution had become the fundamental law and Federalists had won a large majority in the First Congress, however, addition of a Bill of Rights seemed a low priority—well behind creating a new government, getting national finances in order, providing for disposition of national lands, and other such urgent tasks.

The promise of a Bill of Rights might have gone unfulfilled but for the persistence of James Madison, now a congressman from Virginia. He had personal political reasons for taking the lead. Denied a Senate seat by a Virginia legislature dominated by his political adversary, Patrick Henry, and thrown into a congressional district with an Anti-Federalist majority, Madison faced a tough election campaign for a seat in the House of Representatives. (Ironically, his opponent was James Monroe, who later became a close political friend and ally, his Secretary of State, and his successor as President.) Madison's opponents spread the rumor that he was opposed to any amendments to the Constitution. This charge was particularly potent among Madison's Baptist constituents, who were a large and potentially decisive swing vote. Madison composed a letter to George Eve, a Baptist minister, proclaiming his support for "the most satisfactory provisions for all essential rights, particularly the rights of Conscience in the fullest latitude, the freedom of the press, trials by jury, security against general warrants & c." The Baptists shifted their support to Madison.[4]

Having won his seat in the First Congress, Madison drafted a proposed Bill of Rights, differing substantially from the proposals that had emanated from the state ratifying conventions. Among his proposals were two amendments relevant to religious liberty. First, he proposed that Art. I, §9 (the section containing express limitations on the powers of Congress) be amended by adding:

The civil rights of none shall be abridged on account of religious belief or worship, nor shall any national religion be established, nor shall the full and equal rights of conscience be in any manner, or on any pretext, infringed.

Second, he proposed that Art. I, §10 (the section containing express limitations on the powers of the states) be amended by adding:

No State shall violate the equal rights of conscience, or the freedom of the press, or the trial by jury in criminal cases.[5]

Madison's proposals were referred to a Select Committee, which produced a shorter version of the first proposal: "No religion shall be established by law, nor shall the equal rights of conscience be infringed." This proposal led to the longest of all the debates in the First Congress on any provision of the Bill of Rights.[6]

The protection for the equal rights of conscience passed almost unmentioned, but the establishment prohibition encountered serious objection from the Northeast. The first to speak was Peter Silvester of New York, who "feared that [the amendment] might be thought to have a tendency to abolish religion altogether." We do not know the basis for this dire prediction, which seems overwrought. Perhaps Silvester believed public support was necessary for religion to survive. More narrowly, he may have thought that disestablishment would prevent churches from obtaining charters of incorporation—a position that some radical Jeffersonians took in the early decades of the republic. Silvester, whose name is on the charter of St. Peter's [Episcopal] Church in Albany, may have been especially sensitive to the incorporation issue.

Elbridge Gerry, a vituperative Anti-Federalist from Massachusetts, proposed to narrow the establishment provision to prohibit only the establishment of "religious doctrine by law." This would prevent any American reprise of Parliament's Thirty-Nine Articles of Faith, but would presumably allow other elements of establishment. Notably, the localized Massachusetts establishment—unlike that of colonial Virginia—never entailed statewide imposition of doctrine or liturgy. Gerry's proposal would have made the federal constitutional provision congruent with his own state's practice.

Daniel Carroll of Maryland, scion of the leading Roman Catholic family in the nation and whose brother was to become the first Catholic bishop, rose in support of the proposal. He may be seen as the voice of minority faiths in America. At that time, Catholics were less than 2 percent of the population, most of them living in Carroll's own state. He did not parse the words or legal meaning (saying "he would not contend with gentlemen about the phraseology") but proclaimed that "the rights of conscience are, in their nature, of peculiar delicacy, and will little bear the gentlest touch of governmental hand." Note that he viewed "the touch of governmental hand" as *harmful* to the exercise of religion, not as advancing or promoting it. This reflected the increasingly widespread view of many religious Americans that establishment was bad for religion.

Madison rather defensively said he did not know whether the proposed amendment was necessary or not, but it had been demanded by "some of the State Conventions" as the price for ratifying the Constitution. He paraphrased the proposal as follows: "that Congress should not establish a religion, and enforce the legal observation of it by law, nor compel men to worship God in any manner contrary to their conscience." This suggests that the amendment was directed against the "legal enforcement" of religion by law and compulsory worship contrary to conscience. By 1789, those were largely matters of consensus. Even Massachusetts, which continued to compel attendance at worship, did so only when this was not contrary to conscience. Madison clarified that the Necessary and Proper

Clause was the source of the worry that Congress could establish "a national religion" or infringe the rights of conscience. His reference to "a" national religion might be taken to refer to a single established church rather than a multiple establishment.

Next up was Samuel Huntington of Connecticut, who gave a more precise reason for his opposition. While he shared Madison's explanation of the meaning of the provision, Huntington worried that "others might find it convenient to put another construction upon it." He proceeded to describe Connecticut's version of the Congregationalist establishment, in which religious taxes were imposed by means of local "by-laws."[7] Huntington appeared to understand that Madison's proposal did not of itself disestablish religion at the state level, but he speculated that an objector to a state religious tax could get a case into federal court, which might declare it unenforceable. In a passage that is often misunderstood, Huntington spoke of the "blessed fruits" of Rhode Island's prohibition on religious establishment. He was being sarcastic. A Connecticut establishmentarian like Huntington would have had a dim view of Rhode Island—popularly known as "Rogue Island" and a hotbed of populist mischief untempered by sober New England puritanism. Huntington was warning against disestablishment, not praising it. This does not mean he favored a *national* establishment. Rather, he wanted to be sure that the New England establishments would be undisturbed.

Huntington's speech inspired Madison to offer a second defense of the proposal. Again he paraphrased: "He believed the people feared one sect might obtain a pre-eminence, or two combine together, and establish a religion to which they would compel others to conform." Again, he described establishment in terms of compulsion. He suggested that Huntington's concerns could be assuaged by amending the proposal to insert the word "national" before the word "religion."

Samuel Livermore, defender of the New Hampshire Congregationalist establishment, then offered a different suggestion: to replace the Select Committee amendment with one his state ratifying convention had proposed: "Congress shall make no laws touching religion, or infringing the rights of conscience." In other words: The entire subject of religion would be removed from the legislative jurisdiction of the federal government. This was not a separationist proposal, as some modern observers have supposed; it was a states' rights proposal. It would have left the entire topic of religion to the exclusive control of the states.

After Gerry went on a diatribe against Madison's suggestion to insert the word "national"—the term "nation" at that time connoting a unitary nation-state as opposed to a federated republic—Madison withdrew his suggestion in frustration, and the House voted in favor of Livermore's substitute. This was not, however, a sensible proposal, because it would disable Congress from doing anything about religion even within the legitimate scope of its enumerated powers, such as the military, tax, or copyright examples already mentioned. Five days later, without further recorded discussion, the House adopted a new version proposed by Fisher Ames of Massachusetts: "Congress shall make no law establishing religion, or to prevent the free exercise thereof, or to infringe the rights of conscience."

The Ames version of the House proposal went to the Senate, where it underwent what must have been a far-reaching debate. We say "must have been" because at that time, the Senate met in secret and did not allow publication of its debates. All we have is the Senate Journal, which records only motions and votes. Both the establishment and the free exercise parts of the amendment went through major revisions. As to establishment, the Senate initially replaced "no law establishing religion" with "no law establishing one religious sect or society in preference to others." This would have allowed many aspects of religious establishment so long as all religions were on an equal footing. Centuries later, Chief Justice William Rehnquist would champion this "non-preferentialist" interpretation of the Establishment Clause, apparently unaware that the framers considered and rejected it.[8]

A few days later, the Senate adopted a new version: "Congress shall make no law establishing articles of faith or a mode of worship." Much like Gerry's rejected proposal in the House, this would have prohibited an American version of the Uniformity Acts or the Thirty-nine Articles of Faith, but would not have prohibited arrangements similar to those in New England, which compelled support for religion without interference with church doctrine or liturgy.

The House objected, and the amendment went to a conference committee, which produced a version that prohibited laws "respecting" an establishment of religion. Although we have no recorded explanation for the revision, this language perfectly captured both Madison's intention to preclude establishment of a national religion and the concerns of others that it not interfere with their existing state establishments. Most scholars thus conclude that the phrase "no law respecting an establishment of religion" does two things: It broadly prevents any establishment of religion at the federal level—not just establishing articles of faith or modes of worship, and not just preference for one religious sect or society over others, but any and all attempts to enforce religion by law—and it protects state establishments from federal interference.[9]

Confirming this emphasis on federalism, the Senate rejected Madison's proposal to protect the rights of conscience, speech, press, and jury against state governments. Madison had called this "the most valuable amendment in the whole list." Under his theory of the dangers of factions in politics, set forth in *The Federalist* No. 10, the states are more prone to the oppression of factions (including religious factions) than the extended republic because there will be more numerous competing factions at a national level, which will cancel each other out. This found confirmation in the religious circumstances of the day. While different religious denominations were dominant in various states, no one religious group was dominant nationally. Madison lost this debate in 1789, but he arguably won it after the Civil War, when federal constitutional protections for individual freedoms including religion were applied to the states for the first time (see Chapter 4).

In a separate debate, Madison attempted to constitutionalize the exemption of religious objectors from compulsory military service. His proposal read: "No person religiously scrupulous shall be compelled to bear arms." It narrowly passed the House (in amended form) but was rejected by the Senate. Opponents argued primarily that they should "leave it to the benevolence of the Legislature" rather than enshrine a right of conscientious objection in the Constitution. The debate casts ambiguous light on the reach of the Free Exercise Clause,[10] but it makes clear that legislative exemptions from otherwise generally applicable laws were not thought to be an establishment, even when they imposed significant burdens on other people (see Chapter 5). One congressman complained that the exemption would violate the states' Second Amendment right to maintain militias, but no one suggested it would violate the Establishment Clause.

CHAPTER 3

Disestablishment in the States

As described in Chapter 1, nine of the thirteen original states had full-blown establishments of religion until Independence, complete with religious taxes, compulsory church attendance, state control over who was permitted to preach, restrictions on public worship by dissenters, exclusion of dissenters from voting or holding office, and performance of public functions by the churches. The Establishment Clause disabled the federal government from establishing a religion or interfering in a state's establishment, leaving the states free to disestablish at their own pace. The debates over *disestablishment* thus took place entirely in the states. Those debates offer the best evidence of what the founding era meant by "establishment of religion."

THE ARGUMENTS OVER ESTABLISHMENT

During the Revolution, the six states with an Anglican establishment effectively ended tax support for the Church of England—not because of any wellspring of opposition to established religion in the abstract, but because the Anglican Church was so closely wedded to the British monarchy. After Independence, the Anglican Church regrouped as a nonestablished Protestant Episcopal Church, but its churches had been decimated. Anglican ministers had fled or been defrocked; church buildings had been burned or vandalized during the war, and the denomination lacked money to rebuild and rehire.[1] The near-absence of religious teaching in large swathes of the country seemed to many statesmen (many not personally pious) to present a crisis. How would the republican virtues of honesty, thrift, hard work, courage, and self-sacrifice be publicly upheld and communicated to new generations? By contrast, the localized Congregationalist establishments of New England (outside of Rhode Island) emerged from the war with renewed prestige, largely due to their clergy's nearly unanimous support for the patriot cause, with persistent and increasing resistance from dissenters, especially the Baptists.

This set the stage for debates over establishment in almost every state, which lasted from 1776 well into the nineteenth century. Virtually no one wished to establish a single church at the state or, still less, the national level. But in most states (Rhode Island, Pennsylvania, and North Carolina being exceptions) there was significant support for some form of tolerant "multiple establishment," under which citizens would be required to support a church but permitted to decide (within limits) which one to support.

Importantly, by the late eighteenth century, the arguments in favor of establishment were not based on theocratic purposes but on the secular concern to instill the civic virtue necessary for the success of the new republic. George Washington's sentiment was typical: "Religion and morality are indispensable supports" for "the dispositions and habits which lead to *political prosperity*." It was widely believed that "popular" government—meaning republicanism or constitutional democracy—rested on a foundation of civic

virtue: honesty, hard work, thrift, courage, and above all willingness to subordinate one's own interest for the good of the whole.
According to Gordon Wood, a leading intellectual historian of the
founding period, "The eighteenth-century mind was thoroughly
convinced that a popularly based government 'cannot be supported
without *Virtue.*'" It was further believed that, for most people, religious teaching was the most effective means to inculcate this virtue.
Washington (whose own religious commitment was lukewarm)
warned, "Let us with caution indulge the supposition that morality
can be maintained without religion. Whatever may be conceded to
the influence of refined education on minds of peculiar structure,
reason and experience forbid us to expect that national morality can
prevail in exclusion of religious principle." This paean to republican
virtue was recapitulated in countless speeches, bills, preambles to
statutes, and state constitutional provisions. As late as the 1830s,
Alexis de Tocqueville wrote, "Despotism may be able to do without
faith, but freedom cannot. Religion is much more needed in the republic they advocate than in the monarchy they attack, and in democratic republics, most of all. How could society escape destruction
if, when political ties are relaxed, moral ties are not tightened?"[2]

Modern observers sometimes presuppose that disestablishment
was part of a move toward secularization of society, driven by the
idea that traditional religion, in the words of historian Sidney Mead,
"is intellectually at war with the basic premises upon which the
constitutional and legal structures of the Republic rest."[3] Not so.
Opponents of religious establishment almost never disputed that
religion is the foundation for public virtue or that virtue is necessary
for republican government. Instead, they maintained that establishment is unnecessary and even harmful to religion. As Madison
argued in the Virginia legislature, the true question was "not is
Religion necessary, but are Religious Establishments necessary for
Religion?"[4]

The popular movement against establishment was led by the most intensely religious sects, such as Madison's Baptist constituents, who pressured him to support constitutional changes (see Chapter 2). They believed that governmental coercion of religious obligations, such as tithing or prayer, was an invasion of conscience; that establishment of religion runs contrary to the teaching of the Christian faith; and that government financial support undermines the autonomy and vitality of the church. Their arguments against the establishment proposals were, thus, anything but secular. And to a surprising degree, Jefferson's and Madison's arguments against establishment echoed those themes, albeit in a more Enlightenment-inflected register.

To be sure, Jefferson and Madison sometimes expressed skepticism that religion actually performs the civic republican function attributed to it. "The inefficacy of this restraint [religion] on individuals is well known," Madison wrote to his friend. "The conduct of every popular Assembly, acting on oath, the strongest of religious ties, shows that individuals join without remorse in acts against which their [private] consciences would revolt." That is why, at the federal level, Madison advocated reliance on the policy of "supplying, by opposite and rival interests, the defect of better motives"—that is, an extended republic with checks and balances—in lieu of the traditional republican emphasis on "moral [or] religious motives." That did not suggest a preference for secularization, a view Jefferson sometimes expressed, but a realistically cynical attitude toward politics.[5]

Despite the number and variety of these debates, Supreme Court justices have referred to that of only one state, Virginia. The justices assumed that the debates in Virginia offered direct evidence for the historical meaning of the First Amendment. "The provisions of the First Amendment . . . had the same objective and were intended to provide the same protection against governmental intrusion on religious liberty as the Virginia statute," according to the Court.[6] To be sure, the Virginia debates are important and illuminating, not least because Madison and Jefferson are towering figures in the civil libertarian tradition of the United States. But it was a mistake to treat these two sets of debates as the same. Virginia was debating how radical a break to make from its long-standing and highly coercive establishment, while Congress was debating how to prevent the new federal government from disturbing the status quo, including in states with establishments still enjoying the support of their people. These were different questions presenting a different range of perspectives.

Even when discussing the Virginia assessment controversy, Supreme Court justices wrote as if the views of Madison and the absent Jefferson reflected the sum total of the debate—when in fact there were over a hundred substantive petitions on both sides, with over ten thousand signatures. Other than the debates over ratification, this was the largest outpouring of public opinion on any topic during the founding period. Madison and Jefferson were important voices for religious freedom, but as will be seen, they differed between themselves, and their views were not representative of the perspectives of most Americans of the day. In the summer and fall of 1785, the most widely subscribed petition came from evangelicals, especially Baptists. It garnered 4,899 signatures, while Madison's anonymous *Memorial and Remonstrance Against Religious Assessments* garnered only 1,552.[7]

This evangelical petition asserted that the general assessment bill was "contrary to the Spirit of the Gospel, and the [Virginia] Bill of Rights," and continued for many paragraphs in that vein. Interestingly, the preamble to Jefferson's Bill for Establishing Religious Freedom said much the same. It began with the theological proposition "that Almighty God hath created the mind free" and asserted that "all attempts to influence it by temporal punishments or burdens . . . are a departure from the plan of the Holy Author of our religion." The predominant argument among opponents of establishment was that the decision to engage in a religious practice, such as attending worship or contributing to a church, is exclusively a matter between the believer and God; it would be an invasion of God's province for the government to force people to fulfill these sacred duties. This was a long-standing position among evangelical opponents of establishment. The Baptist anti-establishment leader Isaac Backus informed the Massachusetts legislature in 1774 that his coreligionists "are determined not to pay" the church tax "because we dare not render that homage to any earthly power, which I and many of my brethren are fully convinced belongs only to God." Eleven years later, almost identical thinking, even language, found its way into Madison's *Memorial and Remonstrance*: "It is the duty of every man to render to the Creator such homage, and such only, as he believes to be acceptable to him." It is ironic that supporters of establishment by this time largely eschewed religious arguments, focusing instead on civic benefits, but opponents—even Madison and Jefferson—freely invoked scripture and the duty to God.[8]

Madison shared—at least publicly and rhetorically—the evangelicals' premise that humans have a duty to God to worship in accordance with conscience, and that the rights of conscience follow from this theological premise. In the first numbered and most important paragraph of his *Memorial and Remonstrance*, he gave two reasons why the ability to worship God in accordance with conscience "is in its nature an unalienable right." The first reason is secular and accords with an argument made by the philosopher Thomas Hobbes: because it is simply impossible for a person to "follow the dictates of other men" with respect to matters that depend "only on the evidence contemplated by their own minds."[9] It may be possible to force people to say or do things contrary to conscience, but not to force them to believe them. The second reason is theological. Religious freedom "is here a right toward men," but it is also "a duty towards the Creator"—the duty to "render to the Creator such homage, and such only" as the individual believes to be acceptable to God. It follows that religion "can be directed only by reason and conviction and not by force or violence." It is an affront to God, not merely a denial of personal freedom, to interfere with the performance of these duties. Note Madison's language yoking "reason" (an Enlightenment appeal) to "conviction" (a traditional Reformed Protestant appeal). Madison saw no inconsistency between Protestant and Enlightenment conceptions of religious liberty and made it a point to combine them. The idea that religion was inimical to republican government was almost entirely absent from petitions, newspaper articles, and speeches known to us from the Virginia controversy.[10]

Jefferson's arguments against establishment were subtly different, in emphasis and maybe even substance.[11] He wrote in the preamble to his bill that "our civil rights have no dependence on our religious opinions, any more than our opinions in physics or geometry," and he offered no direct argument based on duties to God. This may imply that religious beliefs, like opinions about physics and geometry, are irrelevant to civic matters. That renders Jefferson something of an outlier. Most founding-era Americans, as we have seen, thought the teachings of religion were conducive to civic virtue and thus to good republican citizenship. Even today we see that religious affiliation is a predictor of political beliefs about many matters relevant to government. Our civil rights have no dependence on our religious opinions not because religion is irrelevant to civic life but because in a diverse liberal republic like the United States, our civil rights have no dependence on our adherence to any particular opinions, whatever they are. Madison's emphasis on duties to God offers a more secure foundation for a distinctive freedom of religion, in addition to the broader freedom of opinion that both men espoused, without regard to questionable assumptions about the relation of religion to the civic order.

Madison and Jefferson also had different expectations for the disestablishmentarian future. Jefferson hoped that without coercive governmental support, traditional Christianity would wither and be replaced with a more rational form of the religion. "I rejoice that in this blessed country of free enquiry and belief," he wrote, "the genuine doctrine of one only God is reviving, and I trust that there is not a young man now living in the [United States] who will not die an Unitarian." Madison, who attended a Presbyterian college (Princeton) and whose uncle was an Episcopal bishop, was coy about publicly expressing his own religious sentiments. But like the evangelicals, he believed that religion was more likely to flourish ("in greater purity") without the helping and controlling hand of government. Madison appears to have been the better prophet. By the early years of the nineteenth century, the nation experienced a remarkable upsurge in evangelical Christian belief, practice, and political influence—a phenomenon historians call the Second Great Awakening. In 1819, Madison observed that this had disproved the prediction of some that "religion itself, would perish if not supported by a legal provision for its Clergy." On the contrary, "the number, the industry, and the morality of the Priesthood, & the devotion of the people have been manifestly increased." According to historian Jack Rakove, this upsurge in religious fervor was a "great disappointment" to Jefferson.[12]

For the most part, disestablishment was a negative process: simply repealing the various laws that compelled religious taxes and attendance, prevented dissenting worship, regulated the clergy, and so forth. Because the legal substance of establishment was different in every state, the process and pace of disestablishment varied. Four states (Rhode Island, New Jersey, Pennsylvania, and Delaware[13]) never had a formal religious establishment. Two states (North Carolina and New York) mostly dismantled their establishments with their first state constitutions in 1776–77. Others took decades. Luckily for modern interpretation, some states formally forbade any "establishment" of religion, using that term, and then proceeded to specify what they meant by it. Those provisions are especially illuminating when we seek to know what the founding generation meant by abolishing "an establishment of religion."[14]

Eleven of the thirteen original states (plus Vermont) adopted state constitutions between 1776 and 1780. Almost all of these included protections for the "free exercise of religion" or linguistic variants, such as the right to worship in accordance with conscience. Slightly more than half included prohibitions on religious establishments. For a time, a tolerant establishment coupled with free exercise for dissenters seemed a viable alternative. Because the founding generation did not rigidly bifurcate religious freedom into free exercise and nonestablishment—let alone regard those concepts as being in tension—it is sometimes necessary to look to what we would call free exercise provisions for a full understanding of the extent of disestablishment, and vice versa.

The earliest states to adopt constitutions forswearing establishments of religion were, perhaps not surprisingly, those that had never had establishments. New Jersey was the first, with ratification on July 2, 1776. Its constitutional drafting committee, seven of whose ten members were Presbyterians, declared that "there shall be no establishment of any one religious sect in this province." In the preceding article, the constitution specified that no one could be "compelled to attend any place of worship, contrary to his own faith and judgment, nor . . . obliged to pay tithes, taxes, or any other rates, for the purpose of building or repairing any church or churches, place or places of worship, or for the maintenance of any minister or ministry, contrary to what he believes to be right or has deliberately or voluntarily engaged to perform." What we would regard as "free exercise" provisions were interspersed with these establishment prohibitions, protecting every person's right of "worshipping Almighty God in a manner agreeable to the dictates of his own conscience," while protecting only Protestants in all "civil rights" and the right to hold certain public offices. New Jersey law had never restricted the right of any church to incorporate or to hold property; accordingly, those issues were not addressed. Unfortunately, no records of the deliberations that produced these results have come down to us.[15]

North Carolina, whose establishment of the Church of England was largely notional, adopted a constitution in December 1776 with religion provisions substantially identical to New Jersey's.[16] North Carolina retained its narrow Protestant-only test for state offices.

Pennsylvania, which likewise never had an established church, adopted the most radically democratic constitution of any state. But its provisions addressing religion largely tracked its colonial Charter of Privileges of 1701. Pennsylvania had never imposed religious taxes, required church attendance, or regulated the internal doctrine or governance of its religious societies. The most contentious issue in Pennsylvania was conscientious exemption from the draft.[17]

Delaware also formally foreswore establishment in 1776: "There shall be no establishment of any one religious sect in this State in preference to another." Curiously, and alone among the states, it contained no specification of what this meant in practice. Perhaps this is because colonial Delaware, as an appendage of Pennsylvania, had never imposed religious taxes, attendance requirements, or other elements of establishment. The constitution did provide that "no clergyman or preacher of the gospel, of any denomination, shall be capable of holding any civil office in this State, or of being a member of either of the branches of the legislature, while they continue in the exercise of the pastoral function." Such provisions, which are sometimes mistakenly thought to reflect modern separationist ideas, will be discussed below. Separate legislation permitted all religious societies to hold property in corporate form. This had been forbidden in colonial times.[18]

The remaining states had the more difficult task of dismantling then-existing religious establishments. In New York, where Anglican clergy had been especially strong supporters of the Tory cause, the legislature for some reason thought it had to petition the Continental Congress for permission to delete royalist elements from the Book of Common Prayer. The state's first constitution in 1777 invalidated all laws "as may be construed to establish or maintain any particular denomination of Christians or their ministers." This wording may have reflected the fact that the Dutch Reformed establishment of metropolitan New York, unlike the Anglican one, was not the product of specific statutory law. A separate article protected the free exercise of religion. The future U.S. Chief Justice John Jay, whose ancestors had been oppressed as Huguenots in France, led a movement to withhold civil rights from Catholics unless they abjured transubstantiation and the authority of the Pope, but this was defeated—after seven tries—by liberal forces led by another statesman of Huguenot stock, Gouverneur Morris. Another article confirmed to Trinity Church the valuable land grants it had been given by the king. Trinity Church would remain one of Manhattan's largest landowners for more than a century.[19]

True to its deeply conservative character, South Carolina was slow to alter its church-state arrangements. The state's first constitution, adopted in March 1776 and understood to be temporary, made no reference to laws pertaining to religion, thus leaving its Anglican establishment in place, though wartime exigencies weakened its position. The state's second constitution, of 1778, intended to be permanent, dismantled much of the exclusive one-church establishment but created an intermediate system unique to the Palmetto State. It proclaimed that "the Christian Protestant religion shall be deemed, and is hereby constituted and declared to be, the established religion of this State." Denominations meeting that description were entitled to "equal religious and civil privileges" so long as they comported themselves "peaceably and faithfully" (whatever that means). A broader set of religious faiths—those that espoused belief in "one God and a future state of rewards and punishments"—would be "freely tolerated," though not entitled to full equality. This embraced Catholics and Jews but excluded atheists, polytheists, and universalists. In a more disestablishmentarian spirit, the constitution prohibited taxing anyone "for the maintenance and support of a religious worship that he does not freely join in, or has not voluntarily engaged to support."

Unlike state constitutions adopted earlier, South Carolina addressed churches' legal status and property rights. The 1778 constitution secured the existing property of "all religious societies," expressly mentioning the "Church of England," unbothered by the fact that much Episcopal Church property was the consequence of the colonial establishment. The privilege of incorporation was reserved to denominations that affirmed five specific articles of faith; in practice this limited incorporation to Protestant churches. All monotheists who believed in a future state of rewards and punishment could vote, but officeholding was confined to Protestants. Interestingly, the 1778 constitution prohibited clergy from holding public office, which demonstrates that clergy officeholding bans were not associated with radical disestablishmentarianism. Most of these provisions were eliminated by the state's third constitution, adopted with relatively little controversy in 1790, which embraced the principle that "free exercise and enjoyment of religious profession and worship" would exist "without discrimination or preference."[20]

Despite its prominence in U.S. Supreme Court opinions, Virginia came relatively late to the disestablishment party. In 1776, the commonwealth enshrined a broad free exercise clause in its Declaration of Rights, repealed its compulsory church attendance laws, and enacted a one-year war-time moratorium on taxes to the Church of England, but otherwise left its establishment of the Anglican church in place. Only in January 1786, after establishmentarian forces overreached, did the legislature adopt a disestablishment law, and even then only as a statute. After a lengthy, philosophically complex preamble, the operative portion of Jefferson's Bill for Establishing Religious Freedom contained just three concise provisions:

- "that no man shall be compelled to frequent or support any religious worship, place, or ministry whatsoever,
- nor shall be enforced, restrained, molested, or burthened in his body or goods, nor shall otherwise suffer, on account of his religious opinions or belief;
- but that all men shall be free to profess, and by argument to maintain, their opinions in matters of religion, and that the same shall in no wise diminish, enlarge, or affect their civil capacities."[21]

These provisions were no more radical than the disestablishmentarian measures adopted by other states. All states that disestablished religion did what Jefferson's bill did: They all prohibited compulsory attendance laws and religious taxes. On its face, Virginia's prohibition on compulsory support or attendance was not confined to cases where enforcing these measures would violate conscience, as had been typical of previous provisions in other states. But by 1786, many Virginians likely assumed that these components of religious establishment violated conscience in all cases. Baptists opposed state enforcement even of *voluntary* commitments to give money to a church. Most of the second and third provisions of Jefferson's

disestablishment bill fall more naturally under what modern jurisprudence would categorize as free exercise. Notably, the third provision seems less protective than the Declaration of Rights enacted
ten years earlier; it extends only to opinions and belief, and to speech
professing them, and not to "exercise."

Like Virginia, Maryland ended compulsory taxation for support
of the Church of England in 1776; indeed, it was the first state to do
so. After the war, in 1784, the Maryland Assembly approved a general assessment bill, though it was never put into effect, and the state
retained power over the doctrine and liturgy of the former Church of
Maryland. Both the right of free exercise and the privilege of public
office were limited to Christians. Only in 1810 was the constitution
amended to eliminate the allowance of a general assessment, and
in 1826 the limitation of public office to Christians was struck. It is
ironic that one of the three colonies explicitly founded as a haven
for dissenters (specifically, Catholics) was one of the slowest states
to disestablish.[22]

Georgia had a remarkably inclusive establishment in colonial
times. The colony welcomed Protestant dissenters and Jews, though
it effectively excluded Catholics. Anglicans were never close to a
majority of the population. The Church of England received substantial financial support in the form of glebes (profit-making lands
attached to a parish) and direct subsidies mostly financed through
taxes on alcohol. Interestingly, the colony also made land grants both
to a non-Anglican Protestant church and to a Jewish synagogue—
the only one of the thirteen colonies to grant land to dissenting
faiths. In 1777, the state's first constitution contained a free exercise
clause extending to Catholics and non-Christians but did not prohibit establishment. There were no religious restrictions on voting,
but Protestants alone could serve in the legislature, and clergy also
were excluded. Not until 1798 did the state adopt a constitutional
provision forbidding the imposition of religious taxes.[23]

New England states outside of Rhode Island were the only ones with fully operational religious establishments after 1789, and they gradually adopted disestablishment provisions by the end of the first third of the nineteenth century. Both Massachusetts (1780) and Connecticut (1784) protected conscientious dissenters from the establishment faith from punishment for failing to attend church, but only if they attended their own. As early as 1777, before it was a state, Vermont guaranteed free exercise and forbade any compulsion to "attend any religious worship, or erect or support any place of worship, or maintain any minister," but people still could be compelled to pay tithes for the support of the church to which they belonged, and every territorial parish devoted a plot of public land to the support of the ministry. Only in 1807 were these provisions repealed.[24]

Disestablishment in Connecticut is usually dated to its first constitution, adopted in 1818, which provided that "no preference shall be given by law to any Christian sect or mode of worship." Conspicuously, the drafters rejected a broader prohibition on "preference . . . to *any* religious sect or mode of worship." The constitution eliminated universal taxation for the support of religion, but it empowered religious societies to tax their members, a requirement enforceable in court. Because members were able to withdraw from membership simply by filing a written statement, however, this was effectively, if not formally, the end of compulsory tithes. New Hampshire ended religious taxes the next year. Maine took its first steps toward disestablishment upon separation from Massachusetts in 1820. Massachusetts did not repeal its localized religious tax system until 1833. The move was motivated not so much by a principled opposition to establishment—however loudly and persistently the Massachusetts Baptists made the argument from conscience—as by the fact that in the towns near Boston, Unitarian ministers were more frequently winning elections, thus putting the "First Church" on the village green into the hands of people outside the range of

Protestant orthodoxy. It seemed better, not only to Baptists but also to orthodox Congregationalists, to sever the ties with government and let each church become an independent, self-supporting religious society.[25]

Looking at all of the foregoing provisions, we can identify six essential legal elements to disestablishment (listed roughly in order of adoption):

- Denominational equality;
- Free exercise and/or liberty of conscience;
- Repeal of compulsory religious attendance laws;
- Abolition of religious taxes;
- Autonomy of churches with respect to their doctrine, liturgy, and personnel;
- Stripping the formerly established church of any exclusive public prerogatives or functions such as marriages, recordkeeping, or administration of the poor laws.

Eventually, all states adopted a seventh element: no religious tests for voting or office-holding. This final element took longer—often decades longer—because voting and office-holding were not regarded as civil rights, but rather as political rights that states could regulate as part of their governance structure. Religious tests thus survived for much the same reason that the Fifteenth and Nineteenth Amendments were required to extend the right to vote, even after the Fourteenth Amendment extended constitutional protection to the privileges or immunities of all citizens. Restrictions of political rights on the basis of religion were always in tension with the equal freedom promoted by the Establishment Clause, and in light of today's commitment to religious equality, it makes sense to view them as clear violations of both free exercise and nonestablishment.

SETTLING THE RIGHTS OF THE PREVIOUSLY
ESTABLISHED CHURCHES

One of the most difficult questions in the wake of disestablishment had to do with the legal status of formerly established denominations. How would they be legally organized? What would be their rights to property? How much autonomy would they have? And what role would their clergy play in the political life of the state? Much of this debate centered on the fate of what had been the Church of England.

After the dust of independence and disestablishment had settled, the Church of England sought to re-create itself as the "Protestant Episcopal Church." At the end of the war, especially in Virginia, this church faced the worst of both worlds: It no longer enjoyed the benefit of religious taxes, but its doctrine, liturgy, and clergy discipline were under legislative control, and individual parish vestries were typically elected by all the voters whether or not they were adherents to the church. Formerly an arm of the Crown, the church had no independent legal status, and even ownership of church property was at the mercy of legislative whim. One prominent churchman wrote that the "existing laws which made a part of the old Establishment" would "prove ruinous to the Church" if they were not repealed. At the same time, dissenters continued to complain of the "unjust pre-eminence" of the former Church of England.[26]

Accordingly, in 1784 when the Virginia legislature began debating the future of religion in the state, the Episcopal clergy submitted a petition asking (1) for the repeal of the laws setting the doctrine, liturgy, and clergy qualifications of the church, giving the church the right to govern itself in all these respects; (2) for the church to be made a private corporation, with ownership of then-existing church property and the right to acquire and hold new property by gift or devise; (3) to relieve the church of its civic function of administering public welfare for the poor; and (4) to confine voting for the local vestries to church members. Petitions from the Baptists and Presbyterians supported the last two proposals, and in addition demanded that the right to perform marriages be extended to all ministers on an even basis. The most controversial of these topics were incorporation and property ownership.

Incorporation posed a difficult question because, at the founding, charters of incorporation were acts of special legislation made for public purposes, in which both the governance and the purposes of the corporation were set forth by law and enforceable in court. For this reason, some dissenting churches refused to seek corporate status and viewed the incorporation of established and mainline churches as a form of preference. Yet corporate form was the most convenient way for a church or other perpetual institution to hold property, make and enforce contracts, and generally engage in legal transactions. The alternatives were to be an unincorporated association, which meant that ownership was shared by all the members, or some form of trust, which required placement of church property in the hands of certain individuals. The ultimate solution—first adopted in the South Carolina Constitution of 1778 and a New York statute of 1784—was to adopt general incorporation laws allowing religious societies to incorporate without the need for special legislative acts. General incorporation became the norm for churches decades before it spread to business corporations.[27]

Every state except Virginia eventually adopted general incorporation laws for religious organizations. Virginia vacillated. At the time of disestablishment, the Virginia assembly first issued a charter of incorporation to the Protestant Episcopal Church, but revoked it two years later. The political motivations for the repeal were multifaceted. Lingering resentment felt by Baptists and Presbyterians who thought that incorporation favored the Episcopalians may have played a role, alongside a more general anti-clerical fear that institutional religion would exercise too much power over individual congregants, and an even more general association of corporations with monopoly and privilege. The assembly contemplated a general incorporation act but never managed to overcome objections; indeed, the Virginia Constitution of 1850 explicitly prohibited granting corporate status to churches or religious denominations. Jeffersonians tended to distrust the ability of any artificial entity—religious or secular—to accumulate unlimited amounts of property and to hold it in perpetuity. Accordingly, even some states that permitted churches to incorporate limited the amount and type of property they could hold.[28]

In 1811, James Madison, as President, vetoed a bill incorporating a church in the District of Columbia, on constitutional grounds. He explained:

> The bill enacts into, and establishes by law, sundry rules and proceedings relative purely to the organization and polity of the church incorporated, and comprehending even the election and removal of the Minister of the same; so that no change could be made therein by the particular society, or by the general church of which it is a member, and whose authority it recognises.[29]

Contrary to some interpretations, this did not mean that Madison thought religious societies should be forbidden to incorporate, but only that the government may not decide the terms of internal governance. General incorporation laws solve that problem.

While solving one set of problems about church polity under conditions of disestablishment, these general incorporation statutes created another. Most legislatures presupposed that the corporate structure of a voluntary society would consist of a governing board elected by the members. This happened to accord with the predominant Protestant models of ecclesiastical structure. But as more and more Catholics immigrated to the United States and formed churches, the assumptions undergirding general incorporation laws created massive problems, because the corporate form favored lay leadership over the hierarchical governance dictated by Catholic ecclesiology.[30] Eventually, Catholic churches won the right to incorporate in forms more consonant with their ecclesiology, but this struggle lasted almost a century.

Property that had been acquired under the prior regime posed another quandary. With a few exceptions, only the Church of England in the South and parts of New York, and the local majority church (usually Congregationalist) in New England, had the benefit of property derived from public sources. To expropriate properties held by a church for many years appeared hostile and even antagonistic—as the seizure of religious properties in revolutionary France exemplified. But to allow the formerly established church to retain property purchased at the expense of the general public, or reserved from the era of initial settlement, would be unfair to the dissenting churches that had to purchase property out of voluntary contributions. There was no perfect solution to this problem.

Most states opted to leave all church property where it was at the time of disestablishment. In the states with an Anglican establishment, that gave the Protestant Episcopal Church an advantage. In Massachusetts, the advantage went to whatever church was in possession in 1833—Congregationalists in most places, Unitarians in others. Two states, Virginia and Vermont, initially vested church property in the incumbent church at the time of disestablishment, but later changed their minds. They concluded that it had been wrong to vest in the formerly established church property that had (in large part) been derived from royal grant or mandatory taxation. Both states, however, compromised: They left the Protestant Episcopal Church in possession of church buildings and seized the glebe lands only when the parishes were vacant due to the death or resignation of the parson. The U.S. Supreme Court found these acts of dispossession unconstitutional under general principles of jurisprudence. The Court, in opinions by Justice Joseph Story (himself a sometime president of the Unitarian Church of America), held that "upon a change in government" the legislature has authority to abolish "such exclusive privileges attached to a private corporation as are inconsistent with the new government." Thus, it would have been permissible after the Revolution for the legislature to strip the Protestant Episcopal Church of properties it held as a result of its former exclusive status. But having confirmed the church in its then-existing property by statute at that time, the legislature could not later take it away.[31]

These decisions were not grounded in the religious nature of the property owner and were not based on the First Amendment but rested instead on the Court's vested rights doctrine, most famously articulated in *Fletcher v. Peck* (1810) and *Trustees of Dartmouth College v. Woodward* (1819). Decisions of the Supreme Court did not, however, carry great weight in Virginia, so the Episcopal Church in Virginia lost most of its glebe lands. In Vermont, for a time, there was an attempt to share the benefits of the glebe properties when there were multiple denominations in a town. Alas, but predictably, this led to a "scrambling for the right" and exacerbated religious animosities.[32]

Colleges presented a similar issue. Today, colleges are "public" or "private." There was no such distinction at the founding. All colleges were publicly chartered, most were publicly subsidized by land grants or appropriations, and all were governed by boards of trustees dominated by clergy of the denomination with which the college was affiliated. Of the nine institutions of higher education in the United States prior to Independence, eight were tied to a particular religious denomination and the ninth, the College of Philadelphia, though officially nonsectarian, was heavily Anglican in character. In the early years of the republic, legislatures assumed they had authority to revise collegiate charters to increase political control, but this was not always successful. Jefferson's 1776 proposal to transform William & Mary College into a public institution and to secularize its curriculum died for want of support. In 1779, the Pennsylvania Assembly voided the College of Philadelphia charter with the hope of wresting control from the Anglican trustees. Ten years later, the charter was restored and the legislature declared that its prior action had violated private rights. (Nonetheless, the restored college could not survive and had to merge with the University of Pennsylvania.)[33]

The issue came to a head with Dartmouth College. Dartmouth, a royally chartered institution with the original express purpose of supplying churches in the state with "a learned and orthodox ministry," received extensive support from the State of New Hampshire, including land grants in 1789 and 1807 and sporadic cash grants in the 1790s. After a few decades of secular Enlightenment influence, the Second Great Awakening brought renewed evangelical zeal to the college in the form of a new college president and trustees, as well as revived religious spirit among faculty and students. This was not well received by the anti-clerical Jeffersonian Republicans, who took control of the New Hampshire government in 1816. The legislature amended the collegiate charter and created a new, politically appointed Board of Overseers with power over appointments and curriculum. On litigation up to the Supreme Court, with Daniel Webster representing the trustees, the Court held that corporate charters are contracts that the states have no constitutional right to abrogate. This stripped the legislature of power to seize control of entities in corporate form, be they churches, colleges, or businesses—and thus marked the boundary, existing still today, between public and private power. One legal historian calls the *Dartmouth College* case the "death knell for New England establishment," not because it secularized the affected institutions—it did the opposite—but because it rendered the institutions of civil society, including religious institutions, immune from direct political control.[34]

Seven of the original thirteen states barred clergy from holding certain public offices, most often from serving in the legislature. It is often assumed that the purpose of these provisions—now held unconstitutional—was to safeguard the separation of church from state. That may sound intuitively plausible. But in no state did advocates for disestablishment push for clergy disqualification; it was not part of the disestablishmentarian agenda. On the contrary, as discussed in Chapter 1, clergy disqualification was an inheritance from the prior establishmentarian regimes. Clergy disqualification came to be associated with church-state separation later in the nineteenth century, but it was then repealed in almost every state in the twentieth century, and finally declared unconstitutional by a unanimous Supreme Court in 1978.[35]

THE DEBATES OVER COERCED TITHES

The most frequently debated issue in the years shortly after Independence was whether to provide subsidies to religious bodies through some form of religious tax, or "general assessment." The most famous such debate occurred in Virginia between 1779 and 1786. As discussed in Chapter 1, prior to the Revolution, Virginia had the most rigid, coercive, and comprehensive of the Anglican establishments. All this began to unravel in 1776. The framers of the new state Constitution of 1776 repealed compulsory church attendance laws and adopted a broad protection for the free exercise of religion—championed by twenty-five-year-old James Madison in his first public role—but left the state's establishment otherwise untouched. As chair of the Religion Committee in the late 1770s,

Jefferson proposed a raft of reforms of the religious system, all of which were ignored. During the course of the war, the legislature suspended the payment of religious taxes from year to year, then permanently in 1779. Anglican clergy thereafter relied on the income from glebe lands, which no other religious society enjoyed, plus any voluntary contributions that might be offered, which were relatively meager because Anglicans were not accustomed to making voluntary contributions. Taxes for support of the poor continued to be administered through Anglican vestries.[36]

By the end of the hostilities, religion in Virginia was on the ropes. Not only was religious belief at a low ebb, but—as one visitor to Virginia wrote—churches were "in a ruinous or ruined condition; and the clergy for the most part dead or driven away and their places unfilled." In forty counties, the pulpits of the established church were empty, and there was no source of revenue to attract qualified clergy. The number of Presbyterian clergy in the state doubled between 1779 and 1784, but the demand exceeded the supply, and the shortage of funds was a problem for clergy recruitment even for the Presbyterians, who were not a wealthy group.[37]

Many leading Virginians, whether or not personally religious, believed that the lack of religious instruction was an important source of the increasingly evident lack of public virtue and proposed to remedy the situation by means of a "general assessment"—a tax for the support of religion, with taxpayers permitted to direct their payments to the Christian "teacher" (meaning minister) of their choice. Richard Henry Lee sought to extend the system to *all* "religious teachers," arguing that "true freedom embraces the Mahomitan and the Gentoo as well as the Christian religion," but his motion was narrowly rejected.[38] The assessment proposal, introduced by Patrick Henry, ordinarily a friend to dissenters, squarely rested on the tendency of the "diffusion of Christian knowledge . . . to correct the morals of men, restrain their vices, and preserve the peace of society." It was a more liberal and evenhanded version of the New England system described in Chapter 1 and resembles that prevailing in some Western European nations today. Opposing it was a coalition of Baptists, Presbyterians (after initial vacillation), and disestablishmentarian statesmen led by Madison, who succeeded in defeating the Henry proposal and enacting in its stead Jefferson's Bill for Establishing Religious Freedom, originally submitted to the Assembly (but ignored) in 1779.

Virginia was not the only state to seriously consider restoring financial support for religion. The Maryland Declaration of Rights of 1776 authorized the legislature to "lay a general and equal tax, for the support of the Christian religion; leaving to each individual the power" of determining which denomination would receive the tax, or whether it would go to the poor. This was substantially equivalent to the general assessment proposal voted down in Virginia. After further debate in the legislature in the mid-1780s, this authority was never exercised. In Georgia, a bill "for the establishment and support of the public duties of religion" passed the legislature in 1785 by a lopsided majority. Apparently, however, it too was never put into effect. South Carolina's Constitution of 1778 declared the "Christian Protestant religion" as "the established religion of this State," imposing five articles of faith as a precondition for any church to enjoy this status. At the same time, however, it provided that "no person shall, by law, be obliged to pay towards the maintenance and support of a religious worship that he does not freely join in, or has not voluntarily engaged to support." In South Carolina, therefore, there was an established church with state-specified articles of faith, but no financial support. This was a unique and unprecedented arrangement.

Even in the middle states, which, other than parts of New York, did not have an established religion, legislatures acted favorably on establishmentarian proposals. The New York legislature declared in

1784 that "it is the duty of all wise, free and virtuous governments, to countenance and encourage virtue and religion." The Delaware legislature declared in 1787 that it was their "duty to countenance and encourage virtue and religion, by every means in their power, and in the most expedient manner," and some leaders advocated a general assessment scheme similar to that rejected in Virginia. In 1787 the Continental Congress, by contract with the Ohio Company, set aside land in the Northwest Territory for the support of religion, an arrangement that survived in parts of Ohio until 1968.[39] In 1789, the New Jersey legislature appointed a committee to "report their opinion on what may be proper and competent for the Legislature to do in order to promote the Interest of Religion and Morality among all ranks of People in this State."

Only in New England, however, did an operative system of taxes for religion survive the Revolution. As discussed in Chapter 1, the Revolution only increased the New England clergy's influence. Connecticut maintained its localized system, dubbed "the Standing Order," until the adoption of a state constitution in 1818. This was the system Huntington defended in the First Congress. Similarly, New Hampshire left its old laws on the subject unchanged, despite adopting three new constitutions, and proposing and rejecting a fourth, between 1776 and 1784. This was the system Samuel Livermore surely had in mind when he proposed to keep Congress from passing laws "touching religion." Only in 1819 did the New Hampshire legislature adopt a "Toleration Bill," which provided that "no person shall be compelled to join or support . . . any congregation, church or religious society without his express consent first had and obtained," thus ending the system of compulsory support for religion in the Granite State. Even then, New Hampshire retained its requirement that the governor be a Protestant, which lasted until after the Civil War and was the last vestige of formal establishment in any of the states.[40]

Massachusetts engaged in the most extensive debate over coerced tithes in the nation, other than Virginia. It occupied several weeks of the convention that produced the Constitution of 1780. Over vociferous opposition from Baptists and a few others, Massachusetts reaffirmed its system of localized establishments, indeed tightening the conditions under which dissenters could obtain exemption or direct their taxes to their own church. Under this system, each taxpayer was taxed for the support of "public Protestant teachers of piety, religion, and morality." A taxpayer was permitted to direct his taxes "to the support of the public teacher or teachers of his own religious sect or denomination, provided there be any on whose instructions he attends." Otherwise, the proceeds went "toward the support of the teacher or teachers of the parish or precinct in which the said moneys are raised." In important respects, this system was more restrictive than that voted down in Virginia. With minor modification, this system lasted until 1833.

We must look, then, to the debates in all these states, and not just that in Virginia, for an understanding of the arguments for and against compulsory support for religion. It is a mistake to assume that supporters of religious taxes were "religious" and opponents "secular." Support came from the civic republican tradition as well as from the formerly established churches accustomed to public support. Popular opposition was concentrated among the most intensely evangelical elements of society. Their opposition was largely theological in nature. According to the Baptists and other evangelical opponents of establishment, it is wrong not only to require someone "to furnish contributions of money for the propagation of opinions which he disbelieves," as Jefferson wrote, but also even to require congregants to furnish support for their own churches. Massachusetts observers marveled at the willingness of Baptists to go to jail or have their property distrained for failure to report their contributions to Baptist churches. The reason for this stubbornness was their belief that the support of religion is a duty to God alone, for which believers are not answerable to the state.[41] They insisted that religion must be voluntary not because it is unworthy of public support, but because "nothing can be true religion but a voluntary obedience unto [God's] revealed will."[42] It would be a form of idolatry—Madison called it "an unhallowed perversion of the means of salvation"—for people to conform their religious conduct to the dictates of the state rather than their own reading of scripture.

Supporters of assessments took issue with this perspective. To them, the requirement of paying to support religious instruction was not an effort to enforce a private religious obligation, but instead a means of ensuring the provision of effectual moral instruction for the betterment of society. This was a benefit that would inure to nonbelievers and believers alike, in much the way that public education is thought to benefit the whole of society by raising up good citizens and teaching proper civic values. The petition from Amelia County, Virginia, put it this way:

> As every Man in the State partakes of the Blessings of Peace and Order, which results no less from the Influence of Religion on the Minds of his Fellow citizens, than from the Operation of the laws, every Man should be obliged to contribute as well to the Support of Religion, as to that of Civil Government; nor has he any Reason to complain of this, as an Encroachment upon his religious Liberty, if he is permitted to worship God according to the Dictates of his Conscience . . . .

A Massachusetts advocate of assessment similarly urged that "religion, both in rulers and people [is] . . . of the highest importance to . . . civil society and government, . . . as it keeps alive the best sense of moral obligation, a matter of such extensive utility, especially in respect to an oath, which is one of the principal instruments

of government." While agreeing that compelled worship or attendance at worship would violate conscience, establishmentarians
denied that monetary exactions had any bearing on conscience.
Massachusetts Chief Justice Theophilus Parsons wrote that this
"objection seems to mistake a man's conscience for his money."[43]

This was the crux of the debate. All agreed that the state has
no business enforcing religious obligations, and all agreed that the
state may tax for the support of the common good, but the two sides
disagreed over whether taxes for the support of religious institutions
fell in the former or the latter category.

It is important to stress that, contrary to once-prevailing Supreme
Court doctrine (see Chapter 6), this conscience-based objection to
religious taxes did not imply opposition to the use of public funds
to support social services, such as schools, orphanages, or hospitals
when operated by religious institutions, even if they were imbued
with religious teaching. As Professor Mark Storslee has shown, states
including Virginia uncontroversially made grants to religious institutions for such purposes, and even staunchly separationist groups
like the Baptists sought and received support for such functions.
This was not seen as governmental enforcement of a religious obligation, like tithing or attending church. The conscientious objection was not to the financial assistance of religious organizations,
but to the governmental enforcement of specifically religious duties.
Thus, services that could be performed by secular as well as religious organizations were eligible for public assistance even under
anti-establishment principles.

Contrary to repeated assertions by the Supreme Court,[44] this
was true even of training for the ministry. Nearly every college in
colonial and early republican America provided clerical education.
For many—including William & Mary, Princeton, Harvard, Yale,
and Dartmouth—the training of a "learned and orthodox ministry" was declared to be their foremost purpose for existence. For

example, Harvard College, then a quasi-public institution and recipient of significant public financial support, was chartered under the Massachusetts Constitution of 1780 in terms that expressly recognized the college's role in educating the clergy:

> Whereas our wise and pious ancestors, so early as the year one thousand six hundred and thirty-six, laid the foundation of Harvard College, in which university many persons of great eminence have, by the blessing of God, been initiated in those arts and sciences, which qualified them for public employments, both in church and state . . .

Twenty-one percent of the student body at Princeton from 1776 to 1784, and 13 percent in the next decade, were studying for ministerial careers. Almost all these colleges received public funding.[45] Although Virginia and other states rejected proposals to impose taxes for the support of religious worship and instruction, they frequently and uncontroversially provided state support to schools and colleges that educated aspiring clergy. For example, the Maryland legislature voted to fund Washington College, which educated students in subjects "useful . . . for the service of their country in church and state," including divinity, at the same time it was rejecting a general assessment proposal for support of religion. No one thought these decisions were inconsistent. Baptists and Presbyterians, who opposed religious taxes, received state grants of aid for their institutions of higher learning in a number of states, which trained clergy along with law, medicine, science, classics, and other subject matter. The University of Virginia, founded in 1819 by Thomas Jefferson, was the first public institution not to offer degrees in divinity or theology, but neither the University of Virginia nor any other public university denied the benefits of their education to students who were studying for a clerical career.[46]

Appeals to conscience and the exclusive authority of God over religious observance formed the most common arguments against establishment, but almost as prevalent were arguments that government support is not necessary for religion, and indeed is more likely to be harmful. Dozens of petitions pointed out that the early church thrived not only in the absence of government support but also in the face of persecution. The Hanover Presbytery wrote: "Neither can it be made to appear that the gospel needs any such civil aid. We rather conceive that, when our blessed Saviour, declares his kingdom is not of this world, he renounces all dependence upon state power." Not only was state support not necessary, it was counterproductive. A petition from Rockbridge County, Virginia, declared that "this scheme [the General Assessment Bill] should it take place is the best calculated to destroy Religion that perhaps could be devised." Vermont disestablishmentarians declared that religious taxes were "detrimental to the interests of true Religion" because they had "a tendency to increase the number of hypocrites and infidels" and sowed dissension among denominations. Again, Madison concurred: "the policy of the bill is adverse to the diffusion of the light of Christianity."[47]

Why might this be so? First, if churches receive government money, they will lose their autonomy. As a Presbyterian petition warned:

> If the legislature has any rightful authority over the ministers of the gospel in the exercise of their sacred office, and if it is their duty to levy a maintenance for them as such, then . . . [they may] declare who shall preach, what they shall preach, to whom, when, and in what places they shall preach; or to impose any regulations and restrictions upon religious societies that they may judge expedient.[48]

Even today, many of the most difficult church-state questions involve the relation between the right of religious organizations to public assistance on the same terms as their secular counterparts and the strings that often are attached to that assistance.

Moreover, state financial support was expected to have a stultifying effect. According to Madison, government support tends to "weaken in those who profess this Religion a pious confidence in its innate excellence, and the patronage of its Author; and to foster in those who still reject it a suspicion that its friends are too conscious of its fallacies, to trust it to its own merits." Jefferson made the same point in economic terms, noting that the need to attract voluntary contributions provides "an additional incitement to earnest and unremitting labors for the instruction of mankind." The philosopher-historian David Hume, who thought that enthusiastic religion is a threat to civil society, supported the established Church of England precisely because he thought that guaranteed sinecures dampened the enthusiasm of the clergy and made them less effective, and therefore less dangerous. The revolutionaries in France evidently agreed: They put priests, ministers, and rabbis—those who took an oath of fealty to the new republic—on the payroll.[49]

CONCLUSION

The process was different in every state, but by the end of the first third of the nineteenth century, the states that had inherited a religious establishment from the colonial era had repealed those laws. State disestablishment provisions clarify the sort of laws the Establishment Clause prohibited the federal government from enacting: laws conditioning civil or political privileges on religious belief or affiliation; laws compelling church attendance or tithes;

laws interfering with church doctrine, governance, or administration; and laws authorizing a religious group to perform vital civic functions for the state. The First Amendment placed such laws beyond the federal government's reach from the beginning. It took another constitutional amendment to place them beyond the reach of the states too.

CHAPTER 4

Application of the Establishment Clause to the States

THE ESTABLISHMENT CLAUSE says that "Congress"—meaning the federal government[1]—"shall make no law respecting an establishment of religion." As we saw in Chapter 2, the peculiar language "respecting an establishment" makes clear that the national government may neither establish religion at the federal level nor pass laws affecting state establishments, which about half the states still had at the time. Yet since 1947 the Supreme Court has held that the clause "is incorporated against" the states; indeed, the majority of Establishment Clause cases involve states rather than the federal government. This strikes many as odd. As Justice Clarence Thomas has put it, this seems to "prohibit precisely what the Establishment Clause was intended to protect—*state* establishments of religion."[2] We believe the Court's conclusion that the Establishment Clause now applies to the states is *mostly* correct, but that the Court's reasons have been faulty.

THE BILL OF RIGHTS AND THE FOURTEENTH AMENDMENT

The Bill of Rights as proposed by the First Congress applied only to the federal government. In Madison's original proposal, this was clear because the amendments were appended to Article I, Section 9, which is confined to restrictions on federal power. Madison's proposal to protect the rights of conscience, press, and jury trial against potential violations by state governments, which was rejected, was appended to Section 10, which restricts the states. When the Bill of Rights was converted to a freestanding set of amendments at the end of the document, this created an ambiguity, which was solved by beginning the First Amendment with the words "Congress shall make no law . . .," making clear that these rights applied to the federal government rather than the states. Even so, as recounted in Chapter 2, some members of the First Congress worried that the establishment provision might indirectly undermine the then-existing state establishments of religion in places like Connecticut. That is why the language was revised to forbid Congress from making any law "respecting" an establishment of religion—meaning any law having to do with an establishment of religion. This prohibited two things: (1) any establishment of religion at the national level and (2) any federal interference with state establishments. The Supreme Court repeatedly held in the early nineteenth century that the Bill of Rights applied only to the federal government. One of those cases involved the Free Exercise Clause.[3] There was no doubt or uncertainty about this: The First Amendment Establishment Clause did not restrict the power of the states to establish religion.

In the years between adoption of the Bill of Rights and the Fourteenth Amendment, every state with a religious establishment abolished it, with Massachusetts the last to go, in 1833. The question of protecting state establishments from federal interference thus ceased to have much practical significance. By the time of the

Civil War, there had been a sea change in the way that many states assessed the relationship between Christianity and the law, based on an emerging consensus that the relation of man to God is a matter of conscience rather than legislation.

In 1868, after the Civil War, the Fourteenth Amendment was added to the Constitution. Section One forbids states from making or enforcing "any law which shall abridge the privileges or immunities of citizens of the United States"; from depriving "any person of life, liberty, or property, without due process of law"; and from denying anyone "the equal protection of the laws." Although the evidence is mixed, we are persuaded by the historians who argue that the architects of the Fourteenth Amendment understood Section One to apply the individual freedoms set forth in the Bill of Rights to the states, especially to protect the rights of freedmen and religious dissenters in the South.[4] The slave states of the South had violated almost every freedom enshrined in the Bill of Rights, not only against enslaved persons, who had virtually no legal rights, but also against abolitionists and others who dared to speak out against the Peculiar Institution. For example, as Lyman Trumbull noted when introducing the Civil Rights Act of 1866, southern states had prohibited Black Americans from "exercising the functions of a minister of the Gospel." Senator Henry Wilson remarked in 1864 that the southern states had violated the "great rights" of the First Amendment, which were "essential to liberty." No wonder that the victorious side in the Civil War sought to protect those rights by constitutional amendment.[5]

In its first encounters with the Fourteenth Amendment, however, the Supreme Court rejected the argument that the Amendment applied the rights of the Bill of Rights to the states.[6] That seemed to conclude the matter—for a time. Beginning in the late nineteenth century, the Court began a process of "selective incorporation" of some but not all parts of the Bill of Rights—those understood to protect rights that the justices deemed "fundamental" or "implicit in the concept of ordered liberty."[7] Free speech was "incorporated" in 1925, free exercise of religion in 1940, nonestablishment in 1947, and the right to keep and bear arms in 2010. The most recent addition to the list was the Sixth Amendment's right to a unanimous jury for criminal convictions. The rule now seems to be that all "personal" rights are incorporated.

The Court's textual hook for this incorporation has been the Due Process Clause. As one justice put it: "Some of the personal rights safeguarded by the first eight Amendments against national action may also be safeguarded against state action, because a denial of them would be a denial of due process of law."[8] This is linguistically implausible. By clear negative implication, the Due Process Clause *allows* the deprivation of life, liberty, and property *with* due process of law, meaning proper legislative enactments enforced through proper procedures.[9] It twists the words to say that it prohibits deprivation of liberty even *with* due process.

There is, however, another provision of the Fourteenth Amendment that, by its terms, protects substantive rights against infringement by the states: the Privileges or Immunities Clause. This Clause provides that "No State shall make or enforce any law that shall abridge the privileges or immunities of citizens of the United States." The terms "privileges" and "immunities" are old-fashioned synonyms for what we would call "rights"—privileges being affirmative rights and immunities being negative rights. What are the privileges or immunities "of citizens of the United States"? There are several possible answers to that question, but one linguistically plausible answer is: those rights listed in the Bill of Rights (plus habeas corpus and a few other rights found elsewhere in the Constitution). And indeed, Senator Jacob Howard, who introduced the draft Fourteenth Amendment on the floor of the Senate, explained the Clause in that way, as did Representative John Bingham, the leading drafter in the House.[10] The Supreme Court, however, has stubbornly stuck to its implausible Due Process theory, with the exceptions of Justices Hugo Black, Neil Gorsuch, and Thomas. The majority seem to prefer making mincemeat of the words of the Amendment to admitting that the Court got it wrong in the 1870s.[11]

In fairness, the issue of incorporation is more complicated and contested than this simple account may suggest. There are whole books written on the incorporation issue, and reputable scholars on both sides. We need not get into those complexities here, because no justice of the Supreme Court now questions the applicability of the personal rights of the Bill of Rights to the states, under one clause of the Fourteenth Amendment or another.

THE SPECIAL PROBLEM POSED BY THE ESTABLISHMENT CLAUSE

The Establishment Clause, however, raises a special challenge for the incorporation theory. Even assuming all the personal rights in the Bill of Rights are applicable to the states through the Fourteenth Amendment, how is it possible to incorporate a provision—"no law respecting an establishment of religion"—that strips the federal government of power over state establishments? If the Establishment Clause reserved to the states the power to establish or disestablish religion, as they chose, how could that be "applied" to the states so as to take away the very power the Clause reserves to them? Justice Potter Stewart rightly commented that "it is not without irony that a constitutional provision evidently designed to leave the States free to go their own way should now have become a restriction upon their autonomy."[12] If the Establishment Clause is viewed solely as a jurisdictional provision, reserving a particular subject area to the states, it would not appear to be a guarantee of personal rights, appropriate for incorporation, but instead a federalism provision, enforceable by the states *against* the federal government.[13]

The answer, we think, lies in the dual nature of the establishment protection. The "respecting" language was carefully chosen to accomplish two quite different things: (1) to reserve the states' power to establish religion, or not, and (2) to prohibit Congress from establishing a religion at the national level. The first aspect cannot, by its nature, be "incorporated" against the states. In effect, the first part was simply superseded first by state-level disestablishments and then by the Fourteenth Amendment. Fourteenth Amendment disestablishment aroused little attention and no opposition because by this time no state wished to exercise that prerogative. To be sure, there existed vestigial state practices that were inconsistent with the full scope of disestablishment, but no one at the time was thinking at that level of detail.

The second aspect—that the Clause disabled Congress from "establish[ing] a religion, and enforc[ing] the legal observation of it by law," in Madison's paraphrase—is easily understood as a personal rights provision. It meant that the federal government could not compel religious attendance or support, control religious doctrine or personnel, or do any of the other things that constituted the "church by law established." Broadly speaking, the Establishment Clause prohibited government from regulating religion, from favoring one religion over another, and from compelling persons to engage in religious practices, and the Free Exercise Clause protected the right of all persons to practice the religious faith they freely adopted. Both were, in large part, personal rights, and both could be "incorporated" against the states without logical difficulty. Viewed in this way, it is not at all mysterious that legally significant aspects of the Establishment Clause are applicable to state governments.

There remain, however, a few anomalies. Some aspects of disestablishment do not obviously affect personal rights, such as the prohibition on the use of religious institutions for public functions like recordkeeping, the proclamation of holy days, the formal declaration of religious doctrine, or governmental display of religious symbols. For those who think that the Establishment Clause is strictly limited to coercive government acts, such policies pose a conundrum.

There are two possible answers. First, it could be that some noncoercive acts, such as declaring an official religion, violate the Establishment Clause but no one has standing to challenge them in court. That is not so odd—there are many constitutional violations that never make it to court because no one has standing to challenge them. Second, it could be that the Fourteenth Amendment does not incorporate against the states those requirements of the Establishment Clause that do not protect rights. Under either theory, the states would remain morally and constitutionally obligated to respect the rights protected by the Clause, even if the courts cannot hold them accountable.

THE BLAINE AMENDMENT PUZZLE

This leaves one unresolved historical puzzle. Prior to the arrival of large numbers of Irish Catholics on these shores, government aid to primary education was almost invariably pluralistic, in the sense that aid was provided on more or less neutral terms to any school, no matter what its religious or denominational connection. There were no public schools, in the modern sense, in the early decades of the nineteenth century, and schools were invariably religious in some sense. By the 1870s, however, state-level disputes between Protestants and Catholics over school funding morphed into a national political issue. In the middle of the nineteenth century, some people began to advocate the exclusive support of "nonsectarian" schools—schools that taught common-denominator religious and moral principles but were not connected to the specific tenets of any sect. Protestants, fueled in many cases by nativism and anti-Catholic bigotry, opposed funding Catholic schools as "sectarian," while regarding generically Protestant schools as acceptable. Catholics obviously could not agree: "Nonsectarian" schools were objectionable because they incorporated the King James Bible and Protestant prayers into the curriculum.

In 1875, presidential candidate James G. Blaine proposed a constitutional amendment that would have interfered with state authority over education.[14] It is useful to have the entire text of the proposed amendment at hand for understanding its implications:

> No State shall make any law respecting an establishment of religion or prohibiting the free exercise thereof; and no money raised by taxation in any State for the support of public schools, or derived from any public fund therefor, nor any public lands devoted thereto, shall ever be under the control of any religious sect, nor shall any money so raised or lands so devoted be divided between religious sects or denominations.[15]

This version of the bill passed the House by the requisite two-thirds majority. A more sweeping version got a 28–16 majority in the Senate. This being short of two-thirds, the amendment failed, but it remained a lively political issue for many years.[16]

The puzzle is this: Why would Congress have thought it necessary to amend the Constitution to apply the Religion Clauses to the states if they believed that the Fourteenth Amendment had already done so? We think there is a ready solution. The core of the proposal was its prohibition on religious school funding. Such a prohibition was a departure from the consensus understanding of the religion clauses. Federal, state, and local governments had for decades funded religious schools, never regarding this as an incident of an establishment. A handful of "common school" proponents had argued that principles of religious liberty forbade funding religious schools, but until anti-Catholic and anti-immigrant sentiment came to dominate the debate, most rejected that argument. As recently as the Freedmen's Bureau Act (1865), the bulk of federal aid to education was channeled through "benevolent associations," most of which were missionary societies connected to the various religious denominations. Although some educators were critical of the missionary focus of these schools, to our knowledge they did not frame the issue in terms of church-state separation.[17] The point of the Blaine proposal was to alter this constitutional understanding, effectively to amend the settled meaning of the Establishment and Free Exercise Clauses. It was rhetorically strategic to wrap the controversial change in the comfortable garb of revered constitutional language. The proposal therefore casts no serious doubt on the incorporation thesis, though its failure does suggest that Americans considered—and rejected—an extreme no-funding position.

It is interesting, also, that the Senate amended the proposal to forbid it from being "construed to prohibit the reading of the Bible in any school or institution." Bible reading in public schools had long generated intense Catholic-Protestant animosity. Protestants typically advocated the use of the King James Bible, "without note or comment." Catholics refused to go along, based on their view that the Bible must be read in light of the authoritative teaching of the church. They therefore demanded that Catholic students be permitted to use the Douay translation of the Bible, which contained extensive notes reflecting church teaching, as well as the intertestamental books recognized as canonical by the Catholic Church but not by Protestants. In some states, Catholic students were beaten for refusing to read from the King James Bible.[18] Disputes of this sort led Catholics to create their own school systems—which in turn led to disputes over a fair allocation of school funds, the topic of the Blaine Amendment. The proposed amendment thus should not be seen as a precursor to modern separationism, but as combining anti-Catholic positions on private school funding and public school prayer. Application of the First Amendment to the states was a sideshow.

PART II

. . .

Modern Controversies

CHAPTER 5

The Rise and Fall of the *Lemon* Test

THE SUPREME COURT said almost nothing about the Establishment Clause until the middle of the twentieth century.[1] The only significant debates about the scope and application of the Clause in the nineteenth century were in Congress. As a result, the Supreme Court had no reason to craft judicial doctrine. In *Everson v. Board of Education* (1948), after holding that the Clause applies to the states, the Court relied on a limited swath of founding-era history to determine that the government may not support even the nonreligious activities of religious schools. The Court endorsed Thomas Jefferson's assertion that the Clause was meant to erect a "wall of separation between church and state," emphasizing separationism—one, but only one, of the concerns originally animating the Clause. The Court seemed to embrace two contradictory ideas: that religious institutions must be excluded from public support even when they perform secular functions, simply because they are religious, and that no one may be discriminated against on account of their religion, without seeming to realize that these principles are inconsistent. The four dissenting justices wholeheartedly embraced the "no-aid" view, which eventually came to dominate the Court's thinking—except when it didn't.

Over the ensuing decades, after applying the Establishment Clause to prayer in public schools, tax exemptions for churches, and accommodations for religious dissenters, the Court sought to consolidate its scattershot Establishment Clause jurisprudence into a single "test." In *Lemon v. Kurtzman* (1971), another school-funding case, the Court laid down three rules: A law (1) must have a secular purpose, (2) must have a "primary effect" that "neither advances nor inhibits religion," and (3) may not foster an "excessive entanglement" between government and religion. Failure to meet any of these three rules rendered a law unconstitutional. For three decades, the Court treated the *Lemon* test as a one-size-fits-all doctrine for evaluating establishment claims, applying it to a wide array of factual scenarios. Over the last two decades, the Court has rarely relied on the *Lemon* test, instead crafting more context-specific doctrines in various categories of cases. The rest of Part II of this book is about the doctrines that apply in those contexts, but it is impossible to understand those doctrines without understanding what they replaced, and why.

The *Lemon* test had three strikes against it from the beginning. It was plagued by conceptual ambiguity, overemphasized separationism at the expense of religious freedom, and was a mismatch with the historical understanding of disestablishment. Consider the "secular purpose" requirement. It is important to note that under the *Lemon* test, a law's lack of a secular purpose alone, regardless of its effect on religion, would invalidate it. One of the questions this raises is what counts as a law's purpose? The motivation of those who voted for it? If so, the secular purpose requirement differs from the rule in most other constitutional contexts. Generally, the Court declines to invalidate a government action solely on the basis that the decision makers had an unconstitutional motive. Why declare a law without a secular purpose unconstitutional if it has no effect on religion one way or the other? Moreover, what does it mean to say that a law's purpose is *secular*: Does it mean that it could not be supported by a religious reason? What if the government enacts laws, like the prohibition on murder, that coincide with religious teaching? What if the majority of citizens, based on their religious convictions, think it is wrong for the government to engage in certain activities, like the funding of embryonic stem cell research? The secular purpose requirement of the *Lemon* test raised these questions but provided no coherent way to answer them.

The rule that a law must have the "primary effect of neither advancing nor inhibiting religion" also has ambiguities. First, if a government action has many effects, which one is "primary"? When the government pays for computers or textbooks for a religious school, is the "primary" effect to promote education or to "advance religion"? Just two years after *Lemon*, the Court recognized that the term "primary" calls for "metaphysical judgments [that] are neither possible nor necessary" and reformulated the test to ask whether the government action has "the direct and immediate effect of advancing religion."[2] That was not a mere change in words; it made the test more exacting. It is also oddly asymmetrical with the secular purpose test. If government action has any nontrivial secular purpose it will be upheld, but if it has any "direct and immediate" religious effect it will be struck down.

Second, whether a government action "advances or inhibits religion" depends on the baseline for comparison. Suppose the government institutes a military draft and a religious objector seeks an accommodation. Would granting the accommodation—without granting one for a nonreligious concern, like working on the family farm—"advance religion"? Or would denying the accommodation "inhibit religion"? If the government subsidizes a broad range of activities on a neutral basis, does it "advance" religion to include religious activities that satisfy the neutral criteria? Or would it "inhibit" religion to exclude them? Third, is the "effect" test concerned with the mechanism by which any government action ends up "advancing" religion? If the law allows individuals to use benefits in either a secular or a religious way, on a neutral basis, is it the *government*, or the *beneficiary*, that has advanced religion?

The "secular purpose" and "primary effect" rules both tilt the scales against religious liberty. The secular purpose rule makes it unclear whether citizens and officials can bring religious reasons to bear on policy proposals. Excluding religious voices from public affairs would interfere with rights of religious exercise, speech, press, and assembly. The "primary effect" rule, for its part, could be construed to invalidate laws that attempt to accommodate religious exercise—even though such accommodations by definition exempt only those who dissent from government policy. These implications of the *Lemon* test elevated one purpose of the Establishment Clause—separation of church and state—above individual and corporate religious liberty. Furthermore, they set Establishment Clause doctrine on a collision course with the Free Exercise and Free Speech Clauses of the First Amendment.

The "no excessive entanglement" rule is the most mysterious, but perhaps the most enduring component of the *Lemon* test. What is "government entanglement with religion," and when does it become "excessive"? Over the years, the Court has alluded to several possible conceptions of "entanglement." "Administrative entanglement" occurs when governmental authorities interact with religious institutions. A typical example is when the government monitors private organizations receiving government funds to ensure they are not used for religious purposes. "Political entanglement" occurs when a government decision produces, or results from, political division along religious lines. Another form of "entanglement" occurs when the government is called upon to resolve religious disputes. As

James Madison famously said, the government is an "incompetent judge of religious truth." Some of these ideas bear close resemblance to the historic purposes of disestablishment. Some do not.

Especially in funding cases, the *Lemon* test proved to be unreasonably restrictive and incoherent. As discussed more fully in Chapter 6, state and local governments during the *Lemon* era sought ways to give low- and moderate-income families a broader range of educational choices and to relieve overcrowding of public schools. This became an urgent matter of public policy because public schools in urban areas were often of disastrously poor quality. One might think that the government should be concerned only about educational quality, but the *Lemon* test forced school districts to be "certain" that education supported with public funds was not tainted with religious teaching. At the same time, the *Lemon* test treated governmental attempts to enforce this secularization rule as a forbidden "entanglement." The "effects" and "entanglement" prongs of the *Lemon* test thus created a "Catch-22" (the Court's own description!) that threatened the government's ability to partner with religious providers of public goods, partnerships that had endured for decades or longer. When a court describes its own doctrine as a Catch-22, you know there is a problem.

As each of the following chapters explains, the Court has abandoned the *Lemon* test, one factual context at a time. Instead of a single Establishment Clause test, the Court has developed context-sensitive doctrines. We think this approach better reflects not only the original understanding of the Clause but also the full panoply of concerns originally animating disestablishment, including, importantly, equal religious liberty.

For two decades, the Supreme Court repeatedly ignored the *Lemon* test, even while lower courts continued to feel bound by it, leading to a bizarre situation where different legal principles were applied on appeal to the High Court than had governed the district and appellate proceedings. No wonder almost every Supreme Court Establishment Clause case during this period was a reversal.

Justice Antonin Scalia famously likened the test to "some ghoul in a late-night horror movie that repeatedly sits up in its grave and shuffles abroad, after being repeatedly killed and buried." Scalia's theory as to *Lemon*'s longevity was that "it is so easy to kill. It is there to scare us (and our audience) when we wish it to do so, but we can command it to return to the tomb at will. . . . Such a docile and useful monster is worth keeping around, at least in a somnolent state; one never knows when one might need him."[3]

In 2019, in a case about a public religious symbol (see Chapter 9), a plurality of the Court joined an opinion criticizing the *Lemon* test and its "endorsement test" variation, but Justice Elena Kagan, who joined most of the opinion, refused to make a fifth vote for formally overruling *Lemon*. Scalia's "monster" was badly wounded but not yet dead. Then in 2022, in *Kennedy v. Bremerton School District*, a case about a public high school football coach's after-game prayers, the Court described the *Lemon* test as "ambitious, abstract, and ahistorical" and announced that "this Court long ago abandoned *Lemon*." It is true that the Court had long ago "abandoned" the *Lemon* test in the sense that it had decided its last seven Establishment Clause cases without relying on the test, but it had never uttered the fateful word "overruled." This is significant because lower courts are instructed to follow Supreme Court holdings until expressly overruled. It is not enough that the Supreme Court has decided cases that reject the "reasoning" of the precedent; they must "leav[e] to this Court the prerogative of overruling its own decisions." It is therefore odd, and must be frustrating to lower courts, that the *Bremerton* opinion refrained from saying straightforwardly that the *Lemon* test was "overruled." The reason for its choice of words is probably that the John Roberts Court does not wish to be seen as contemptuous toward stare decisis, and it had already explicitly overruled one iconic

case that term, *Roe v. Wade*. Nonetheless, whatever word was used—
"abandoned" rather than "overruled"—it is safe to say that Scalia's
"monster" has now been slain.[4]

What replaces *Lemon*, though, is uncertain. The *Bremerton*
opinion states that "in place of *Lemon* and the endorsement test,
this Court has instructed that the Establishment Clause must be
interpreted by 'reference to historical practices and understandings.'" That points to a methodology—some combination of originalism and long-standing practice[5]—but it is not a "test" that will
bring consistency to lower court opinions. In cases like *Bremerton*,
which involved allegations that the coach's prayers violated the
Establishment Clause, it is hard to know what "historical practices
and understandings" courts could consult: There were no public
schools at the founding, and therefore no public school football
coaches, and until 1962 it was not thought unconstitutional for
teachers to lead their students in prayer. In our view, *Bremerton* correctly held that the coach was free to pray in his private capacity
after the games, so long as he did not push students to join him. The
relevant legal principles come from the *School Prayer* decisions and
the state action doctrine, not from historical practices and understandings about teachers or coaches or football games.

In the remainder of this book, we will describe how the historically informed purposes of the Establishment Clause give guidance
in a variety of contexts.

CHAPTER 6

Accommodation of Religious Exercise

ACCOMMODATIONS OF RELIGION, as defined by Justice William J. Brennan, are governmental policies that "exempt, when possible, from generally applicable governmental regulation individuals whose religious beliefs and practices would otherwise thereby be infringed, or [create] without state involvement an atmosphere in which voluntary religious exercise may flourish."[1] They are as old as the republic—older, actually—but in the context of today's culture wars they have become one of the most controversial features of Establishment Clause law. This is partly because the increasingly sharp divide between secular and religious elements of our culture has made the facilitation of religious exercise seem partisan and problematic, in ways that were not true in the past. Perhaps more importantly, some of the most conspicuous forms of religious accommodation in recent years—though far from the most common, numerically—have involved religiously motivated resistance to triumphs of the cultural left with respect to hot-button issues like abortion, same-sex marriage, and transgender rights. For many, there is simply no room for exceptions or accommodations on matters of that magnitude.

There are both civil libertarian and pragmatic reasons to accommodate religious conscience. First is the general respect our society has for religious conscience and the diversity it entails. As Madison wrote in his most famous statement on religious freedom, "The duty of every man to render to the Creator such homage, and such only, as he believes to be acceptable to him . . . is precedent both in order of time and in degree of obligation, to the claims of Civil Society."[2] A diversity of religious faiths, free to practice their beliefs even if divergent from prevailing norms, is a hallmark of liberal democracy. Moreover, as a pragmatic matter, accommodating dissenters makes it easier to build coalitions to enact legislation in the face of social divisions. Without accommodations, dissenters will have the incentive to fight legal change with all the force they can muster, but they may relax their efforts if they will remain free to conform their own behavior (and that of their churches) to their own beliefs. Finally, it may be more trouble than it is worth to coerce conscientious objectors. It would be expensive to prosecute and punish Quakers for refusing to go to war. Why not offer them the alternative of noncombat service? Why attempt to force the Little Sisters of the Poor to pay for abortions? Given the strength of their conviction, they are unlikely to comply, and the punishment only gets in the way of their good works. In short, accommodations often are a win-win solution for the problem of ineradicable conscientious differences. Government policies do not always have to be universally enforced to be effective. It is one thing to oppose accommodations when they would result in material harm to others, but sometimes opposition stems from indignation at the dissenters' refusal to conform to the will of the majority. In those cases, the anti-establishment principle warns against using the power of the state to enforce conformity.

ACCOMMODATION OF RELIGION AT THE FOUNDING

Throughout our history, courts have struggled to decide whether the principle of free exercise of religion entails the right to an exemption from a general law that would otherwise require believers to violate contrary religious commands—that is, a right enforceable in court. In the decades between Independence and the Civil War, about half the state courts faced with the question answered "yes" and about half answered "no."[3] Today the answer seems to be "sometimes."

From the beginning, though, legislatures and executive officials have exempted religious believers from general laws where they thought any damage to the public weal from those exceptions was outweighed by the importance of religious freedom. As Washington wrote to the Society of Quakers, "In my opinion the Consciencious [*sic*] scruples of all men should be treated with great delicacy and tenderness, and it is my wish and desire that the Laws may always be as extensively accommodated to them, as a due regard for the Protection and essential Interests of the Nation may Justify, and permit."[4] During the early republic there were relatively few conflicts between legal requirements and religious exercise. Americans, who were overwhelmingly Protestant, disagreed on matters of theology and modes of worship but largely agreed about morality and how the law should enforce it. Even still, religious minorities sometimes needed an accommodation and the government often provided one, on such matters as oath requirements, compulsory jury service, sabbath laws, the priest-penitent privilege, marriage laws, and import restrictions. Such accommodations were never seen as an establishment of religion. Indeed, since accommodations enabled people to carry out beliefs *contrary* to the majority, they were in a sense the *opposite* of an establishment, promoting diversity and dissent rather than uniformity. Even courts that declined to extend religious accommodations under state constitutional provisions invariably noted that principles of disestablishment did not stand in the way of the legislature providing such accommodations by law.[5] As Professor Douglas Laycock has put it, "There is virtually no evidence that anyone thought [religious accommodations] were constitutionally *prohibited* or that they were part of an establishment of religion."[6]

The leading example is exemption from compulsory military service, which was common in colonial law, enacted by the Continental Congress during the Revolution, supported publicly by Washington and Madison, constitutionalized in some state constitutions, and incorporated in every federal conscription statute in American history. When first challenged as an establishment during World War I, the Supreme Court responded, unanimously:

> We pass without anything but statement the proposition that an establishment of a religion or an interference with the free exercise thereof repugnant to the First Amendment resulted from the exemption clauses of the [draft statute] because we think its unsoundness is too apparent to require us to do more.[7]

The First Congress's debate over draft exemptions, during consideration of the Bill of Rights, provides the best evidence of the founders' attitude toward religious accommodations. Following a suggestion by James Madison, the House Select Committee proposed to include within what is now the Second Amendment the provision "no person religiously scrupulous shall be compelled to bear arms." This would have constitutionalized the draft exemption for religious objectors as a matter of federal law. The proposal narrowly passed the House and was rejected in the Senate, where the debate was not recorded. In the House, much of the debate centered on whether objectors should be required to "pay an equivalent"—meaning to pay a sum sufficient to hire someone else to take the objector's place. This did not bear on the legitimacy of accommodations but only on the form that the accommodation should take. This form of the amendment was rejected on the ground that "those who are religiously scrupulous of bearing arms, are equally scrupulous of getting substitutes or paying an equivalent." Several days later, the Select Committee version was amended to read "no person religiously scrupulous shall be compelled to bear arms in person," which left the question of substitutes to legislative discretion. No one expressed the view that either version of the exemption would constitute an establishment of religion, though one member suggested it would violate the right of the people to bear arms. Egbert Benson of New York gave the most extensive analysis of the ground for opposition. "[I] would always leave it to the benevolence of the Legislature," he said. "No man can claim this indulgence of right. It may be a religious persuasion, but it is no natural right, and therefore ought to be left to the discretion of the Government." Benson's argument counts against the claim that the Free Exercise Clause demands a draft exemption, but also against any claim that the Establishment Clause prohibits it.[8]

The same First Congress made provision for hiring military chaplains. This is an accommodation of a different sort—where the government so controls a particular institutional or physical environment that its affirmative assistance is needed to enable people trapped in that environment to practice their faith. The military, prisons, and schools are classic examples. When troops are stationed in some distant place far from their homes—perhaps in a country without churches that could tend to their religious needs—soldiers will be unable to worship if the army does not provide ministers, buildings, and necessary religious paraphernalia. In 1775, during the Revolutionary War, the Continental Congress created the Chaplain Corps, providing one chaplain for each regiment. After ratification of the Constitution, Congress continued the Chaplain Corps, and it has been a routine part of the military ever since. This kind of accommodation might appear to violate ordinary church-state separation in ways that would never be tolerable in ordinary circumstances. The government selects, hires, and pays clergy; the government erects places of worship; the government determines which faiths are numerous enough to warrant the cost of accommodation. None of this would be permissible in ordinary civil society, but Congress judges that the alternative, which is denial of the chance to worship to thousands of military personnel, would be a more serious affront to First Amendment values. When challenged in court hundreds of years later by Harvard students with time on their hands, a federal court of appeals upheld the practice of military chaplaincies as an accommodation.[9]

The First Congress also appointed legislative chaplains for the House and the Senate. This is harder to justify, especially now that the capital city is filled with religious institutions of every description, which members of Congress are free to use. It is possible that legislative chaplaincies were thought compatible with the Establishment Clause because they were not an exercise of Congress's power to enact "law," which is all that the First Amendment covers, but instead an exercise of each House's power to choose its officers, like sergeants-at-arms, clerks, and the like. In any event, the Supreme Court eventually upheld the legislative chaplaincy on purely historical grounds, without serious attempt to analyze why it might be constitutional under general principles.[10]

ACCOMMODATIONS OF RELIGION IN THE MODERN ERA

Accommodations have been a normal part of the religious-political landscape for most of our history. In 1992, a scholar counted over 2,000 accommodations in federal and state law, targeting specific religious practices. His study illustrates the breadth and diversity of accommodation laws:

> In the United States Code, for example, exemptions exist in food inspection laws for the ritual slaughter of animals, and for the preparation of food in accordance with religious practices. The tax laws contain numerous exemptions for religious groups and allow deductions for contributions to religious organizations. Federal copyright laws contain an exemption for materials that are to be used for religious purposes. Antidiscrimination laws, including Title VII, the Fair Housing Act, and the Aid to the Disabled Act, contain exemptions for religious organizations. Ministers are automatically exempt from compulsory military training and service. Aliens seeking asylum can do so on the grounds that they will suffer religious persecution if returned to their home countries and gambling laws contain an exemption for religious organizations. Those in the military may wear religious apparel while wearing their uniforms, subject to limitations imposed by the Secretary of Defense. And . . . federal drug laws contain an exemption for the religious use of peyote by members of the Native American Church.[11]

After the Court drastically reduced the availability of constitutionally required accommodations under the Free Exercise Clause in *Employment Division v. Smith* (1992), attention shifted to the legislative sphere. Congress and some twenty-one states enacted generalized accommodation laws, and some state supreme courts stuck with pre-*Smith* interpretations of free exercise. The Religious Freedom Restoration Act (RFRA) provides an accommodation from any federal law that substantially burdens religious exercise unless the law is the "least restrictive means" of "achieving a compelling government interest." The Religious Land Use and Institutionalized Persons Act (RLUIPA) imposes a similar compelling interest requirement on both state and federal agencies with respect to land use decisions and the treatment of prisoners. Title VII of the Civil Rights Act of 1964 requires employers to make "reasonable accommodations, short of undue hardship" for the religious needs of their workers. The National Environmental Protection Act, the Native American Graves Protection and Repatriation Act, and the National Historic Preservation Act provide some (though inadequate) protection for Native American sacred sites. Accommodations of religion are thus extremely common—some targeted at particular threats to particular religious practices and some much more general.

Starting in the 1960s, however, lawyers began to argue that legislative accommodations that are not required by the Free Exercise Clause violate the Establishment Clause. Sometimes they sought to extend the accommodations to nonreligious conscientious objectors, and sometimes their object was to strike down the accommodation for everyone. The *Lemon* test (discussed in Chapter 5) provided potent ammunition against accommodations. Interpreted woodenly, as courts were wont to do in the 1970s and 1980s, each of the three parts of the Lemon test seemed to categorically bar accommodations:

- Accommodations have no nonreligious purpose and undermine the "secular purpose" of the general law by creating exceptions based exclusively on religious objections.
- The "effect" of accommodation laws is to favor religion over nonreligion by conferring a benefit (exemption from general law) on an explicitly religious basis.
- Accommodation laws typically involve an "entanglement" between government and religion because they require officials to assess the nature and sincerity of religious claims.

On closer examination, this critique was highly implausible. If correct, it would condemn the Free Exercise Clause itself. The Free Exercise Clause lacks any "secular purpose"—unless protection for religious freedom is itself a secular purpose. It protects only the free exercise of "religion," and therefore can be derided as a religious preference. And by requiring government to consider how government action affects religion, it entails entanglement between government and religion. If *Lemon*'s condemnation of accommodations were an accurate interpretation of the Establishment Clause, then the two halves of the religion provisions of the First Amendment would be at war with one another.

This seeming inconsistency inspired the first of many pushbacks against the *Lemon* test. In the mid-1980s, the Department of Justice filed a series of briefs arguing that the *Lemon* test was ill-suited to the evaluation of accommodations of religion.[12] The arguments attracted the attention of Justice Sandra Day O'Connor. In a case involving a moment-of-silence law, she pointed out that "it is disingenuous to look for a purely secular purpose when the manifest objective of a statute is to facilitate the free exercise of religion by lifting a government-imposed burden. Instead, the Court should simply acknowledge that the religious purpose of such a statute is legitimated by the Free Exercise Clause." As to the effect of an accommodation law, she urged that "courts should assume that the 'objective observer' is acquainted with the Free Exercise Clause and the values it promotes."[13]

It took just a few years and a few discordant cases before the full Court embraced this way of looking at religious accommodations. In 1987, in *Corporation of Presiding Bishop v. Amos*,[14] a case involving a provision of Title VII of the Civil Rights Act of 1964 exempting religious organizations from the prohibition of employment discrimination on the basis of religion, the Court unanimously rejected applying the *Lemon* test to accommodations. The case was brought by a janitor in a church-owned gymnasium, who argued that the exemption was unconstitutional insofar as it extended to employees whose jobs were of a nonreligious nature. Based on *Lemon*, the lower court agreed.

The Supreme Court did not. "This Court has long recognized that the government may (and sometimes must) accommodate religious practices and that it may do so without violating the Establishment Clause." It rejected the idea that the "secular purpose" rule of the *Lemon* test requires that "the law's purpose must be unrelated to religion." The Court affirmed that "it is a permissible legislative purpose to alleviate significant governmental interference with the ability of religious organizations to define and carry out their religious missions." It did not matter that religious organizations might not have a constitutional right to an accommodation of this breadth; it was sufficient that the law, without the accommodation, would impose a "significant burden" on religious exercise, which the legislature chose not to impose. That would seem to green-light accommodations of religion, at least with respect to the first part of the *Lemon* test.

The Court outright rejected the argument that accommodations are invalid because they single out religion for protection not accorded comparable secular entities. Acknowledging that some of its precedents had "given weight to this consideration," the Court announced that "where, as here, government acts with the proper purpose of lifting a regulation that burdens the exercise of religion, we see no reason to require that the exemption comes packaged with benefits to secular entities." The Court also insisted that the effect of an accommodation law must be judged against the baseline of the religious organization's rights prior to the enactment of the law from which the exemption is granted. Because "the Church's ability to propagate its religious doctrine . . . [is no] greater now than it was prior to the passage of the Civil Rights Act in 1964," the Court could not "see how any advancement of religion achieved by the Gymnasium can be fairly attributed to the Government, as opposed to the Church." This is one of the most important points in the decision. Statutes and policies regulating religious activities but also making accommodations from those regulations must be evaluated as a whole. If the government tells building owners they may not enlarge their facilities (as happened in *City of Boerne v. Flores* [1997]) but then exempts churches, churches are no better off than they were before enactment of the regulation.

The *Amos* majority easily dismissed the "no excessive entanglement" rule in one sentence: "It cannot be seriously contended that [the religious exemption] impermissibly entangles church and state; the statute effectuates a more complete separation of the two and avoids the kind of intrusive inquiry into religious belief that the District Court engaged in in this case." As Justice Brennan explained more fully in his concurring opinion, the Title VII exemption eliminated any need for the government to figure out which jobs within a religious organization are religious and which are not, a religion-sensitive question the government is not competent to resolve (see Chapter 10). As the *Amos* case illustrates, it is often true that either course—exempting or not exempting religion from regulation—will entail some degree of involvement between regulators and churches (or religious individuals). Given that entanglement will be present either way, it does not make sense to interpret the *Lemon* test as a thumb on the scales against accommodation.

Having reinterpreted each of the three parts of the *Lemon* test in a way that renders the test compatible with religious accommodations, the Court stated that it "need not reexamine" the *Lemon* test itself. No longer would that test be a wrecking ball for any and all governmental efforts to alleviate burdens on the exercise of religion. This became all the more important three years after *Amos*, when the Court reinterpreted the Free Exercise Clause to eliminate most constitutionally mandated religious exemptions from general laws. After that decision—*Employment Division v. Smith* (the "Peyote Case") (1990)—virtually all accommodations became a matter of legislative discretion rather than judicially enforceable constitutional command. If *Amos* had left in place the interpretation of the *Lemon* test under which nonconstitutionally required accommodations were vulnerable to Establishment Clause challenge, it would have been the end of the nation's long tradition of religious accommodations.

It must be stressed, however, that the *Amos* decision did not give a stamp of approval to all accommodations. "At some point," the Court cautioned, "accommodation may devolve into 'an unlawful fostering of religion.'" Because "these are not such cases," the Court did not offer any guidance about what those limits might be. In a series of cases over the next few years, the Court explored various challenges to particular features of religious accommodations, eventually announcing a new three-part test bearing no resemblance to *Lemon*.

Cutter v. Wilkinson (2005),[15] another unanimous decision, upheld the federal Religious Land Use and Institutionalized Persons Act. The statute entitles individuals confined in prisons, hospitals, and other such facilities to accommodations from policies that substantially burden their religious exercise unless the government can show that those policies achieve a compelling public interest in the least restrictive manner. Writing for the Court, Justice Ruth Bader Ginsburg declined to apply the *Lemon* test, instead concluding that the law is constitutional for satisfying three principles:

- the accommodation "alleviates exceptional government-created burdens on private religious exercise";
- is neutral *among* religions; and
- "take[s] adequate account of the burdens a requested accommodation may impose on nonbeneficiaries."

The scope of these principles is somewhat unclear.

Alleviation of burdens. By definition, religious accommodations are designed to alleviate burdens on religious exercise—and thus to restore believers to roughly the same set of incentives and disincentives they would have faced in the absence of the legal obligation. In *Texas Monthly, Inc. v. Bullock* (1989), the State of Texas exempted religious publications from sales tax. It argued that the exemption alleviated the burden such a tax would place on free exercise. The Court disagreed, reasoning (we think correctly) that a modest, nondiscriminatory tax on all publications cannot realistically be seen as a *substantial* burden on the exercise of religion. In addition, ordinarily, tax exemptions for religious property are part of a broader set of exemptions for nonprofit and charitable activities. A religion-only tax exemption is economically equivalent to a religion-only subsidy, which violates long-standing Establishment Clause norms.

The *Cutter* Court's use of the adjective "exceptional" to describe the burden on religious exercise necessary to justify an accommodation, however, came out of nowhere[16] and is too stringent a standard. In prior cases and legislation, the necessary burden on religion was described as "substantial" or "significant." The Court provided no reason to depart from precedent on this point, and, to our knowledge, no lower court has latched onto the adjective "exceptional" to hold an accommodation unwarranted.

A better way to think about this concern, we think, is to ask whether an accommodation goes beyond *accommodating* religious activity to affirmatively *incentivizing* it. When an accommodation has little or no value to a nonadherent—for example, the right to wear a yarmulke with a military uniform or the right to fast during Ramadan—there is little reason to worry that it would create an incentive for affected individuals to change religious beliefs (or to feign them). But when an accommodation would have value to anyone—such as a draft exemption or tax exemption—courts are understandably warier that an accommodation might have the effect of pressuring people to change (or pretend to change) their religion in order to claim the exemption. This concern has sometimes affected how courts have interpreted accommodation laws. Courts sometimes read accommodation laws broadly to include similar conscientious objections that are based on nonreligious beliefs. In two cases during the Vietnam era, the Court extended the statutory draft exemption beyond its terms to two objectors whose bases for objection, while undoubtedly sincere and heartfelt, were arguably nonreligious. A plurality of justices did so, however, as a matter of statutory interpretation rather than constitutional demand. Lower courts have treated groups, like the Washington Ethical Society, that resemble churches in form and function but have a nontheistic philosophy as religious organizations for purposes of property tax exemptions, and the Equal Employment Opportunity Commission (EEOC) has (correctly, in our view) treated atheism as a religion for purposes of employment discrimination protections. Moreover, the Supreme Court has consistently rejected free exercise claims for tax exemptions, even when the arguments otherwise seem powerful, presumably because of the risk of creating incentives for either religious observation or insincere claims.[17] None of these decisions were decided squarely on Establishment Clause grounds, but the Court was sensitive to the ways that an accommodation might operate to distort the incentives for certain forms of religious exercise, which is an establishment concern.

Denominational neutrality. Of the three *Cutter* principles, the requirement of neutrality among religions is the clearest and most deeply entrenched. One of the original elements of disestablishment in every state was the requirement of denominational neutrality (see Chapter 3). But it is also subject to possible misinterpretation. Only those who observe a sabbath need to take off a particular day of the week; only those with dietary restrictions need special meals. We think it would be a misinterpretation of *Cutter* to hold that specific accommodations for particular religious practices violate this stricture merely because they are of religious significance only to one or a handful of faiths. Legislatures typically respond to known conflicts and cannot be expected to craft accommodations for future and unknown hypothetical situations. For that reason, the Court's decision in *Kiryas Joel v. Grumet* (1994),[18] cited with favor in *Cutter*, was in our view wrongly decided (at least on this ground). In that case, the New York legislature, responding to what seemed to be a unique situation involving the disabled children of a small Hasidic community, created a new public school district to accommodate them. The Court held that this was an unconstitutional establishment on the ground that there was "no assurance that the next similarly situated group seeking a school district of its own will receive one." In our view, there can be no denominational discrimination until a similarly situated group is denied similar treatment, at which point the legislature should be permitted to choose between extending the accommodation to the new group or ending it for everyone.

A recent case where the Court failed to protect against denominational preference is *Dunn v. Ray*.[19] In that case, Alabama prison officials refused to allow a prisoner facing execution, Domineque Ray, to be accompanied into the death chamber by a clergy member of his religion (which happened to be Islam). The prison allowed Christian ministers but no other clergy members into the execution chamber. Non-Christians thus faced the choice of being attended by a Christian minister or no clergy at all. The Court denied Ray's request on the ground that he filed it too close in time to the scheduled execution. Justice Kagan, dissenting, had the better view, that the prison's policy "goes against the Establishment Clause's core principle of denominational neutrality."

Impact on nonbeneficiaries. Cutter's third requirement, that an accommodation must take "adequate account" of burdens it may impose on nonbeneficiaries, has proven to be the most controversial. Some scholars and a few judges have argued that instead of requiring the government to *take account* of burdens on third parties, accommodations that impose more than a minimal burden on third parties should be forbidden altogether. That has become the leading Establishment Clause argument against accommodation of religion in recent years.

THE THIRD-PARTY HARM ARGUMENT

Until recently, the majority of claims for religious accommodation came from nonmainstream groups whose claims fit easily within the minority-rights focus of the Warren and Burger Courts, such as draft resisters, Native American religious practitioners, Jewish sabbatarians, Amish farmers, or Muslim women opposed to full-facial photographs. That remains true of the vast majority of accommodation claims; the most common claims come from prisoners and from institutions fighting exclusionary zoning regulation. But the most *conspicuous* accommodation claims in the past ten years have involved religious traditionalists who seek to avoid compulsory support for abortion, contraception, same-sex marriage, and similar progressive causes. The political backlash has been ferocious. Opponents of these accommodations have advanced a novel argument against them: that accommodations of religion violate the Establishment Clause if they have the effect of imposing more than minimal harm on nonbeneficiaries. As one pair of scholars put it: " 'Religious liberty' does not and cannot include the right to impose the costs of observing one's religion on someone else."[20]

At a high level of abstraction, that is quite right. If I engage in a religious practice, such as observing a sabbath, I should be the one who bears whatever cost may accompany it. I have no right to ask my fellow citizens to alter their conduct or give up any of their property to facilitate my sabbath observance. But that is not the question posed by modern regulatory exemption cases. They do not require bystanders to give up rights to make it easier for believers to exercise their religion. Instead, they ask whether the government may exempt religious practitioners from burdens imposed by the government for the benefit or protection of others. When believers seek accommodation from legislative or regulatory burdens of this sort, they are not trying to shift the cost of their religious practice to someone else, but to prevent the government from making their religious exercise more difficult or impossible, for the secular benefit of others. As Justice Brennan explained for the Court in *Texas Monthly*, religious accommodations are generally permitted when they are "designed to alleviate government intrusions that might significantly deter adherents of a particular faith from conduct protected by the Free Exercise Clause."[21]

Consider a hypothetical. In order to make abortions more widely available, the legislature passes a law requiring all obstetricians to provide abortion services on the same terms as live births, on pain of losing their professional license. Under current Free Exercise doctrine, such a requirement would seem to be neutral and generally applicable, and thus not to violate the Free Exercise Clause. But what if, two years later, the legislature passed an exemption for doctors holding the sincere religious belief that abortion is the taking of innocent human life? Would that accommodation be unconstitutional under the "third-party harm" principle? Arguably it would. Women seeking to obtain an abortion from an exempted doctor would be forced to go elsewhere, which might be humiliating as well as inconvenient, and in some cases could increase the medical risks of the procedure. They would be harmed. But is it logical to say that the Establishment Clause, which exists to protect the rights of dissenters to follow beliefs contrary to the majority, requires this result? Whose beliefs are being imposed on whom?

We do not mean to imply that the doctors in this hypothetical are constitutionally entitled to an accommodation (absent other facts that might support such a claim), but only that the legislature is not precluded from providing it. Under *Cutter*, legislators are required to consider how severe the burden on conscientious anti-abortion physicians would be, and how much of an imposition on abortion patients an accommodation would be, but the result of that inquiry is not foreordained. Assuming the underlying law is neutral and generally applicable, the First Amendment would not force one answer or the other. To put the point more generally: when the government enacts regulations for the secular benefit of some, but at the cost of burdening the ability of others to freely exercise their religion, it is permissible for the government to carve out a religious accommodation, even if the result is not to benefit as many third parties as would be benefited without the accommodation. This is an example of what the Court has called the "play in the joints" between the Establishment and Free Exercise Clauses. The strong version of the third-party harm requirement would eliminate this legislative discretion.

The nation has from the beginning fostered a tradition of generous religious accommodations, even when the costs, real or apparent, to third parties were high. In *Amos*, an employee lost his job. In *Cutter*, prison funds that could have been spent on nonreligious activities or prison security were spent on accommodating the religious needs of members of what the petitioners called "nonmainstream" religions. During the Vietnam War alone, 170,000 young men were sent to fight and potentially die in place of religious objectors.[22] Most religious accommodations have a cost, and many of those costs are borne not only by the government or society as an abstract entity but also by identifiable third parties. Under current doctrine, all the Establishment Clause requires with respect to third-party harm is that the government take "adequate account" of the burdens that an accommodation may impose on others. With one possible exception (discussed below), the Court has yet to confront an actual, nonhypothetical accommodation enacted by a legislature that fails this test. This is not surprising. The beneficiaries of an accommodation are by definition dissenters from government policy that presumably commands majority support, and democratic theory suggests that they are unlikely to have the political clout to impose disproportionate costs on the rest of society.

Behind the arguments over third-party harm is a confusion about baselines. Most advocates of a constitutional rule that would prohibit any accommodation that results in nontrivial harm to third parties assume that the proper baseline should be the entitlements of regulatory beneficiaries in the absence of accommodation. Under that assumption, almost any accommodation, by definition, causes them harm—meaning it reduces the value to them of the regulation. Some defend this "social welfare" baseline on the ground that there is no such thing as private conduct that exists free of government regulation. Others admit that there is no neutral way to set the baseline, arguing instead that the question should be whether the accommodation is worth the harm imposed. The result of this is that whether third parties have a right and believers don't—or whether believers have a right and third parties don't—depends entirely on the perspective of the beholder. While this kind of interest-weighing is essential for the legislative branch, it should not be converted into a *constitutional* restriction under the rubric of a "no third-party harm" rule. The weighing of private harms is a paradigmatic question of policy, rather than a question of law.

The only Supreme Court decision that rests on something like the third-party harm theory confirms this view of the baseline question. In *Estate of Thornton v. Caldor, Inc.* (1984), the Court considered a Connecticut law that gave all private employees the right to not work on their designated sabbath. Applying the *Lemon* test, the Court ruled that the statute "impose[d] on employers and [other] employees an absolute duty to conform their business practices to the particular religious practices of the [accommodated] employee by enforcing observance of the Sabbath the employee unilaterally designates."[23] Note that the decision hinged on the "absolute" character of the accommodation, and not the mere existence of some third-party harm. Moreover, unlike the typical religious exemption case, this statute did not lift a newly wrought governmental burden on religious exercise, but rather created a new right against a burden imposed by a private employer.

The case was in fact more complicated than the Court let on, because Connecticut had recently repealed its Sunday closing law, which for hundreds of years had afforded many of those workers the freedom to rest on their sabbath day, if it was Sunday. The new statute was more liberal than the prior regime: It allowed businesses to open on Sunday, it continued the protection for Sunday-sabbath observers against being required to work on their day of rest, and for the first time it provided the same degree of protection for non-Sunday sabbatarians. But the sabbath protection law taken in isolation—which on its face "arm[ed] Sabbath observers with an absolute and unqualified right not to work on whatever day they designate[d] as their Sabbath"—was heavy-handed and may have gone too far. In any case, *Caldor* was a completely different kettle of fish from the typical modern religious accommodation, which lifts a government-imposed burden on religion, rather than creating a government-imposed burden on third parties in the name of religious exercise.

FACILITATING RELIGIOUS EXERCISE THROUGH MEANS
OTHER THAN EXEMPTIONS

Another familiar form of accommodation does not involve an exception to a law, but rather adjusts the schedule of public affairs or regulates the use of government property to enable religious believers to exercise religion in contexts where they might not otherwise be able to do so. A familiar example is the provision of chaplains in the military, in prison, and in similar confined environments. A recent case involved a charter school in Minnesota with a largely Muslim student body. The school arranged its schedule so that there would be a break between classes so students could pray at the times appointed by their religion, closed the school during the Eid holidays, and served no food in its cafeteria that violated Muslim dietary restrictions. These arrangements were challenged as an establishment of religion, and the school was bankrupted before the courts could decide the case.[24] Accommodations of this sort were easy to attack under the *Lemon* test: Their only purpose is to enable believers to worship; that is also their primary effect; and the adjustment of government operations to religious needs falls within the definition of entanglement. But it is hard to see why they transgress any genuine principle of nonestablishment.

In *Zorach v. Clauson* (1952), the Court's first religious accommodation case, the Court turned back a challenge to a public high school "release time" program, which allowed students on a voluntary basis to leave school premises for a period to receive religious instruction in the denomination of their choice off the premises of the school. Opponents argued that the program violated the Establishment Clause, largely on the theory that "the weight and influence of the school is put behind a program for religious instruction." The Court reasoned that the state "may not coerce anyone to attend church, to observe a religious holiday, or to take religious instruction. But it can close its doors or suspend its operations as to those who want to repair to their religious sanctuary for worship or instruction." Further, the opinion said that "when the state encourages religious instruction or cooperates with religious authorities by adjusting the schedule of public events to sectarian needs, it follows the best of our traditions. For it then respects the religious nature of our people and accommodates the public service to their spiritual needs."[25]

In *Bear Lodge v. Babbitt* (10th Cir. 1999), a lower court rejected an Establishment Clause challenge to federal rules attempting to discourage rock climbing in Devils Tower National Monument in Wyoming. This extraordinary rock formation is sacred to the Cheyenne River Sioux and other tribes and is used for ceremonies during the month of June, which also happens to be the best month for rock climbing at the site. The purpose and effect of the rule was clearly to protect and promote the use of federal property for the religious worship of a particular group and thus to "favor religion over non-religion." But the Court rejected the challenge, without even reaching the merits, on the ground that no plaintiffs' First Amendment rights were injured—an emphatic rejection of the theory that third parties whose secular interests are subordinated to religious accommodation are constitutionally wronged. Presumably, in some contexts, the dedication of public land to religious uses of a single denomination could raise Establishment Clause concerns, but when the government has taken title to land that is vital for the exercise of religion, it is not unconstitutional to adjust its land use plan to make that religious exercise possible, even at the expense of some secular uses. By the same token, in *Lyng v. Northwest Indian Cemetery Protective Association* (1988), tribes brought suit against the Forest Service to prevent construction of a logging road that would disrupt their religious uses of forest land. In a controversial decision that may not have been correct, a 5–4 majority rebuffed their free exercise claim—but Congress then stepped in and gave the tribes the relief they had failed to get in court. Under the *Lemon* test, this congressional action seemed to lack any secular purpose; it had the effect of favoring religious uses of government property over secular uses and deeply entangled the government in the process of analyzing and evaluating anthropological evidence regarding the connection between religious practices and the land. There were clear third-party harms to the economic interests of the logging companies. But no one challenged the statute under the Establishment Clause, and rightly not.[26]

In light of this long-standing practice and precedent, it is generally permissible for governments to accommodate religious exercise even when the accommodation specifically targets religion, even when the accommodation is not required by the Free Exercise Clause, and even when it imposes some burdens on third parties. Efforts to invalidate religious accommodations in the name of the Establishment Clause have been almost uniformly rejected, and this has been a good thing for religious freedom and diversity.

CHAPTER 7

No-Aid Separation, Neutrality, and Religious Schools

JUSTICE ROBERT JACKSON warned that "no deeper division of our people could proceed from any provocation than from finding it necessary to choose what doctrine and whose program public educational officials shall compel youth to unite in embracing."[1] That has not kept Americans from trying. Although there were no public schools at the founding, by the second third of the nineteenth century there were major efforts to compel all children to accept their schooling from "common schools" controlled by governmental authorities—schools that would inculcate the common values, virtues, and loyalties thought necessary to citizens of the American republic. If that sounds similar to the purposes of religious establishments in the years following Independence, that is because they *were* similar. Both systems involved compulsory attendance, compulsory financial support, government control over doctrine, and sometimes even—until blocked by the Supreme Court in 1925—legal prohibition of alternatives. For most of that time—over 150 years—the ideology of the common schools was largely Protestant and patriotic, with the objective of "Americanizing" the waves of Catholic and Jewish immigrants flooding to these shores. After the *School Prayer Cases* of the early 1960s (see Chapter 8), the common schools became more secular, sometimes aggressively so, and in recent decades some have become heavily tinged with left-progressive ideology. Dissenters from the common school ideology, whatever it happened to be, either had their children educated into beliefs they did not share or were forced to forfeit the benefits of a free public education and pay tuition for private school.

Ironically, when the Supreme Court first brought the Establishment Clause to bear on these issues, after World War II, it interpreted that Clause to stifle religious pluralism and to foster religious uniformity—exactly the opposite of the historic purposes of the First Amendment. In the last two decades the Court has done a U-turn, producing the most extreme doctrinal about-face in all the volumes of U.S. Reports.

A BRIEF HISTORY OF RELIGION AND SCHOOLS

Public education was essentially unknown to the framers of the First Amendment, though some early statesmen, such as Benjamin Rush, urged the creation of public schools for the formation of republican character. Most colonies and states did, however, subsidize colleges like William and Mary, Columbia, Transylvania, Rutgers, Bowdoin, and Harvard. These institutions met the educational needs of the sons of well-to-do families, providing a basic classical education plus preparation for the three learned professions: law, medicine, and the ministry. With the exception of the University of Pennsylvania, which was nominally nonsectarian but in practice tied to Anglicanism, all were affiliated with one or another religious denomination. Nowhere was this thought to present an establishment problem—even in states that had fully disestablished religion. Even denominations such as the Baptists and Presbyterians, which were in the vanguard of disestablishmentarianism (see Chapter 4), sought and received legislative grants for support of their colleges and seminaries. As Professor Mark Storslee has shown, state support for education was not thought to violate the principle against coerced tithes, even if the education had religious components and was conducted under denominational auspices.[2] Even the most vocal opponents of the Virginia assessment, for example, supported public subsidies for denominational schools even as they dismantled the old establishment.

Primary education was haphazard, private, and almost invariably religious. Families able to pay for the education of their young did so; the poor were educated, if at all, through a combination of private philanthropy and government grants. Almost all primary schools before 1830, even those partially financed by towns, were conducted under religious auspices, often by clergy. Americans agreed that education was essential for developing the republican virtues necessary for the success of the nation's experiment in self-government, and virtually everyone agreed that the basic moral teachings of Christianity were essential for developing republican virtue. Governmental financial support for education, especially in the more religiously diverse big cities, typically took the form of grants to private schools for the education of the poor. Many of these schools were religious. Between 1800 and 1830, New York provided public funds to Presbyterian, Episcopalian, Methodist, Quaker, Dutch Reformed, Baptist, Lutheran, and Jewish schools; to an African Free School; and to the "Free School Society," a nonsectarian (but not nonreligious) school. These arrangements were not challenged as "establishments" under either state or federal constitutions.[3]

So central was religion to education in the early republic that when Stephen Girard bequeathed his considerable fortune to the City of Philadelphia in trust for the creation of a school for white orphan boys on the condition that no member of the clergy "of any sect" be permitted entrance, lest they pollute the scholars' impressionable minds with sectarian dogma, his family contested the will on the ground that subjecting orphans to an education bereft of religious instruction was contrary to the "public law and policy" of the Commonwealth of Pennsylvania, hiring Daniel Webster to make that argument. Although the suit was ultimately unsuccessful, the Supreme Court devoted ten days to oral argument.[4]

The federal government had no role in education outside of the territories, the District of Columbia, Indian country, and the military academies. Notwithstanding the Establishment Clause, schools supported by the federal government were no less religious than those supported by the states. The same Congress that enacted the Bill of Rights re-enacted the Northwest Ordinance, which provided that "Religion, morality and knowledge being necessary to good government and the happiness of mankind, schools and the means of education shall forever be encouraged."[5] The federally funded schools in the District of Columbia included basic instruction in Christianity and were often run by religious organizations or ministers. Even more striking, from the founding through the Civil War, the federal government worked with tribal governments to send paid Christian missionaries to build and operate schools. Presidents Washington, Jefferson, Madison, and Monroe all approved ad hoc partnerships with specific missionaries for this purpose, never hinting at an establishment issue. The practice became a fully fledged program with the so-called Civilization Funds Act of 1820, which specified that money be given to teachers of "good moral character," a requirement that is facially neutral among religious groups and between religious and nonreligious groups. In practice the vast majority of the funds went to Christian missionaries of various stripes—from Baptists to Catholics—in accordance with the preferences of tribal governments. No one in Congress or elsewhere is known to have raised an Establishment Clause objection. The reason? The use of public funds for education, unlike support for a church, did not coerce people to fulfill their duty to God. It simply used tax dollars to pursue a legitimate government interest in education. Americans took it for granted that basic instruction in Christian morality was a component of a proper education.[6]

Controversies about the funding of religious schools did not arise on a broad scale until the middle of the nineteenth century. The disputes differed in detail from place to place but generally shared the same dynamics. A state or city had been funding denominational schools, many of them charity schools, alongside newer "nonsectarian" schools. The nonsectarian schools distinguished themselves from denominational schools by teaching the basics of Protestant Christianity through prayers, Bible readings, and hymns, without fussing about the doctrinal issues that divide Protestant groups. Perhaps the earliest of these was the Free School Society in New York City, but the most influential were the common schools spearheaded by Horace Mann in Massachusetts—the first state system of "public schools" in the modern sense. Playing to the lowest common religious denominator, these schools concurred that religious instruction and practice were essential for a proper education, but they believed that their curriculum was sufficiently "nonsectarian" that it ought to satisfy anyone. Catholics and conservative evangelicals (not to mention Jews and free-thinkers), of course, disagreed. Catholics could not condone reading from the King James Version of the Bible without church sanctioned commentary, and conservative evangelicals wanted more instruction in Christian doctrine. Some accused Mann, a Unitarian, of co-opting the common schools for the teaching of his own brand of Christianity.[7]

The first movement by nonsectarian schools to monopolize government funding arose in New York City in the early 1820s. The Free School Society opposed a grant to a Baptist school and then, with Mayor DeWitt Clinton on its board, successfully lobbied to eliminate funding for all denominational schools. The Society advanced, among others, an argument that funding religious schools violated inchoate principles of separation of church and state.[8]

The main bogeyman of the nineteenth-century no-aid movement, though, was Catholic education. Seen most charitably, common school advocates believed that the primary mission of education should be to foster political unity, social stability, and republicanism; that prayers and Bible reading were essential to achieve these objectives; and that Catholicism tended to be divisive, backward, and authoritarian. As Professors John Jeffries and James Ryan (now President of the University of Virginia) recount in their *Political History of the Establishment Clause*, "[a] generalized Protestantism became the common religion of the common school. . . . Early common schools featured Bible reading, prayer, hymns, and holiday observances, all reinforced by the exhortations of the teacher and the pervasive Protestantism of the texts." They explain that "civic leaders assumed 'that Americanism and Protestantism were synonyms and that education and Protestantism were allies.'"[9] And there was a darker side. Apart from race, anti-Catholicism is the oldest and deepest prejudice in the Anglo-American mindset.[10] Many Protestants saw the Catholic religion as inimical to republicanism, and its Irish and other adherents as culturally and ethnically inferior to Anglo-Saxons. One all-too-typical opponent of funding Catholic schools charged that in those schools immigrant and other Catholic children "will be instructed mainly into the foreign prejudices and superstitions of their fathers, and the state, which proposes to be clear of all sectarian affinities in religion, will pay the bills!"[11] Whether from animus or republicanism, the nineteenth-century movement to defund "sectarian" schools was based on religious discrimination—in favor of nonsectarian Protestantism and against everything else.[12]

Catholics understandably complained that "nonsectarian" schools were effectively Protestant. An 1840 petition from Catholic parents in New York described the curriculum in the public schools:

> The term "Popery" is repeatedly found in them. This term is known and employed as one of insult and contempt towards the Catholic religion, and it passes into the minds of children. . . . Both the religious and historical portions of the reading lessons are selected from Protestant writers, whose prejudices against the Catholic religion render them unworthy of confidence in the mind of your petitioners, at least in so far as their own children are concerned.[13]

Catholics insisted that it was unfair for the government to subsidize schools that indoctrinated students in generic Protestantism without offering equal funds for Catholic schools. Taxing Catholics to subsidize Protestant schools while making them pay for their own schools amounted to taxing them twice. Protestants complacently responded that the common schools should be acceptable to everyone because, after all, they were "nonsectarian."

This dispute opened up a culture war on two fronts: whether publicly funded schools should permit (or require) students to read the King James Version of the Bible, and whether the government should fund religious alternatives to the public schools. By this time, Roman Catholics were almost the only religious group with its own schools; Protestants rallied around the largely Protestant public schools, and Jewish schools were a thing of the future. In 1844, nativist claims that Catholics were trying to remove the Bible from public schools incited riots in Philadelphia that killed fourteen, injured dozens, and left two Catholic churches reduced to ash. This was just a skirmish in a broadening conflict that prompted the organization of the nativist American ("Know-Nothing") Party. These views were not confined to anti-Catholic zealots; they were in the mainstream. In 1869 the National Teachers Association (forerunner of today's National Education Association) resolved both that "the appropriation of public funds for the support of sectarian schools is a violation of the fundamental principles of our American system of education" and that "the Bible should not only be studied, venerated, and honored . . . but devotionally read, and its precepts inculcated in all the common schools of the land."[14] The no-aid movement was thus premised not on the claim that it would violate a constitutional provision for the government to fund any religious instruction and exercise, but rather that it would violate an unwritten principle of the separation of church and state for the government to fund the religious instruction and exercise of a particular dissenting brand of religion. It was a soft establishment of generic Protestantism.[15]

After the Union victory in the Civil War, Congress appropriated money to educate the newly emancipated freedmen of the South. Almost simultaneously with the Fourteenth Amendment, Congress enacted a statute instructing the Freedmen's Bureau to work through private "benevolent associations" whenever the latter provided suitable teachers. Most of these associations were missionary societies from the North, some interdenominational and some affiliated with particular religious denominations. Public funds went to Presbyterian, Methodist, Baptist, Congregationalist, and other religious educational societies. Although some educators were critical of the missionary focus of these schools, the issue was rarely framed in terms of church-state separation.[16] Because the Freedmen's Bureau was enacted by the same political figures who drafted and brought about the ratification of the Fourteenth Amendment, through which the Establishment Clause was made applicable to the states (see

Chapter 4), this embrace of public funding for religious schools would seem to have particular significance for modern constitutional interpretation. But the experience had little effect on the later debate over aid to nonpublic (mostly Catholic) schools, and the Supreme Court never cite it before 2020.

As Reconstruction moved toward its close, the question of aid to religious schools became a contentious national issue for the first time and assumed a constitutional dimension. Opponents of aid to "sectarian" schools did not, for the most part, argue that it violated the First Amendment. Instead, they sought to amend the federal and state constitutions to render public aid to sectarian schools unconstitutional while entrenching the practice of "nonsectarian" prayer and Bible reading in the public schools. In 1875, President Ulysses S. Grant brought the issue to the national political stage in a speech to the Army of the Tennessee. He stated that "if we are to have another contest in the near future of our national existence I predict that the dividing line will not be Mason and Dixon's but between patriotism and intelligence on the one side and superstition, ambition and ignorance on the other." He urged his listeners to "encourage free schools and resolve that not one dollar of money appropriated for their support no matter how raised, shall be appropriated to the support of any sectarian school." "Resolve," he went on, "that neither the State nor the Nation, nor both combined, shall support institutions of learning other than those sufficient to afford to every child growing up in the land the opportunity of a good common school education, [u]nmixed with sectarian, pagan or atheistical tenets. . . . Keep the church and state forever separate."[17]

Congressional Republicans introduced a constitutional amendment, called the "Blaine Amendment" after presidential aspirant James G. Blaine. In its Senate version, the proposed amendment would have done three things. First, it explicitly applied the Establishment and Free Exercise Clauses and Article VI's prohibition on religious tests for office to the states. Second, it provided that no public funds or property could be "used for the support of any school, educational or other institution under the control of any religious or anti-religious sect, organization, or denomination, or wherein the particular creed or tenets of any religion . . . shall be taught." Third, it made clear that the foregoing language "shall not be construed to prohibit the reading of the Bible in any school or institution."[18] The proposal attained only a 28–16 majority in the Senate, which was short of the required two-thirds majority.

Implications of the first provision for the "incorporation" of the First Amendment against the states were discussed in Chapter 4. More illuminating for present purposes are the second and third provisions. The language—prohibiting public subsidy for the teaching of "the particular creed or tenets of any religion," while allowing "the reading of the Bible"—was carefully crafted to reflect the conviction that the "common" elements of religion and morality (i.e., nonspecific generic Protestantism) could (and should) be taught, but "particular creed or tenets" (i.e., Catholicism) must not. President Grant's not-so-subtle references to "superstition, ambition, and ignorance" on just "one side" of the religious divide were reinforced on the floor of the Senate by choice quotations from an 1864 papal encyclical designed to show the authoritarian and anti-republican character of Catholic doctrine.[19] Significantly, the proposed amendment applied only to schools. Throughout the nineteenth and twentieth centuries, religiously affiliated colleges, hospitals, orphanages, adoption agencies, charities, and similar institutions routinely received public funding—which shows that the debate was not about church-state separation in general, but specifically about primary education, where the Catholic-Protestant division was most stark.

At the heart of the debate was disagreement over the difference between "religion" and "sectarianism." Supporters of the amendment believed that children "can be taught religion without being taught the particular tenets or creed of some denominations." Opponents countered that this was an impossibility, and that the common schools were themselves effectively "sectarian." Even the choice of which version of the Bible would be read, they argued, is "sectarian." Unless all religious and moral education were eliminated from the schools, which few regarded as possible or desirable, the only way the purposes of education could be achieved without "favoring one sect rather than another" was to fund all educational institutions "pro rata according to the number they supported."[20]

Although the Blaine Amendment never achieved the necessary two-thirds vote in both houses of Congress, it served as the model for so-called "little Blaine Amendments" in the states. Indeed, Congress demanded the inclusion of such provisions as a condition to statehood in the Dakotas, Montana, Washington, and New Mexico. By 1890, some twenty-nine states had enacted limitations on religious school funding in their state constitutions.

The attack on Catholic schools intensified in the early decades of the twentieth century. In 1922, Oregon voters approved a referendum requiring all school-age children to attend public schools— effectively outlawing private alternatives. The referendum was backed by—among other organizations—the Ku Klux Klan, which focused on the role of public schools to "Americanize" immigrants, many of whom were Catholic or Jewish. The law was challenged by a Catholic school and a private military academy. In *Pierce v. Society of Sisters*,[21] the Supreme Court unanimously held the law unconstitutional on the ground that it "unreasonably interferes with the liberty of parents and guardians to direct the upbringing and education of children under their control." In ringing terms, the Court stated that "the fundamental theory of liberty upon which all governments in this Union repose excludes any general power of the state to standardize its children by forcing them to accept instruction from public teachers only." The Court did not cite the Establishment Clause, but the idea that the government lacks power to "standardize" its children bears a striking resemblance to the disestablishmentarian ideal. Yet *Pierce* was, in a sense, an uncomfortable compromise. The state could not *compel* dissenting families to send their children to the government's schools, but it made those schools available for free, out of tax dollars extracted from the entire population. Groups who sought an alternative more compatible with their beliefs were forced to pay out of their own pockets, through tuition and voluntary contributions. In this period, though, it was not federal constitutional law that barred Catholic and other nongovernmental schools from receiving state aid. It was mostly politics, supplemented by state constitutional law in many places. That began to change after World War II, when the federal courts first got involved.

THE SUPREME COURT GETS INVOLVED

After World War II, overt anti-Catholicism began to wane, giving way to the familiar triad of Protestant-Catholic-Jew made famous by Will Herberg.[22] President Dwight Eisenhower found it politically advantageous to name an Irish Catholic (William Brennan) to the Supreme Court, and John F. Kennedy was elected the nation's first Catholic president in 1960. Catholics gained political power, especially in the urbanized states of the Northeast and Midwest. Legislatures began to respond, by extending public support to the secular components of Catholic education. We believe these moves should have been greeted as a step away from Protestant hegemony and educational uniformity—in other words, toward *disestablishment*. Instead, many elements of the civil liberties community reacted with alarm. We believe the fundamental error was to view the Establishment Clause as about benefitting religion, rather than enlarging the scope of individual religious choice.

The first Establishment Clause challenge to government aid to private religious education reached the Supreme Court in 1947.[23] Ewing Township, New Jersey, had only two high schools: one public and one Catholic. It passed an ordinance reimbursing parents for the cost of public transportation to the two schools. A taxpayer challenged the payments as a "law respecting an establishment of religion," and the case, *Everson v. Board of Education*, ascended to the Supreme Court.[24] Lacking relevant precedent, the Court turned to history for guidance. It ignored the history of aid to religious schools just recounted; ignored the language and history of the First Amendment (Chapter 2); and ignored the controversy and conflicting precedents about application of the Bill of Rights to the states (Chapter 4). It turned, instead, to the 1784–85 fight in Virginia over Patrick Henry's proposal to tax all citizens for the support of churches (discussed in Chapters 1 and 3). The Court recognized the Virginia controversy was over "the imposition of taxes to pay ministers' salaries and to build and maintain churches and church property," but the moral it adduced from the episode was far broader. Relying heavily on Madison's *Memorial and Remonstrance* and Jefferson's successful *Bill for Establishing Religious Freedom*, the Court concluded that the founders believed that "individual religious liberty could be achieved best under a government which was stripped of all power to tax, to support, or otherwise to assist any or all religions." The Court allowed a narrow exception for the provision of basic public services, such as fire and police protection. The justices split 5–4 over whether this exception should include the subject of the *Everson* litigation, reimbursement for public transportation. All of them, though, agreed that the Virginia assessment controversy was the touchstone for interpreting the Establishment Clause and averred that it is the Court's task to "ke[ep] high and impregnable" the First Amendment's "wall between church and state."

The Court was not wrong to consult the Virginia controversy, which was one of the most sustained and thoughtful of all the debates over disestablishment. But it was wrong to regard the Virginia bill as the same, in principle, as the New Jersey law. The Virginia bill's express purpose was to promote religion; the New Jersey statute's purpose was to promote education, or perhaps safe transportation, and to equalize the treatment of families making different educational choices. The money under the Virginia proposal was earmarked for specifically religious uses: church buildings and ministers' salaries (with minor exceptions). The money under the New Jersey law was designated for a secular use, transportation, and was distributed neutrally, not favoring religious over secular recipients or vice versa. The Virginia money went to religious institutions; the New Jersey money went to parents. Most importantly from an historical point of view, the argument against the Virginia bill rested on the principle that no one should be compelled to attend or support religious worship, because this was a duty to God and not the business of government. No one at the founding, to our knowledge, took the position that education was not the business of government, even if it contained religious elements or was conducted by religious institutions. Indeed, the same people who opposed the Virginia bill voted in favor of subsidizing colleges run by various religious denominations. The principle that underlay most opposition to the Virginia bill was not that religious institutions may not work with the government to provide public goods, but that duties to God may not be coerced. In Madison's words, "It is the duty of every man to render to the Creator such homage, and such only, as he believes to be acceptable to him."[25] It is hard to see how using tax dollars to pay for bus transportation to an accredited school coerces a duty to God.

The result was a confusing, 5–4 opinion that combined sweeping and absolutist no-aid rhetoric ("no tax in any amount, large or small, can be levied to support any religious activities or institutions, whatever they may be called, or whatever form they may adopt to teach or practice religion") with a holding that the New Jersey program is constitutional. (It "does no more than provide a general program to help parents get their children, regardless of their religion, safely and expeditiously to and from accredited schools.") Either principle—no-aid separationism or neutrality—if taken to its logical conclusion, would swallow up the other. Yet the Court offered no suggestion about how to square the principles. The majority hinted that the New Jersey program "approaches the verge" of what is permitted under the Establishment Clause but supplied no grounds for identifying where that "verge" might be.

The four dissenters exhibited no such ambivalence. To them, the Establishment Clause is "unrelentingly absolute." It "broadly forbids state support, financial or other, of religion in any guise, form or degree. It outlaws all use of public funds for religious purposes." They recognized the impossibility of distinguishing between the secular and the religious components of a religious school's budget. It did not matter, they asserted, that bus transportation is secular in nature, for "transportation, where it is needed, is as essential to education as any other element. Its cost is as much a part of the total expense . . . as the cost of textbooks, of school lunches, of athletic equipment, of writing and other materials; indeed of all other items compassing the total burden." Similarly, they recognized that the idea of neutrality toward all institutions performing a public function, if accepted as matter of principle, would swallow up any pretense at no-aid separation. "If that is true and the Amendment's force can be thus destroyed, . . . then I can see no possible basis, except one of dubious legislative policy, for the state's refusal to make full appropriation for support of private, religious schools, just as is done for public instruction."[26]

The *Everson* dissenters avoided the anti-Catholic rhetoric that had been so large a part of earlier no-aid advocacy, but the same was not true of public commentary on the decision. No less a figure than John Dewey, the leading American philosopher of education, wrote in *The New Republic*:

> The Roman Catholic hierarchy . . . has attempted for many years to gain public fiscal aid and its program has been advanced through active lobbying for school lunches, health programs and school transportation facilities for Catholic schools. . . . It is essential that this basic issue be seen for what it is, namely, as the encouragement of a powerful reactionary world organization in the most vital realm of democratic life with the resulting promulgation of principles inimical to democracy.[27]

Twenty years passed until the next case, *Board of Education v. Allen* (1968). It presented the same stark choice between principles, and the Court majority made a similarly unconvincing attempt to square the circle. New York passed a law under which public school districts would "lend" free textbooks to students in grades seven through twelve, no matter what schools they went to. The textbooks all came from the same list approved for use in the public schools. The majority recognized that textbooks are closer to a school's pedagogical mission than bus rides but did not think that distinguished the case from *Everson*. The textbooks were secular, they were supplied to all schoolchildren on the same basis, and (because textbooks otherwise would be the financial responsibility of the parents) the program benefited the children, not the schools. (Of course, the same could be said of tuition, but the majority did not comment on that.) The dissenters rang most of the same chimes as had the dissenters in *Everson*, but their opinions returned to the anti-Catholic tropes that the *Everson* dissenters had largely avoided. Justice Black's dissent commented: "The same powerful sectarian religious propagandists who have succeeded in securing passage of the present law can and doubtless will continue their propaganda, looking toward complete domination and supremacy of their particular brand of religion."[28]

There was, however, an important difference between the transportation subsidies of *Everson* and the free textbooks of *Allen*, which none of the justices seemed to notice. By their nature, bus rides have no pedagogical content; they cannot be religious and they cannot be secular. Textbooks, by contrast, are a primary means of conveying content and shaping ideas. The textbooks used in common schools, such as the *McGuffy Reader*, had been central to Catholic complaints about pervasive Protestantism. Not surprisingly, Catholic schools typically used their own textbooks, especially in subjects like history, ethics, and literature, where religious perspectives are most likely to be important. The transportation subsidies in *Everson* thus had no effect on the pedagogical character of the schools. The textbook subsidies in *Allen* had the inevitable effect of homogenizing what was taught in public and religious schools. Of course, religious schools could refuse the textbooks and thus retain their pedagogical autonomy—which, after all, was the original reason for their existence—but at a significant cost. Cash-strapped schools almost always succumbed. In effect, the textbook program was a bribe for religious schools to secularize their curriculum.

THE ERA OF LEMON AND NYQUIST:
ALMOST ALL AID HELD UNCONSTITUTIONAL

For a fifteen-year period, the Supreme Court moved progressively closer to the no-aid position of the *Everson* and *Allen* dissenters. The most important analytical step came in *Lemon v. Kurtzman* (1971),[29] a case about salary supplements for teachers of secular subjects in nonpublic schools. Chief Justice Warren Burger's opinion sought to unify Establishment Clause doctrine in one three-part test, which was the subject of Chapter 5. Most directly pertinent for the schools issue was the interaction between the doctrines of effect and entanglement. Under the "effects" test, the Court held that the state had to be "certain" that no religious instruction creeped into the funded aspect of the program, which meant *all* of the teaching by teachers who received public subventions had to be strictly secular, even though more than 80 percent of their pay came from private sources. At the same time, the Court held that "monitoring and surveillance" to enforce that this no-religious-elements requirement constituted "excessive entanglement" between church and state. The Court later described this combination of rules as a "Catch-22."[30] If governments take steps to enforce secular use restrictions, the program violates the entanglement prong, and if they don't, it violates the effects prong. Catch-22. This made subsidies to defray the costs of teacher salaries—by far the largest element in budget of a school—impossible. The Court explained that textbooks were okay under this test because, once inspected to ensure no religious content, they would not change, and thus required no monitoring or surveillance.

Two years later, in *Committee on Public Education v. Nyquist* (1973),[31] the Court went still further. New York enacted two types of aid to nonpublic education: grants to schools to defray up to half the cost of the heat, electricity, and building maintenance of nonpublic schools in low-income areas, and tax credits and reimbursements for the cost of tuition to low-income families using nonpublic schools. It was thought that both halves of the program would withstand scrutiny under the precedents of *Everson*, *Allen*, and *Lemon*. Payments for heat, electricity, and maintenance require no monitoring or surveillance to ensure they are devoid of religious content. Like the bus rides in *Everson*, they have no ideational content. And tuition assistance benefits the child, not the school, like the textbooks in *Allen*. Nonetheless, the Court struck down the entire program. The heating, electricity, and maintenance grants were invalid because "no attempt is made to restrict payments to those expenditures related to the upkeep of facilities used exclusively for secular purposes." Note the analytical shift from whether the aid is itself secular in nature to whether the aid benefits or supports activities with a religious component. That approach would have produced a different result in *Everson*, since the bus rides took children to all their courses—but neither *Everson* nor *Allen* was overruled. The Court also rejected the argument that the tuition subsidies merely ensured "comparable benefits to all parents of schoolchildren," reasoning that "this argument would prove too much, for it would also provide a basis for approving through tuition grants the complete subsidization of all religious schools . . . a result wholly at variance with the Establishment Clause."

Under the *Lemon-Nyquist* doctrine, the Court invalidated a wide array of programs meant to help students of modest means: salary supplements for private school teachers; grants to schools for facilities maintenance and safety; grants and tax credits to families for tuition; provision of nonreligious instructional materials such as maps, periodicals, charts, and films; use of public school personnel to provide speech and hearing therapy and English instruction on private school premises; and reimbursement for transportation for field trips to museums. At the high-water mark in 1985, the Court held unconstitutional a long-standing federal program under which public school teachers went on the premises of religious schools to provide remedial English and math tutoring to individual students on the basis of objective criteria of economic and education deprivation, as well as a similar program in which public school teachers taught extracurricular programs (music, art, foreign languages) not previously available at the school.[32]

During the same period, the Court continued to approve other forms of aid to religious institutions, creating glaring logical inconsistencies with the doctrine applied to primary education. First, the Court by an 8–1 vote held constitutional tax exemptions and tax deductions for churches and other religious institutions on the ground that these tax laws did not "single out" religious recipients for special benefits but instead "granted exemption to all houses of religious worship within a broad class of property owned by nonprofit, quasi-public corporations, which include hospitals, libraries, playgrounds, scientific, professional, historical, and patriotic groups." Thus, the neutrality theory prevailed in the domain of tax benefits even as the no-aid theory increasingly dominated direct grants. Second, the Court declined to apply *Lemon*'s "Catch-22" to religious universities, charities, hospitals, or service organizations—indeed, to any religious organizations other than primary schools and houses of worship. Concluding that these institutions were not "pervasively sectarian," the Court held that they could be trusted not to divert aid (even cash grants) to the religious aspects of their operations without the need for intrusive monitoring and surveillance. Thus, without proof of specific religious uses of public funds, aid to religious institutions other than schools violated neither the effects nor the entanglement parts of the *Lemon* test. Most conspicuously, the federal government provided direct tuition grants under the GI Bill and the Pell Grants program for students to attend the college or university of their choice, be it the University of Illinois, Notre Dame, Brigham Young, or Cardozo—even though, under *Nyquist*, tuition grants to attend religiously affiliated high schools were strictly forbidden. Third, even for primary schools, the Court never overruled *Everson* or *Allen*, and indeed haphazardly extended those precedents to a few inherently "neutral and nonideological" forms of aid, such as school lunches and standardized tests. These categories proved malleable and unpredictable. Noting that the Court permitted the provision of books but not maps, Senator Daniel Patrick Moynihan asked on the floor of the Senate: "What will they do with atlases, which are maps in books?" This quip, which Chief Justice Rehnquist quoted during an oral argument, probably did more to bring down the whole incoherent edifice than any arguments based on history or precedent.

The more fundamental problem was that the premise of the no-aid position lacked any grounding in the purposes of the Establishment Clause. The Establishment Clause was never intended to require unequal treatment of religious institutions, but to prevent the use of government power to impose or induce religious uniformity. The *Lemon-Nyquist* line of cases, taken as a whole, reduced religious choice and educational diversity. School choice should have been seen as a step toward disestablishment and away from the era of Protestant hegemony. As long as religious schools satisfied objective criteria of educational quality, it should have been a matter of constitutional indifference whether they also imparted religious instruction in accord with the wishes of the families who chose to attend them.

NEUTRALITY TOWARD RELIGIOUS SCHOOLS: FORBIDDEN, PERMITTED, REQUIRED

With astonishing speed, the Court repudiated this entire inconsistent and discriminatory line of doctrine. In all the annals of U.S. Reports, there is no example of a more complete volte-face in constitutional doctrine.

The change came in three stages. First, starting in the late 1980s, the Court began to reject no-aid absolutism in favor of neutrality theory. The first decisions were a pair of as-applied challenges brought by individuals with highly sympathetic cases. It may be that these personal claims had a more powerful pull on the justices than more abstract cases about state legislation. The first, *Witters v. Department of Services for the Blind* (1986),[33] was brought by Larry Witters, a blind young man who was barred from using a state scholarship on the ground that he wished to study for the ministry at a religious college. The state claimed that allowing him to use the scholarship for that purpose would violate the Establishment Clause—a conclusion seemingly supported by the precedent of *Nyquist*. Somewhat surprisingly, the Supreme Court reversed unanimously, in an opinion by Justice Thurgood Marshall, largely on the ground that the scholarship was "made available generally without regard to the sectarian-nonsectarian, or public-nonpublic nature of the institution benefitted, and is in no way skewed toward religion." The Court also noted that "importantly," a victory for Witters would not likely lead to any "significant portion" of the aid "flowing to religious education." Five justices, concurring, took the position that as long as the terms of eligibility were neutral, it should not matter what percentage of the aid went to religious uses.

Witters was followed by a case in which a deaf student was denied the services of a sign-language interpreter because he chose to attend a Catholic school, which meant that the interpreter would be tasked with conveying prayers and religious teaching as well as the rest of the curriculum. Again the Court reversed. It then held on Free Speech Clause grounds that the University of Virginia could not refuse student activity funding to a student publication solely because it had a religious perspective.[34] Each of these opinions attempted, unpersuasively, to distinguish the *Lemon-Nyquist* line of precedents without overruling any of them.

This first stage ended with a bang. In *Agostini v. Felton* (1997), the Court overruled the two 1985 decisions invalidating programs where public school teachers went on the premises of religious schools to teach remedial English, math, and extracurricular secular subjects.

In *Mitchell v. Helms* (2000), the Court overruled two more precedents from the 1970s, repudiated the doctrinal category of "pervasively sectarian" institutions, and backed away from the idea that
schools had to be "certain" that secular forms of aid could not pos-
sibly be diverted to religious uses. Finally, in *Zelman v. Simmons-
Harris* (2002), a clear majority explicitly replaced no-aid theory with
neutrality. In a case involving vouchers for low-income children
seeking alternatives to the failed public school system of Cleveland,
Ohio, the Court held that tuition aid programs may include religious
schools so long as the terms of the program are neutral between religious and secular schools and government funds flow to private religious schools only as the result of independent decisions of families,
not the government—a holding the Court euphemistically described
as a "refinement" of *Lemon*'s effects test.[35] The Court effectively
overruled the tuition assistance portion of *Nyquist*, stating, "We now
hold that *Nyquist* does not govern neutral educational assistance programs that, like the program here, offer aid directly to a broad class
of individual recipients defined without regard to religion."

As this cascade of overrulings indicates, the decisions from
Witters through *Zelman* amounted to a sea change from the *Lemon-
Nyquist* era. During that era, the reigning principle was one of no-aid
separationism, with occasional unpredictable departures. Since
Zelman, the reigning principle has been its opposite: that aid programs that treat religion neutrally and allow individual choice do
not violate the Establishment Clause. The Establishment Clause is
not to be interpreted as a thumb on the scale against religion, but as
ensuring private choice and diversity through neutrality.

The second stage, after *Zelman*, might be called the period of
"permissible neutrality." No longer would neutral funding programs be invalidated on the ground that they provided aid to religion, but states were generally free to discriminate against religious

schools for the purpose of enhanced "separation." Plaintiffs argued that the Free Exercise Clause forbade discrimination against otherwise eligible recipients on the basis of their religiosity, unless such discrimination was required under the Establishment Clause, but the courts were unreceptive to that argument. The key case was *Locke v. Davey* (2004).[36] The facts were almost identical to *Witters v. Department of Services*. Joshua Davey won a state-funded scholarship, under objective criteria, to assist academically gifted students with postsecondary educational expenses, but the State of Washington refused to allow him to pursue a degree in devotional theology at a religious college. This time, unlike in *Witters*, the State justified the refusal not on the basis of an ostensible Establishment Clause requirement to do so, but on the basis of a state constitutional provision. The question, therefore, was not whether the Establishment Clause permitted the State to provide the scholarship on a neutral basis, but whether the Free Exercise Clause required it to do so—a legal question not raised in *Witters*. In a 7–2 opinion, the Court sided with the State, holding that the decision whether to include devotional theology degrees in the scholarship program was within the State's discretion—what it called the "play in the joints" between the strictures of the Establishment and Free Exercise Clauses. The dissenters complained that the decision conflicted with free exercise cases forbidding the states from singling out religion for unfavorable treatment.

This stage did not last long. In *Trinity Lutheran v. Comer* (2017),[37] Missouri had a program under which schools and day care centers could receive, at state expense, rubberized playground surfaces, using recycled tires from yet another state program. A daycare program operated by Trinity Lutheran Church qualified under the objective criteria but was denied the benefit because it was a church, on the ground that even neutral aid to religious schools violated a "little Blaine Amendment" in the state constitution. By a 7–2 vote, the Court reversed, holding that "the exclusion of Trinity Lutheran from a public benefit for which it is otherwise qualified, solely because it is a church, is odious to our Constitution all the same, and cannot stand." Neutrality toward religion, it now appears, is not only permissible but also mandatory. But the reach of the *Trinity Lutheran* decision was not clear. Perhaps it applied only to forms of aid that are inherently neither religious nor secular, like rubberized playground surfaces. This would replicate the legal categories of *Everson*, only this time asking whether neutral treatment is required rather than whether it is permitted.

That question was answered three years later in *Espinoza v. Montana Department of Revenue* (2020).[38] *Espinoza* involved a state program that gave taxpayers a tax credit for donations to scholarship funds for K-12 schools. Administrators of the program refused to allow parents whose children attended religious schools to receive the scholarships, invoking a "little Blaine Amendment" in the state constitution. Unlike *Trinity Lutheran*, which involved aid of an inherently secular nature, the scholarships would support all the activities of the school, including religious instruction. Nonetheless, the Court held that Montana's discrimination against religious schools, solely because of their religious status, violates the First Amendment.

The Court has thus come full circle, from holding that neutral funding programs are unconstitutional when they support religious activities, to holding that states have discretion whether to fund religious schools on a neutral basis, to holding that discrimination against an otherwise eligible school on the basis of its religious status is unconstitutional. *Espinoza* was also the first majority decision to call out the prior discrimination against "sectarian" schools for its anti-Catholic origins. The Court labeled the Blaine Amendments as "born of bigotry" and stated that they "arose at a time of pervasive hostility to the Catholic Church and to Catholics in general." States can no longer rely on those provisions to favor nonreligious institutions over religious ones. Finally, in *Carson v. Makin* (2022), the Court rejected a state's claim that it could withhold funds from an otherwise eligible school on account of the religious "uses" to which the aid would be put, as opposed to its religious "status." The Court correctly perceived that this was a distinction without a difference. Religious "status" is determined by religious actions.

Importantly, the Court has not held—and almost certainly will not—that governments are obligated to fund private schools. It simply held that when a state aids secular private schools, it may not discriminate against otherwise eligible schools on the ground that they are religious.

Readers may feel a sense of whiplash. Only a few decades ago, the Supreme Court held in case after case that states were constitutionally forbidden from including religious schools in general programs of public funding (with minor and confusing exceptions). Now the Court is holding that states are constitutionally forbidden from excluding schools from such programs on the ground that they are religious. What was constitutionally required is now constitutionally forbidden. There has been no more abrupt doctrinal one-eighty in the annals of U.S. Reports. But in truth, the period of no-aid-separationism was brief and, we believe, misguided from the start. The first case to strike down a program of neutral aid was decided in 1971. The ensuing decisions were confused and contradictory. As early as 1983, the Court accepted the idea of neutral school aid in the form of tax credits. The last no-aid case was in 1985, less than fifteen years after the first. The rhetoric of no-aid separationism attempted to link the modern doctrine to the disestablishmentarianism of the founders, but this was an error of history. Your authors believe that the current Establishment Clause doctrine, in which neutrality is the reigning principle, is truer to the history and theory of disestablishment in America. Wealthy families have long enjoyed the benefits of school choice, either by moving to a well-funded school district with excellent schools or by paying for a private alternative. Thanks to the decline in anti-Catholic prejudice in state legislatures and the Supreme Court's change of doctrine, that privilege can be enjoyed by a broader segment of the population.

CHAPTER 8

Prayer, Bible Reading, and Coercion

AMERICANS WERE STARTLED in 1962 to learn that prayer in public schools violates the Constitution. The practice was deeply entrenched, was beloved by millions, and had endured since public schools had been created. The practice was not merely regional: In a 1960 survey, over 40 percent of public schools nationwide reported classroom prayer or Bible reading, and the Supreme Court's first prayer case arose in New York. (One of your authors remembers Bible reading, though not prayer, in his first-grade class in suburban Louisville.) Much of the country exploded in anger, with 70 percent of those polled disapproving of the decision, according to Gallup.[1] Yet the following year, the Court doubled down on its holding, reiterating its condemnation of public school prayer and extending it to Bible reading and presumably all other religious exercises.

This was the Court's finest hour with the Establishment Clause. It is easy for the Court to do the right thing—actually, it is even easy for the Court to do the wrong thing—when it will be praised for so doing and admired for its courage when no courage was required. It is harder to act in the face of public opposition and long-standing practice.

Assuming that school prayer is coercive, it is at odds with a basic tenet of disestablishment, on which evangelical and enlightenment opponents of establishment at the founding fully agreed: that the government may not compel the performance of religious duties, such as attendance at worship services. Every state with an established religion required church attendance, and every state repealed those requirements as part of disestablishment. (See Chapters 1 and 3.) *Engel v. Vitale* (1962) and *Abington Township v. Schempp* (1963) thus illustrate how the principles of historic disestablishment can be applied, convincingly, to modern circumstances. The few seconds devoted to prayer at the beginning of the school day may not be a worship service, but it differs only in length and degree.[2]

But *is* the practice coercive? Students in *Engel* and *Schempp* were given the right to leave the room while the religious exercises were taking place. The school district thus defended the practice on the ground that the prayer was voluntary. The Court disagreed, noting that the "indirect coercive pressure" on reluctant students "is plain." That seems obviously correct. Schools are an inherently coercive environment. Attendance is compulsory, alternatives are costly, and the atmosphere is one of obedience. Children with minority beliefs—atheists, Jews, sometimes Catholics, members of other minority religions—faced a choice between conformity and the embarrassment and intimidation of dissenting in the presence of their classmates. Even if teachers and school authorities did not *directly* coerce students, classmates have their own methods of enforcing uniformity. The father of the plaintiff children testified that his kids would be "labeled as odd balls" if they exercised their supposed right to leave the room during the prayers, and that standing out in the hall carried the stigma of punishment. Any veteran of middle school can empathize.

Contrary to myth, public school prayer does not go back to the founding, for a simple reason: There were no public schools as we understand them at the founding. Public schools in anything remotely resembling the current system first came into being in the early 1830s, and compulsory education in the last half of the nineteenth century.

Nor can defenders of the practice draw support from that fact that, when public schools were created, they included prayer and Bible reading as a matter of course. Far from representing a consensus understanding about what practices were permissible in a world of disestablishment, school prayer and Bible reading sparked religious controversy and complaints of religious oppression from the earliest days of public education.

The "common school" movement, as its name implied, was a self-conscious attempt to inculcate a common set of values on an increasingly diverse population. Advocates unapologetically used the term "Americanization." As discussed in Chapter 7, the principal mission of common schools was never merely to teach the "three Rs" but to inculcate the morals and ideals necessary to citizens of a republic. Horace Mann, the inspirational leader of the common school movement, explained that the schools should "draw the line between those views of religious truth and of Christian faith which are common to all, and may, therefore, with propriety be inculcated in school, and those which, being peculiar to individual sects, are therefore by law excluded." The Bible (King James Version) was an important part of the daily schedule, and other materials, such as the *McGuffy Reader*, were infused with Protestant theological and moral themes. From a Catholic or a Jewish perspective, "nonsectarianism" was Protestantism in disguise. Educational historian Carl F. Kaestle describes the "ideology" of the common school movement as centering on "republicanism, Protestantism, and capitalism." Indeed, the common schools used almost every one of the tools of the now-defunct religious establishment: compulsory attendance, compelled contributions, governmental control over the message, and suppression of alternatives.[3]

Despite its unpopularity, the Court's holding was thus firmly grounded in the history and rationale of disestablishment: "Government in this country, be it state or federal, is without power to prescribe by law any particular form of prayer which is to be used as an official prayer in carrying on any program of governmentally sponsored religious activity." Just so. But along the way, the Court unfortunately made it sound like coercion was irrelevant to the analysis. This led to confusion in religious liberty doctrine for decades, ironically threatening the right of public school teachers and students to pray on their own.

THE ROLE OF COERCION

Having explained that the practice of vocal prayer in the environment of a public school is coercive—albeit "indirectly" so—and that the vice in the practice is the assumption of a government power to "prescribe by law any particular form of prayer," the Court proceeded to announce that coercion did not actually have anything to do with the decision. Momentarily forgetting how coercive the practice of classroom prayer actually is, the Court observed that "the fact" that observance of the prayer by the students "is voluntary" does not free the practice "from the limitations of the Establishment Clause, as it might from the Free Exercise Clause." It proceeded to explain:

> Although these two clauses may in certain instances overlap, they forbid two quite different kinds of governmental encroachment upon religious freedom. The Establishment Clause, unlike the Free Exercise Clause, does not depend upon any showing

of direct governmental compulsion and is violated by the enactment of laws which establish an official religion whether those
laws operate directly to coerce nonobserving individuals or not.

This statement was passing strange. First, it was accompanied by
no citation of authority. In then-recent cases, the Court had summarized the Establishment Clause as "forestal[ling] *compulsion by
law* of the acceptance of any creed or the practice of any form of
worship," and its holdings in three previous Establishment Clause
cases had turned on the presence or absence of coercion.[4] Nor did
the Court give any explanation why its statement about the irrele-
vance of compulsion to an Establishment claim might be true. The
historical evidence it recounted (at length) squarely contradicted
the conclusion. The statement was also dictum—irrelevant to the
case—since the Court concluded that coercion, at least "indirect"
coercion, had been present.

Yet this doctrinal diktat—that the Free Exercise Clause requires
coercion as an element of violation and the Establishment Clause
does not—distorted interpretation of both Clauses for decades.
The statement was wrong about the Establishment Clause, wrong
about the Free Exercise Clause, and wrong about the relation between them.

The Establishment Clause. If the Court had merely said that there
are some contexts in which coercion is not a necessary element in an
Establishment Clause claim, this would have been unobjectionable
and historically accurate. As explained in Chapter 1, one of the six
elements of historical establishments was denominational discrimination, or "sect preference." If the government favors one religion
over another in the provision of material benefits or privileges—for
example, if Congress adopted a rule that only Protestants could be
selected as military chaplains[5]—this would almost certainly be an

establishment of religion even if no religious conduct is coerced. Similarly, an official proclamation of religious doctrine by law would likely violate the Clause even if there were no compulsive sanction. (Parliament's adoption of the Thirty-nine Articles of Faith was the centerpiece of the establishment of the Church of England, and even the narrowest version of the Establishment Clause debated in the Senate of the First Congress forbade enactment of "articles of faith.") But the *Engel* dictum was taken to mean that coercion is categorically irrelevant to Establishment Clause cases. That is wrong in the vast majority of contexts.

As discussed in Chapter 2, in the debates in the First Congress concerning the First Amendment, James Madison, the principal draftsman and proponent, said that he "apprehended the meaning of the words to be, that Congress should not establish a religion, and enforce the legal observation of it by law, nor compel men to worship God in any manner contrary to their conscience." Upon further questioning, Madison stated that he "believed that the people feared one sect might obtain a preeminence, or two combine together, and establish a religion to which they would compel others to conform." The lengthy preamble to Jefferson's *Bill for Establishing Religious Freedom* contains a dozen references to coercion, compulsion, imposition, punishments, and other synonyms for coercion, and its operative paragraph provides that no man shall be "compelled" to frequent or support any religious worship. Not every element in the historic establishments of religion involved coercion, but most did—and the closest analogue to the *School Prayer Cases* certainly did.

Free Exercise. Nor is the *Engel* dictum an accurate statement of the scope of the Free Exercise Clause. Modern free exercise law is primarily focused on whether a law is "neutral and generally applicable." If it discriminates against religion, it is subject to strict scrutiny, without any inquiry into whether it was coercive. Take, for example, one of the Court's most recent free exercise decisions, *Espinoza v. Montana Department of Revenue*, discussed in Chapter 7.[6] In that case the state government concluded that the state constitution allowed families using secular private schools to take advantage of a tax-preferred subsidy program, but not families using religious private schools. Obviously, the state's action burdened the families' ability to exercise their religion, but it did not coerce them one way or the other; it was a discrimination-against-religion case, not a coercion case.

The Relation Between the Clauses. Perhaps the most insidious implication of the *Engel* dictum was to subordinate the Free Exercise Clause to the Establishment Clause, and thus to destroy the neutrality of the combination. As a result of the *Engel* dictum, any government action favorable to religion raises an Establishment Clause problem whether any person is coerced by it or not, but government action unfavorable to religion can be challenged only when it involves direct coercion. This systematically favors secularization. Mere government approval—maybe even just "endorsement"—of religion is a constitutional problem, but government disapproval of religion does not raise an issue unless it is coercive. Indeed, after *Employment Division v. Smith* (1990), even coercive action against religious exercise cannot get to court unless the law is discriminatory as well as coercive.

Even some of the justices noticed the danger that the doctrine was one-sided, though not precisely identifying the cause. Justice Arthur Goldberg wrote a separate concurrence (joined by Justice John Marshall Harlan II) warning that

> untutored devotion to the concept of neutrality can lead to invocation or approval of results which partake not simply of that noninterference and noninvolvement with the religious which

the Constitution commands, but of a brooding and pervasive devotion to the secular and a passive, or even active, hostility to the religious. Such results are not only not compelled by the Constitution, but, it seems to me, are prohibited by it.[7]

Over the next few decades, the Court would encounter cases where the existence, or lack, of coercion would seem central to whether there was a violation of the Establishment Clause and would quietly walk away from the *Engel* dictum.

NONCOERCIVE OFFICIAL PRAYERS

The Court did not confine its dictum to the context of schools, or even to captive audience situations. On the face of the opinion, its holding extended to "any program of governmentally sponsored activity." But this was contrary to widespread practice going back to the founding and extending to the present day. In George Washington's first inaugural address, he stated:

It would be peculiarly improper to omit in this first official Act, my fervent supplications to that Almighty Being who rules over the Universe, who presides in the Councils of Nations, and whose providential aids can supply every human defect, that his benediction may consecrate to the liberties and happiness of the People of the United States. . . . In tendering this homage to the Great Author of every public and private good I assure myself that it expresses your sentiments not less than my own; nor those of my fellow-citizens at large, less than either.

Washington identified this prayer as an "official act"; it was not merely personal. And he purported to be tendering this "homage" on behalf of all Americans. On the other hand, the prayer was as nonsectarian as the language of the late eighteenth century would permit. It was monotheistic, but not identifiably Christian, and not even necessarily biblical. Although we cannot rule out the likelihood that there was some unrecorded private grumbling, the prayer was not denounced as an establishment of religion. The obvious difference is that no one was required to attend, and as adults, the audience was under no pressure to conform.

In light of the sharp denominational differences between Protestant sects in the eighteenth and early nineteenth centuries, one might expect public prayer to have inspired sectarian squabbles. More typical was the tone struck by Sam Adams at the Continental Congress. When one of the members moved to open with prayer, several distinguished members, including John Jay, later the first Chief Justice of the Supreme Court, objected on the ground that "we were so divided in religious Sentiments, some Episcopalians, some Quakers, some Anabaptists, some Presbyterians and some Congregationalist, so that We could not join in the same Act of Worship." Adams, a staunch Congregationalist, "arose and said that he was no Bigot, and could hear a Prayer from a Gentleman of Piety and Virtue, who was at the same Time a Friend to his Country." He suggested a local Episcopal priest to open the body in prayer.[8] In Georgia, the same Baptist minister who led the charge against religious taxes in 1785 delivered the opening prayer at the 1795 state constitutional convention.[9] This is strong evidence that legislative prayer was not seen as establishment.

Since Franklin Roosevelt, presidents have invited members of the clergy to offer the inaugural prayer. Joe Biden, our second Roman Catholic president, invited a Catholic priest. The priest addressed his prayer to "gracious and merciful God" and quoted from the first American Catholic bishop, Pope Francis, and the Book of James. Every president has also proclaimed Thanksgiving as a day of prayer, though Jefferson ceased the practice in his second term and Madison privately expressed regrets. It was not the prayer itself he regretted, but calling on the American people to observe a day of thanksgiving, prayer, and fasting in accordance with a congressional resolution. "Altho' recommendations only, they imply a religious agency," he wrote in an unpublished memorandum.[10]

From the beginning, Congress has begun its proceedings each day with a prayer. As president, Jefferson allowed religious groups to use the Capitol and various other government buildings for worship services, at a time when the newly created Washington City had no church buildings. He also invited local clergy to conduct meetings in the Rotunda of the University of Virginia for students who wished to attend.

It is therefore not surprising that the Court gradually reintroduced the idea of coercion as an important part of Establishment Clause analysis. In more recent decisions involving prayer at public school events—a middle school graduation ceremony and a New Mexico high school football game—the Court made clear that, under the circumstances, the prayer was "in a fair and real sense obligatory." In a case involving a prayer at the start of a city council meeting in upstate New York, the Court stated for the first time that the Establishment Clause "must be interpreted by reference to 'historical practices and understandings.'" It approved the prayer on the ground that no one was "compelled" to attend or participate; that "no faith was excluded by law, nor any favored"; and that there was "a vanishingly small burden on taxpayers."[11]

Legislative prayers are not without their problems. It is difficult to achieve neutrality among faiths, and there is a distinct whiff of using religion as a political prop. Our point is more general: the only principled way to explain the pattern of cases about public prayer is to distinguish those that involve coercion from those that do not.

More important than these ceremonial occasions was the Court's recognition that students in public school have the right to engage in religious activity on equal terms with other student-organized activity. This was not always so. Until the mid-1980s, every court of appeals to address the question held that it was unconstitutional under the Establishment Clause for high school student clubs to engage in voluntary religious activities like prayer or Bible reading on the premises of the school. A Third Circuit opinion was typical: "Since it is the public schools which provide the most prolonged and involved contact which our youth enjoy with the State, and indeed, for many, the public schools may appear as an institutional symbol for the government in general, any practice which communicates sanction by the school of religious activity amounts to an Establishment Clause violation."[12] During the same period, lower courts concluded that it would violate the Establishment Clause to allow a teacher to read silently from a Bible during silent reading period, for students to distribute religious materials to other students on school grounds, for a student to be allowed to write a research paper about Jesus Christ, and for a college professor to offer an optional lecture called "evidences of God in human physiology." The fact that all these religious activities were entirely voluntary—indeed, that they were conducted in the teeth of opposition from school authorities—was dismissed as irrelevant under the Establishment Clause. To allow religious activities on school premises was a form of "support" for or "endorsement" of religion, and in violation of the First Amendment.[13]

Congress took the first step toward reversing these cases. It passed the Equal Access Act, which forbade public schools from discriminating against voluntary student groups on the basis of the "religious, political, or philosophical content" of their speech.

Lower courts held the Equal Access Act to violate the Establishment Clause, but the Supreme Court reversed, emphasizing the importance of voluntariness. The Court has extended this principle to all manner of religious activity within the context of governmentally sponsored programs as a requirement of the Free Speech Clause of the First Amendment, so long as there is no favoritism and no realistic danger of coercion. The result is that schools may not sponsor prayer that pressures students to comply, but neither may they restrict the free exercise of religion by teachers and students.

When the religious observer is an authority figure, the line between private religious observance and indirect coercion can be hard to draw. A 2022 decision, *Kennedy v. Bremerton School District*, is illustrative. A public school football coach, a devout Christian, would offer a prayer in the locker room before games, use religious imagery as part of his inspirational exhortations to the team, and—most conspicuously—drop to his knees at the end of a game, on the fifty-yard line, to offer a silent but very public prayer. The problem, of course, is that even if students are not required to join in, they might very well do so to curry favor with the coach. After five years of this, the school district got wind of the practice and decided to intervene. By the time the case got to the Supreme Court, the coach had agreed not to offer the locker room prayer, not to include religious references in his inspirational talks, and to wait until his team had left the field and were doing other things before offering his fifty-yard-line prayer. Nonetheless, the school district suspended him from his job when he persisted in offering his postgame silent prayer. The coach sued under the Free Exercise Clause, but the lower court rejected his claim, holding that it would violate the Establishment Clause to allow him to engage in this prayer.[14]

In the Supreme Court, the case was one of the most controversial of a controversial term, but the controversy was more over what facts were at issue than the underlying principle. Not all religious acts by teachers while they are on duty present danger of coercion, and some are central to the teacher's right of free exercise. A teacher surely may wear identifiably religious garb, such as a hijab, yarmulke, or cross; a teacher surely may offer a silent prayer of thanks for lunch in the cafeteria, even if students are able to see; a teacher may surely attend worship services even if the students are aware of that fact. That a popular teacher may be a role model is not a sufficient basis for forcing the teacher to forego private acts that manifest his or her religious faith. The Supreme Court's decision in favor of the coach in this case did not greenlight acts that have coercive effect, and it left in full force the principles of the *School Prayer Cases*. The dissenters' complaint was not really with the legal holding, but with the majority's refusal to analyze the fifty-yard-line prayer in the context of the coach's earlier, more problematic, conduct. They contended that the coach's prior course of conduct remained relevant, and presented a real risk of coercion. Perhaps the real question is whether religious acts by authority figures should be presumed to be personal (and protected) in the absence of proof of coercive effect, or the opposite. The line will often not be clear.

CHAPTER 9

. . .

Conflicts Over Symbols

PUBLIC RELIGIOUS SYMBOLS are relatively rare in the United States compared with other parts of the world, perhaps because the austere Protestantism that was so dominant in the early years disdained crosses and religious images as vestiges of "popish" idolatry. (For example, Puritans did not celebrate Christmas.) The most common public manifestations of religion are found in place names—Providence, Rhode Island; Zion, Illinois; Corpus Christi, Texas; Saint Paul, Minnesota—which (oddly) have never been challenged in court. The seal of the city of Zion and an aircraft carrier named for Corpus Christi were challenged, but not the city names themselves. There are a fair number of crosses on public land, most of them associated with memorials to the departed, most often to veterans. San Jose, California, boasts a statue of the Aztec god Quetzalcoatl (upheld by a federal district court). Religious images often are part of artwork solemnizing civic buildings. The most famous are Moses and Mohammed on the frieze of the Supreme Court's courtroom, beloved of lawyers arguing against too strict an interpretation of the separation of church and state. (As the marshal cries, "God save the United States and this Honorable Court!") Most common today are nativity scenes, menorahs, stars, Christmas trees, and other symbols of the holiday season.

No one even *thought* to challenge the public display of religious symbols under the Establishment Clause until the 1950s. No symbols case got to the Supreme Court until the early 1980s. Since then, litigation over religious symbols has proliferated. For reasons that somewhat elude your authors, cases over nativity scenes, Ten Commandments monuments, crosses, and even Christmas trees and menorahs seem to excite popular passions more than seemingly more consequential Establishment Clause issues about matters like educational alternatives for disadvantaged children or shuttering houses of worship for nearly a year during a pandemic. Symbols are, by definition, merely symbolic. But apparently they matter a lot. Here's a theory: Who gets to control public space is a visible signal of who has power in our culture. Can Christians post replicas of the Ten Commandments in public courtrooms or include Christmas music in the high school choir repertoire? Can secularists insist on removal of religious trappings from public spaces in December or force a city in Maryland to chop the arms off a veterans memorial cross in a busy intersection? The cases—or more precisely, the Supreme Court's decisions in the cases—are the real prize, more important than the symbols themselves.

Almost no one admires the Supreme Court's decisions on the constitutionality of government-sponsored religious symbols. From its first foray into the field in 1984, the Court's decisions have been highly fractured, often governed by the thinking of one or two swing justices. No one is satisfied. Secularists believe any public religious symbol demeans the citizenship of nonbelievers. Believers think the cases trivialize and threaten traditional religion. Commentators of all stripes find them inconsistent and incoherent.

The Court has recently proposed an approach that, though theoretically unsatisfying, may have the salutary effect of focusing lower

courts on symbols cases that actually entail a live political controversy. Reducing the number of cases may lower the temperature.

DO THESE CASES BELONG IN COURT?

It is far from obvious that religious symbols should be regarded as a
question of constitutional law in the first place. No one—to the best
of our researches—ever claimed at the founding that the display
of religious symbols was a form of religious establishment.[1] To the
contrary, Americans across the spectrum used biblical language and
imagery to give emotional depth to their words and messages. When
Benjamin Franklin and Thomas Jefferson, both of whom were religiously unorthodox and disestablishmentarian, were appointed to
a committee to design a seal for the new nation, they chose a scene
from the Bible—Moses leading the Jewish people across the Red
Sea—with the words "Rebellion to Tyrants Is Obedience to God."[2]

The seal officially adopted in 1782 likewise had religious imagery: an eye representing "the Eye of Providence" surrounded by "Glory" above the motto *Annuit Coeptis*—"He [God] has favored our undertakings."[3] And one of the earliest monuments in the nation's capital—the Washington Monument (begun in 1848)—has inscribed in Latin at its apex "Praise be to God."

No one suggested that the Bill of Rights was offended by these symbols.

President George Washington's 1789 Thanksgiving Day Proclamation recommended "a day of public thanksgiving and prayer" for the "Supreme Being['s]" role in "the foundations and successes of our young Nation." A church service was part of Washington's first inaugural, but no member of Congress refused to attend because of separationist concerns. Washington's personal addition to the oath of office—"So Help Me God"—was controversial in some quarters, but not because it was a religious reference. It was because that was the way the king ended his oath. The Constitution was dated "the Year of our Lord" and exempted Sunday from the count of days for the president to sign legislation. And no less disestablishmentarian a president than Jefferson allowed various denominations to use the Capitol and other federal buildings for weekly worship services—which he even attended. To be sure, early leaders such as Washington were generally scrupulous to use broad, nonsectarian language, but this was a matter of statesmanship and civility, not of constitutional law.

Some of these religious references drew criticism—but only when they sought to influence actual practice by the people. Passive symbols passed without controversy. Jefferson, for instance, declined to proclaim days of thanksgiving, explaining in a private letter that prescribing "religious exercises" was "an act of discipline" that interfered with the right of "every religious society . . . to determine for itself the times for these exercises, & the objects proper for them, according to their own particular tenets." Madison, long after retirement, regretted issuing proclamations "recommending thanksgiving & fasts" because "the members of a Govt. as such . . . can not form an Convocation, Council or Synod, and as such issue decrees or injunctions addressed to the faith or the Consciences of the people."[4] Putting aside the fact that Jefferson and Madison were clearly in a minority about this, their objection might extend to such modern practices as the National Day of Prayer, but not to the display of passive symbols on government property.

Even if the Establishment Clause addresses religious symbols, it is doubtful that the proper forum for resolving disputes about them is the courts. Not every important constitutional question is "justiciable." Outside of religious symbols litigation, the Supreme Court has consistently held that litigants lack standing to challenge government practices when their only claim of injury is mere offense, or "psychological discomfort." In the race discrimination context, where public display of Confederate symbols on state flags and other prominent locations is a far more unambiguous insult to the equal citizenship status of Black Americans, the courts have not intervened. Those symbols have instead been challenged, often successfully, in the political arena. The Supreme Court has never explained why there should be a special rule for religious symbols, and we think it would have been better if the Court had never entered this minefield.

Perhaps the most egregious example is *Salazar v. Buono*,[5] a case involving a cross erected by a local VFW post in 1934 in the Mojave Desert, on federal park land some forty miles down a dirt road. A sign, no longer present, stated that the cross was erected "In the Memory of the Dead of All Wars." Now the cross is most remembered as a symbol of pointless and expensive culture-war litigation. A former park employee of the Mojave Desert Preserve filed a lawsuit after he retired and moved to Oregon. The case went twice to the Ninth Circuit, which ordered it removed, in conflict with the United States Congress, which passed a statute ordering it restored and protected. At the order of the court, the cross was encased in a wooden box so that passersby could not see that it was a cross, and at one point it was stolen by vandals apparently inspired by the constitutional challenge. If ever there was a case where the wisdom of enforcing standing rules was made evident, this was it.

As a practical matter, however, your authors do not suggest that now—after forty years of entertaining and deciding religious symbols cases—the Court should completely withdraw from the fray, either on grounds of substantive Establishment Clause law or on standing grounds (though many lawsuits should probably be tossed). A total abandonment of the field would be seen as a dramatic retreat from constitutional protections for religious minorities and would likely create more divisiveness and interreligious ill will than it would solve. As will be seen below, the Court has recently arrived at a more irenic, if less principled, resolution to the conflict.

THE COURT'S STRUGGLES TO FIND A COHERENT STANDARD

The Supreme Court has struggled to identify a coherent principle for deciding religious symbol cases. Its first such case, *Lynch v. Donnelly*, arrived in 1984.[6] *Lynch* involved a Christmas holiday display cosponsored by the City of Pawtucket, Rhode Island, and its downtown retail merchants' association. The display featured Christmas trees, wreaths, candy cane poles, Santa Clauses, cut-out bears, and—memorably—a talking wishing well. A focal point of the display was a nativity scene, which was the subject of the litigation. Plaintiffs argued that the nativity scene was a "sectarian" element with no secular purpose and with the primary effect of benefiting religion, and asked the Court to remove it. A 5–4 majority refused. Although this was the first time any government action that did not affect the plaintiffs in any concrete way (other than annoying them) and did not involve the expenditure of public funds had ever been challenged in the Court under the Establishment Clause, neither the majority, written by Chief Justice Burger, nor the dissents, written by Justices Brennan and Harry Blackmun, paused to ponder why the plaintiffs had standing to sue or whether a "passive symbol" should be governed by the same constitutional analysis applied to such issues as school aid or accommodations. They just trundled forward under the three-part *Lemon* test, reaching opposite conclusions.

How would the *Lemon* test answer the case? The secular purpose was obvious from the identity of the retail merchants' association as sponsor: to draw shoppers to downtown stores, where they would spend money. The effect on religious belief or practice was almost certainly negligible, and there was no evidence of "entanglement." But no less an authority than Justice Brennan thought just the opposite. He thought it was an easy case under the *Lemon* test—against the nativity scene.

Justice Sandra Day O'Connor, new to the Court, realized that religious symbol cases presented a novel question and that the *Lemon* test is unsuited to answering it. She propounded a theory that the central purpose of the Establishment Clause is to prevent the government from conveying messages of "endorsement" or "disapproval" of religion. "Endorsement," she explained, "sends a message to nonadherents that they are outsiders, not full members of the political community, and an accompanying message to adherents that they are insiders, favored members of the political community. Disapproval sends the opposite message." The endorsement test has several seemingly insuperable difficulties, discussed below, but at least the approach is connected to a plausible understanding of the purposes of disestablishment: to create equality of citizenship among persons of all faiths, including atheism or no faith at all. It bears at least an affinity with the prohibition on "sect preference," which was part of the historic disestablishment.

As a practical "test," though, the endorsement test proved to be singularly unhelpful. Justice O'Connor advised courts to determine whether "the challenged governmental action is sufficiently likely to be perceived by adherents of the controlling denominations as an endorsement, and by the nonadherents as a disapproval, of their individual religious choices." But what if—as is almost always the case—people have *different perceptions*? Some citizens of Pawtucket regarded the nativity scene as a sectarian intrusion, while others enjoyed it as a typical part of the holiday season, no less appropriate than the Santa Clauses. Some thought removal of the nativity scene, just because it was religious, would be hostile, not neutral, toward religion. (The Mayor said removing the crèche would be "taking Christ out of Christmas.") Instead of asking how actual people perceived the nativity scene—an inquiry that would reveal only division—Justice O'Connor said to consult the view of a "reasonable observer" conversant with the history and context of the display. But which, among the conflicting perceptions, was the "reasonable" one? If divorced from the actual perceptions of real people, the endorsement test reduces to the "eye-of-the-beholder"—in other words, the judge. Justice O'Connor herself concluded that the Pawtucket nativity scene was not an endorsement, but the dissenting justices along with many scholarly commentators were unpersuaded. Given O'Connor's background, some joked that her reasonable observer test was really a "reasonable Episcopalian test."

Still, a slender majority of the Court thought that the endorsement test would offer a path through the quagmire. Predictably, it did no such thing. The first test of the new approach came in two cases from Pittsburgh, Pennsylvania, one involving a nativity scene on the steps of the county courthouse and the other a large menorah in a city park nearby, accompanied by a still larger Christmas tree and a sign saying "salute to liberty." The Court fractured three ways. Four justices thought both the nativity scene and the menorah were permissible, three justices thought both symbols were impermissible, and two justices—O'Connor and Blackmun—thought the nativity scene was impermissible but the menorah was fine. Why was a nativity scene constitutional in Pawtucket but not in Pittsburgh? The key, according to Justice Blackmun's controlling opinion, was that the Pawtucket nativity scene was surrounded by the Santa Clauses, candy canes, and a talking wishing well, which leached the nativity scene of its religiosity, while the Pittsburgh nativity scene was alone (if you ignore the menorah, tree, etc., displayed nearby). Predictably, the decision pleased no one. Secularists thought the government should not be sponsoring nativity scenes anywhere, no matter how festooned they might be with holiday kitsch. Religious people did not like the thought that their holy symbols could be seen in public only when diluted with the trappings of materialism.

As a result of these indeterminate decisions, more and more cases were brought to challenge religious symbols around the country—not just in holiday displays but in municipal seals, statuary, and other artwork. It was difficult in these cases for the cities to prevail: Whatever purpose governments might have for seals, symbols, holiday displays, or artwork, plaintiffs could always demand to know why that purpose could not be achieved without the religious imagery—just as Justice Brennan had argued that the festive and commercial purposes of the Pawtucket holiday display could have been met by the Santa Clauses, etc., without a nativity scene. Moreover, because victorious plaintiffs are entitled to attorney fees if they prevail while defendants bear their own litigation costs, cash-strapped municipalities very frequently settle the cases and remove the symbols, whether or not they really make religious minorities feel like outsiders to the political community.

In a brace of cases involving Ten Commandments displays, the Court again fractured 4–4 with a single justice—Stephen Breyer—voting opposite ways and thus commanding the majority in both. Justice Breyer stressed that the purpose of the Establishment Clause is to reduce divisiveness across religious lines. The distinction between the two displays, in his view, was that the granite monument outside a courthouse in Texas had been there for many decades without raising a commotion, while the framed copies of the Commandments in two Kentucky courthouses were recent additions, installed by politicians making jingoistic speeches. The latter fostered religious divisiveness while the former did not.

Finally, in 2019, in a case out of Maryland, the Court for the first time put together a 7–2 majority, jettisoning the *Lemon* test and the endorsement test, and embracing something akin to Justice Breyer's approach. More on that below.

The endorsement test is the Court's most thoughtful attempt to find a neutral solution to religious symbol cases. Unfortunately, it presents insuperable logical and practical problems. The Court seems to have abandoned it.

1. The test confuses endorsement with preference. Justice O'Connor's formulation of the test assumes that "endorsement" is tantamount to a message "that religion or a particular religious belief is favored or preferred."[7] That is not necessarily so. Think of ethnic festivals. When Chicago has a Polish festival in the summer, featuring Polish food, Polish beverages, Polish music, Polish dancing, and lectures on Polish literature and history, it is no doubt "endorsing" the role of Polish immigrants to American and Chicagoan life, but does it make Dutch or Tamil people feel like second-class citizens? The federal government maintains a spectacular Museum of African American History and Culture in a prominent location on the National Mall, right next to the Washington Monument. The presence of this museum must surely convey a message of affirmation to African Americans, but it would be a mistake to think that it sends any messages that Americans of other races are "outsiders, not full members of the political community." Congress passes hundreds of resolutions every year praising various people, products, activities, and events—some of them religious—which no doubt make people affiliated with those things feel good, which is why representatives bother to sponsor them. But do these endorsements carry a message of disapproval for everything else? When Congress declares November 14 to be National Pickle Day, are olive eaters demoted to second-class citizens? It is possible to endorse any number of beliefs, practices, people, places, or things without casting aspersions on others. In a pluralistic society, the better course is to broaden public celebrations to recognize more religious traditions rather than to extirpate them all.

2. *There is a difference between not erecting a symbol and demolishing one that is already in place.* Much discussion of religious symbol cases seems to proceed as if the question before the courts were whether it is good or bad for the symbol to be displayed. That is never the question. The question is whether the symbol should be *removed*, which is quite a different proposition. Only recently has the Court recognized this problem. When a symbol is of long standing, the Court observed in *American Legion v. American Humanist Ass'n* (2019),[8] "removing it may no longer appear neutral, especially to the local community for which it has taken on particular meaning." More pointedly, the Court observed that a "government that roams the land, tearing down monuments with religious symbolism and scrubbing away any reference to the divine will strike many as aggressively hostile to religion." By the same token, erecting a religious symbol for the first time can be—perhaps intentionally—an act of majoritarian triumphalism, inconsistent with the values if not the letter of the Establishment Clause. Alabama state Judge Roy Moore's provocative erection of a two-and-a-half-ton granite monument to the Ten Commandments at the state supreme court building was an obvious poke in the eye to "secular humanists" and propelled him to national prominence and nomination to the United States Senate. It also succeeded in making the Ten Commandments, which once had been a relatively uncontroversial symbol of the sacred origins of law, into a polarizing symbol of religious disputation. This is not to say that all newly erected religious symbols are of this sort. A cross

was erected on the site of the 9/11 attacks to honor the dead and has not been regarded as an insult to non-Christian faiths.

The symbolic significance of departures from the status quo is not a problem for Establishment Clause cases about concrete harms to people affected by government action—such as whether to deny families tuition assistance if they choose a religious school or to shield a religious group from liability under the discrimination laws. In such cases, the legal rights of one side or the other are redressed in a material way, and any symbolic message the decision might communicate to the public is purely secondary. But in the symbol cases, the message is all that is at stake. The courts need to be attentive to the fact that departure from a long-established status quo will often affect the message, perhaps dramatically.

   3. The test lacks a baseline for judging approval or disapproval. The "reasonable observer" test provides absolutely no guidance to lower courts or municipalities about which symbols square with the Establishment Clause and which do not. To tell decision makers to make a "reasonable" judgment is to tell them to do what they think is right. It is a Rorschach test; it tells a lot about the test taker but nothing useful about the observed phenomenon. The endorsement "test" is thus not truly a "test" for identifying what symbols violate the Establishment Clause. It is really just an argument for why religious symbols might be thought to raise an issue under the Establishment Clause. But by creating the appearance of being a test, it does some concrete damage. The reasonable observer standard by definition identifies one view as being the most or only "reasonable" one. Thus, an unsuccessful challenger to a religious symbol, like the plaintiffs in *Lynch*, will not only lose on the merits, but in the process their point of view is labeled less than "reasonable." It would be better for the Court to acknowledge openly that there are many reasonable perspectives and explain why it chooses one over another in a particular case.

Plaintiffs in symbols cases have an implicit baseline for judging the appropriateness of religious symbols in government space: There should be none.[9] In every case, they will demand to know why a secular symbol would not have accomplished the government's purpose just as well. The effect, over time, is to denude the public square of all religious symbols. But neutrality and secularism are not the same thing. The baseline for evaluating neutrality is not a secular blank slate to which any addition of a religiously expressive element is a sectarian intrusion. The Establishment Clause was not intended to secularize society any more than it was to Christianize it. Its purpose was to prevent the government from using its power to mold the society into any particular religious shape; it was to leave the degree and nature of religious practice to the free choice of the people, as nearly as is possible.

THE COURT'S RECENT RESOLUTION

In 2019, the Supreme Court for the first time reached near-consensus in a religious symbols case. While the decision lacks theoretical rigor, it promises a practical end to most of the squabbling over religious symbols. *American Legion v. American Humanist Ass'n* involved a ninety-four-year-old war memorial in Bladensburg, Maryland. Inspired by the military cemeteries for American soldiers in Europe, with their dramatic rows of white crosses, the memorial takes the form of a large Latin cross with various patriotic inscriptions. It towers above the surrounding countryside. It was designed by a local citizens' commission shortly after World War I to honor the community's fallen soldiers, and was completed by the efforts of the American Legion, a private veterans' group. The property is now owned and maintained by the state. Applying the *Lemon* test, the lower court ordered that the cross be dismantled or—remarkably—that its arms be lopped off.

In an opinion written by Justice Alito and joined by Chief Justice Roberts and Justices Breyer, Kagan, and Kavanaugh, the Court distinguished between "retaining established, religiously expressive monuments, symbols, and practices" and "erecting or adopting new ones" and held that the "passage of time gives rise to a strong presumption of constitutionality." Two more justices, Thomas and Gorsuch, indicated agreement with the general approach but did not join the opinion for the Court because they thought the plaintiffs lacked standing to sue and thus that the Court lacked jurisdiction. There were only two dissenters. The meaning is clear: Lower courts may no longer apply the nebulous *Lemon* factors to overturn religiously expressive monuments, symbols, or practices that were created in the past. The Court did not state what "test" will apply to the erection of new monuments, but it appears likely that the key question will be whether they go beyond acknowledging the role that religion plays in the lives of the people to effectively declare one religion to be superior or officially privileged, or to declare a minority religious view to be false or unworthy of respect.

The Court's emphasis on the "passage of time" might not appear to have persuasive theoretical grounding. Why would a new symbol be more likely to reflect an establishment of religion than an old one? But the approach has three distinct practical virtues. First, historical longevity leaves in place symbols that are less likely to be the product of religious division today, and therefore less likely to affect religious sentiment one way or the other. If the religious character of society changes, it can use the ordinary political process to amend its public symbols to reflect those changes. In a pluralistic society, this is more likely than not to lead to changes to public symbols that are incremental and inclusive.

The passage-of-time approach also solves the departure-from-status-quo problem with a more judicially manageable test. Lower courts will be able to apply it, and doing so will not send a signal that *the Court* "endorses" one side's perception of a symbol's meaning over the other's. And finally, because the vast majority of religious symbols in the United States are of long standing, the approach will dry up most litigation, which has proven to be divisive rather than helpful. Because the decision commanded seven votes, including two justices from the liberal-progressive wing, there is every reason to believe that the decision will prove stable over the foreseeable future. That is a considerable improvement over the Court's prior, fractured attempts to police religious symbols, which were neither principled, nor consistent, nor helpful. The new approach may lack elegance, but hopefully it will put an end to a divisive body of law.

CHAPTER 10

. . .

Church Autonomy

THE SEPARATION OF church and state is a two-way proposition. The state may no more control the church than the church may control the state. While much that churches do in the world is subject to regulation, the internal governance of religious organizations is off limits. As Thomas Jefferson explained, "The government of the United States [is] interdicted by the Constitution from intermeddling with religious institutions, their doctrines, discipline, or exercises."[1] As we saw in Chapter 3, in addition to ending government compulsion with respect to duties to God and official preferences for one (or more) religious faiths over the others, disestablishment invariably guaranteed a right of self-governance to religious institutions. Consistent with that original vision, the Supreme Court has long recognized "a spirit of freedom for religious organizations, an independence from secular control or manipulation, in short, power to decide for themselves, free from state interference, matters of church government as well as those of faith and doctrine."[2]

Overt government control over internal church matters ended with disestablishment, but even today legal regimes enacted for other purposes sometimes have the effect of intruding into matters of internal church governance. The two most prominent sources of intrusion are employment law and the application of property law to church splits. In both areas, we will begin with the relevant history and move to current controversy.

CHURCH EMPLOYMENT

As we saw in Chapter 1, a central feature of the establishment of religion was control over the selection and discipline of the clergy. The effect on the Church of England, especially in the American South, was ruinous—creating a servile and poorly compensated clergy under the thumb of royal governors and the planter aristocracy. Clergy licensing laws also hampered the efforts of dissenting churches, like the Baptists, to evangelize and compete with the settled ministry. Church historians credit the extraordinary expansion and flourishing of American religion in the Second Great Awakening to the competition set off by disestablishment. Unlike the funding issue, which tended to divide dissenters from Anglicans and Congregationalists, almost all religious factions shared the disestablishmentarian drive to end government control over clergy selection. As the Baptists of Ashfield, Massachusetts, said in a 1768 petition: "If we may not settle and support a minister agreeable to our own consciences, where is liberty of conscience?"[3]

Each of the states that first maintained an establishment and later adopted a state constitutional amendment forbidding establishment of religion—South Carolina, New Hampshire, Connecticut, Maine, and Massachusetts—adopted at the same time an express provision that all "religious societies" have the "exclusive" right to choose their own ministers.[4] The South Carolina Constitution of 1778, for example, declared that "the people of this State may forever enjoy the right of electing their own pastors or clergy."[5] The New Hampshire Constitution of 1784 stated that "religious societies, shall at all times, have the exclusive right of electing their own public teachers."[6] This demonstrates that church autonomy over its choice of clergy was an element of disestablishment.

Not surprisingly, therefore, when the issue of government involvement in clergy selection first surfaced at the federal level, Secretary of State Madison, after consulting with President Jefferson, declared in ringing terms that "the selection of ecclesiastical individuals" is entrusted entirely to the churches. After completion of the Louisiana Purchase, Roman Catholic Bishop John Carroll, in imitation of European practice, consulted the Secretary of State about whom to appoint to lead the church in the new territory. Madison responded that the appointment of church "functionaries" was "entirely ecclesiastical," and that he would adhere to "the scrupulous policy of the Constitution in guarding against a political influence in religious affairs."[7] Notice that Madison used the broad language of "functionaries" and "religious individuals" instead of the narrower language of clergy, bishop, or minister.

Today the most common form of governmental regulation of church employment stems from antidiscrimination laws. This is not a new development. It arose immediately after adoption of the Fourteenth Amendment, when the first civil rights laws were passed. These debates have particular significance for constitutional interpretation because, as explained in Chapter 3, it is through the Fourteenth Amendment that the Religion Clauses now apply to actions of state and local governments. An early version of what became the Civil Rights Act of 1875[8] extended the anti-discrimination prohibitions of the Act to "church institutions" in common with railroads, inns, theaters, schools, and most other public conveyances and meeting places.[9] This is much like the application of the current federal employment discrimination law, Title VII, to a church. After a number of senators objected on First Amendment grounds, churches were excised from coverage.

Senator Frederick Frelinghuysen of New Jersey[10]—later floor leader for the Civil Rights Act—argued that its application to the inner workings of church institutions was "an infringement of the Constitution." He raised a series of hypothetical applications of the provision, which would be equally applicable to Title VII:

> Now, the Japanese, in California, see proper to make nationality, we will suppose, a part of their religion, and to exclude all who do not belong to their people from their worship; or, the Huguenots of South Carolina might form a religious society, and one of their regulations be that no one should be a member unless a descendant of the Huguenots; or, the Scotch Presbyterians might declare that none shall be connected with their church unless producing a certificate from the church at home; or, the Africans might form a church making emancipation an essential to membership.

The Act's "equal rights" mandate in such instances, he said, would impose "a restriction upon the perfect freedom of religious worship" by denying a church the "liberty to exclude those who do not meet the requirements stated."

Other supporters of the Act likewise objected to the provision on constitutional grounds. Senator Matthew Carpenter of Wisconsin explained that the Act's application to churches was "in violation of the spirit of the Constitution . . . and is in conflict with what [the framers] believed they had secured." According to him, "the debates in the Convention on that subject, and [] the Federalist, and [] the political literature of that day" established that "they who framed the Constitution of the United States intended to, and thought they had, carefully excluded the whole subject of religion from Federal control or interference." In making this argument, Carpenter explained that the Religion Clauses were not directed solely "against the establishment of a particular faith to the prejudice or exclusion of others," but also barred certain laws that apply "equally upon all and compel[] all to observe its precepts." Thus, it did not matter that the proposed Civil Rights Act was neutral and generally applicable to all denominations.

Similarly, Senator Oliver Morton of Indiana, a radical supporter of civil rights, argued that "people have a right to say how they will worship, what they will worship, and with whom they will worship; and, if they have a right to say how they will worship, and with whom they will worship, then under the Constitution of the United States you cannot pass this provision with regard to churches." Still other senators objected to the provision on religious liberty grounds without explicitly invoking the Constitution.[11] The Supreme Court has made no reference to any of this history in its decisions, but those decisions are nonetheless consistent with it.

Employment discrimination law has the potential to intrude upon church autonomy in three important ways. First—and most blatantly—the prohibition on discrimination on the basis of religion, if applied to religious groups, would strike at the core of freedom of association, the right of any group (religious or not) to coalesce on the basis of their shared ideas and purposes. As applied to secular entities, the prohibition on religious discrimination is of course essential and valuable, but it is a category error to apply religious discrimination laws to religious organizations. A synagogue must not be forced to hire gentiles as rabbis, or to admit non-Jews to their congregations. Such exclusion is not a product of bigotry, but of the fundamental right to worship with fellow believers. Accordingly, from the beginning, Congress has exempted religious organizations from the prohibition of discrimination on the basis of religion (though not all state discrimination laws do so). This exemption—Section 702(a) of

Title VII of the Civil Rights Act of 1964—applies to all employees of all religious organizations, but it only exempts them from liability for discrimination on the basis of religion.

Second, some bases of employment discrimination law, if applied to some positions within the church, would directly conflict with religious doctrine. Most obviously, the prohibition on discrimination on the basis of sex, if applied to religious groups with an all-male clergy—such as Orthodox Judaism, Roman Catholicism, some Protestant denominations, Orthodox Christianity, Islam, and some Native American religions—would violate their freedom to worship in accordance with their own view of their duties to God.

Third, even religious groups with no such restrictions on the sex of their clergy can be affected by such laws, because a claim of discrimination would entail a civil investigation (by court or regulatory agency) of whether a candidate for the ministry was passed over in favor of a less qualified candidate of a different race or sex. This would require the state to determine who is most qualified to serve as a minister—something it is no business of the state to decide.

Accordingly, the Supreme Court held unanimously in *Hosanna-Tabor Evangelical Lutheran Church & School v. EEOC* that religious groups have an absolute right to choose their "ministers" and are immune from suit for discrimination against a ministerial employee. This is not merely a defense in court: The Constitution altogether "bars such a suit."[12] In contrast to the statutory exemption from religious discrimination laws, this constitutional immunity is applicable to all types of discrimination, but it is confined to those employees who communicate the church's teaching, conduct worship, or have other sensitive roles analogous to clergy. Although called the "ministerial exception," it extends beyond persons formally ordained as clergy, and in three cases it has been applied by the Supreme Court to teachers of religious classes in religious schools.[13] The reach of the immunity is hotly contested and is the subject of frequent litigation, because of the fear that too expansive a definition of "minister" would exempt ordinary employees of religious enterprises—such as nurses at hospitals affiliated with religious denominations—from the protection of employment discrimination laws.

CHURCH PROPERTY DISPUTES

Many religious faiths regard their form of church organization as a matter of doctrine, compelled by their reading of scripture or other authority. If the state imposes a legal form antithetical to the church's own doctrine, this is a severe imposition on their right to worship in accordance with religious conscience and conviction. As recounted in Chapter 3, almost all states struggled with what legal structure religious societies would take after disestablishment. Corporate form was the most convenient, but some religious groups could not, consistent with their beliefs, seek a corporate charter. Moreover, during the founding period, corporations were a quasi-public category. Legislatures granted corporate charters on a case-by-case basis to entities serving the public good, and those charters limited the corporations' purposes and specified the corporations' form of organization. The practice of granting corporate charters to churches thus had the odor of special legislation and seemed to invite governmental control over the church's mission and internal workings. Recall President Madison's veto of a congressional statute chartering a religious corporation in the District of Columbia on these grounds (Chapter 3). The solution was general incorporation laws, in which churches could obtain a corporate charter as a matter of legal right, without needing special legislative authorization.

But general incorporation laws presented two difficulties. First, because of the widespread distrust of corporations in the Jacksonian era, the right to incorporate was often conditioned on a restriction of the amount of property the corporate entity could own. Maryland limited church landholdings to two acres; North Carolina prohibited churches from owning profit-producing property in excess of 200 pounds in revenue per year. Second, the most familiar corporate form placed control of the property in trustees elected by the membership. This form accorded with most Protestant churches, but it was antithetical to the hierarchical ecclesiology of the Catholic Church and some other denominations. The canons of the Roman Catholic church require that title to most church property be vested in the bishop—not in lay trustees. Yet a number of states in the mid-nineteenth century passed statutes requiring that religious corporations be controlled by lay boards elected by the congregation. In part this was due to the wave of anti-Catholicism that swept the nation in the mid-nineteenth century, in part it was driven by the desire of some Catholics for greater democratization of their church, and in part it just seemed natural and normal. Conflicts between lay trustees and the Catholic hierarchy raged in cities all over the United States for about seventy-five years before the bishops prevailed. Today, almost without exception, the Catholic Church may organize its property as it sees fit.[14]

It was hard enough to figure out how to adjust civil property and trust law to conform to the ecclesiological differences among various religious organizations, but it has proven all but impossible to find and follow neutral principles for the resolution of church splits. If individual congregations—whose members typically paid for and maintained the church property—decide to sever ties with the denomination, which side keeps the property? In recent years, as several large mainline Protestant denominations have divided over issues such as biblical interpretation and same-sex marriage, litigation over the ownership of church property has occurred in almost every state, costing millions of dollars and inflicting untold emotional (and maybe even spiritual) injury on believers whose sacred spaces are wrenched away from them. When legal title to the property is vested in the denomination or the hierarchy, the answer is simple: The denomination keeps the property. But if legal title is vested in the local congregation or its trustees, the courts are almost evenly split over which side prevails.

These cases are as old as the republic.[15] For roughly 150 years, the dominant approach in common law jurisdictions was the "English rule," which required courts to award the property to whichever faction of the church had adhered to the intent of the original donor, which almost always meant that courts had to determine which group had adhered to "the true standard of faith" for that denomination. Although this approach is now understood as plainly unconstitutional, it was based on a common-sense intuition about donor intent: Donors give to the church they believe in, and allowing a church to use that donated property to propagate a substantially different doctrine would do violence to the original donors' intent.

The English rule raised several difficulties, which we now recognize as insuperable constitutional objections. First, it required civil courts to decide which faction is correct about church doctrine. Second, the assumption that donors are focused on doctrine may not always be true. Some may care more about tradition and community. In a conflict between doctrinal consistency and institutional continuity, some donors might prefer the latter. I am a lifelong Presbyterian, they might say, and I am going to stick with the denomination even if it has abandoned its long-held teaching on predestination (or whatever is the issue of the day). Even more seriously, the English rule would penalize any major evolution of church doctrine, lest the church lose its property to a faction of traditionalists. Think about the acceptance of female ministers in many denominations, or the abandonment by the LDS Church of its erstwhile racial limitations on the priesthood. Why should courts assume that church doctrine is frozen in time?

Whatever the answer may be to these questions, one thing is certain: It is not the government's business to decide them. As Madison wrote in his *Memorial and Remonstrance*, the notion that "the Civil Magistrate is a competent Judge of Religious truth" is "an arrogant pretension falsified by the contradictory opinions of Rulers in all ages."[16] If the courts choose the winners in these conflicts, the effect is an establishment of the religion that they favor over the one they reject.

In 1872, in *Watson v. Jones*, involving a church split over the issue of slavery, the Supreme Court rejected the English rule as a matter of federal common law. In ringing terms, the Court declared "unquestioned" the "right to organize voluntary religious associations to assist in the expression and dissemination of any religious doctrine."[17] In a series of cases in the twentieth century, the Court constitutionalized *Watson*'s rejection of the English rule. No longer would courts decide for themselves which faction was most true to the faith. These decisions constitutionalized two related principles: first, that civil courts should not decide ecclesiastical questions, and second, that churches have a First Amendment right to be free from state interference in their internal affairs. The first derives primarily from the Establishment Clause, barring civil "entanglement" in religious matters, and the second derives primarily from the Free Exercise Clause, protecting the right of believers and religious institutions to order their affairs in accordance with their own convictions. These related principles are essentially the same as those articulated by the Court in *Hosanna-Tabor*. Significantly, the Court recognized that religious freedom is not merely individual but also institutional, and that the First Amendment protects the right of religious communities "to decide for themselves, free from state interference, matters of church government as well as those of faith and doctrine"—what students of religion would call "ecclesiology"—as well as "theology."

Unfortunately, it is not that easy. In many internal church controversies, for example, challenges by members to decisions of the church, such as excommunication, there is no question who the church is. Under *Watson*, the courts will defer to the governing authorities of the church and not second-guess their decisions, even if those decisions appear (to the outsider) to violate church rules or norms. But in church split cases, both sides lay claim to being the relevant church. How can secular courts know which side they should defer to?

There are two basic approaches. One divides the universe of church organizational schemes into two categories: hierarchical denominations and congregational denominations. If the denomination is hierarchical, the court will defer to the highest church tribunal, and if the denomination is congregational, the court will defer to the congregation. This is called the "deference" approach. The other approach, usually called the "neutral principles doctrine" (Justice Brennan called it, more accurately, the "formal title doctrine"),[18] looks to the formal legal documents governing ownership of property—deeds, trusts, corporate charters, and the like—to determine what body owns the property.

The main problem with the deference approach is that not all denominations fall into one of the two clear categories of hierarchical or purely congregational. The "hierarchical" label best fits the Roman Catholic Church, where local parishes are subject to strict, ascending levels of authority—from priests, to diocesan bishops, to the Pope. Typically, Roman Catholic parishes hold property in the name of the diocesan bishop—thus ensuring hierarchical control. At the other end of the polity spectrum, Quakers and Independent Baptists exemplify the classic "congregational" model. There are no religious bodies connecting individual congregations to each other. They recognize no ecclesiastical authority outside of the congregation. But many religious polities fall somewhere between the two, or change over time. Familiar examples include "mainline" Protestant denominations such as Methodists, Presbyterians, and Lutherans.

Other religious groups cannot be located on a hierarchical–congregational spectrum at all. This is particularly true of non-Christian religious organizations, which often do not share the Christian notions of "assembly" and "membership" that underlie the hierarchical–congregational dichotomy. Examples include Hindu temples, Islamic mosques, Sikh temples, and some Jewish groups. For these groups, a hierarchical–congregational categorization makes no sense.

In short, the blanket assumption that all churches are either hierarchical or congregational, and that all hierarchical churches share the same ideas of "implied consent," is a poor fit for many church polities. The true nature of a church's polity is a complex, nuanced factual question that civil courts are ill equipped to resolve. Often the issue that divides the congregation is who has the authority to speak for the church, a question that is irreducibly theological.

The second problem with the deference approach is that it systematically favors hierarchical forms of governance by treating mixed cases, those that are not "strictly congregational," as hierarchical. In practice, this has allowed the national denominational bodies of the Presbyterian and Episcopalian churches to assert ownership over local church buildings, even though those denominations have never regarded themselves as hierarchical. This thumb on the scales in favor of one polity over another violates the "sect neutrality" fundamentals of disestablishment.

That is why your authors believe that the neutral principles approach is most consistent with Establishment Clause principles. As the Supreme Court explained in *Jones v. Wolf*, the neutral principles approach "free[s] civil courts completely from entanglement in questions of religious doctrine, polity, and practice." Critically, it "shares the peculiar genius of private-law systems in

general—flexibility in ordering private rights and obligations to reflect the intentions of the parties"—and thus "accommodate[s] all
forms of religious organization and polity."[19] Hierarchical churches
can—and do—frame their property deeds to make the bishop or
other hierarchical authority the owner of the property. Congregational
churches can vest the property in their local governing body. And
intermediate ("connectional") churches can decide for themselves
where the property goes in the event of a split. Some churches provide for hierarchical authority while the church is united but give
local congregations secession rights, with their property, in the event
of irreconcilable differences.

All but four states have faced the choice between these two approaches, and they have divided roughly evenly. Unfortunately, the
Supreme Court has repeatedly denied petitions to resolve this conflict, perpetuating uncertainty, cost, and acrimony. Much like child
custody disputes after divorces, there is no perfect solution—but
unlike child custody disputes, there is no possibility of joint custody.
It is all or nothing. If, as we believe, half the states are favoring hierarchical over nonhierarchical forms of church governance, that is a
grave violation of Establishment Clause principles, which only the
Supreme Court can redress.

CHAPTER 11

. . .

Conclusion

Neutrality Beyond the Establishment Clause

AT THE NATION's founding, religion was the focal point of cultural division. Most founding-era (non-native) Americans were Christians, but do not be fooled: The divisions between Baptists and Anglicans, Quakers and Presbyterians, New Lights and Old Lights—not to mention Catholics and Protestants, the bitterest divide—were every bit as intense as the divisions among far more diverse Americans today.

In addition to matters of theology and modes of worship, Americans divided over the important question of religion's place in public life. The most common view at the founding was that religion is necessary for civic virtue. Washington called religion and morality "the firmest props of the duties of men and citizens." Others regarded religion as irrational and divisive. Thomas Jefferson, at least in private, worried that "sectarian dogmas" spark division and society would do well to cabin their influence on public affairs.[1] These conflicting dispositions continue to assert their influence today, with many reading the Establishment Clause to entrench one or the other. As this book has endeavored to show, neither of these views is consistent with the founders' understanding of disestablishment. The reason Americans rejected established religion was that they had come to believe that the government should not be in the business of promoting religious uniformity. As the Supreme Court would later say, "We sponsor an attitude on the part of government that shows no partiality to any one group and that lets each flourish according to the zeal of its adherents and the appeal of its dogma." The Establishment Clause is agnostic about religion. It favors neither the secular nor the religious, but instead reflects the idea that the nation's public life should reflect the type and degree of religiosity of the people themselves, a religiosity shaped as little as possible by government.

How the Establishment Clause accomplishes this remarkable blend of religious freedom and neutrality cannot be understood without reference to the kinds of laws that characterized an establishment of religion. England and colonial governments relied on a set of interrelated legal elements to foster religious uniformity: (1) government control over doctrine, governance, and personnel of the church; (2) compulsory church attendance; (3) compulsory financial support; (4) prohibitions on worship in dissenting churches; (5) use of church institutions for public functions; and (6) restriction of political participation to members of the established church. The states that inherited religious establishments dismantled them, purging their laws of these elements one by one. The Establishment Clause made sure that the federal government never adopted them, and the Fourteenth Amendment later applied parallel strictures to the states.

The Supreme Court's enforcement of the Clause over the years has been erratic and sometimes misguided. For over a century and a half, the Court said almost nothing. Then, based on an inaccurate and incomplete account of the history, the Court developed a three-part "test"—the *Lemon* test"—which directed courts to ask whether a law had a secular purpose, had the primary effect of advancing or inhibiting religion, or fostered government entanglement with religion. Each part of this "test" was not only ambiguous and manipulable, but in many cases it was also at odds with the underlying purposes of the Clause to promote religious neutrality, religious freedom, and church autonomy. In the 1980s, some of the justices began to question the wisdom of the *Lemon* approach, and for almost two decades the Court decided Establishment Clause cases without reliance on *Lemon*—while leaving the "test" formally in place to govern lower court adjudication, with the result that almost every Establishment Clause case was a reversal. More recently, the Court has abandoned *Lemon* as a one-size-fits-all test in favor of context-specific rules. The rules differ somewhat depending on the context, but they all are an effort to implement the principles underlying the historical understanding of the Establishment Clause, ensuring the government maintains religious neutrality and interferes with personal and corporate religious freedom as little as possible. Indeed, the Court has increasingly understood that in some sorts of cases—especially those involving religious symbols—sometimes the course that most promotes neutrality and freedom is for the Court to stay its hand.

The freedom ensured by the Establishment Clause has facilitated the development of the most religiously heterogenous society the world has ever known. Such diversity entails value pluralism—deep disagreement about important moral issues, the government's role in solving social problems, and even what constitutes a social problem in the first place.[2] This value pluralism undoubtedly creates cultural and political conflict. Some consider pluralism, for this reason, to be destabilizing. In recent years, Americans have become increasingly politically polarized, each side distrusting, even fearing, the other, and this polarization has in many cases been fueled by religious disagreement. The fear is driven, we think, more by apprehension that the "other side" will seize control of state power and use it to stamp out dissent than by any real desire on the part of most to create uniformity of opinion. The "other side," you see, is ruthless and aggressive, and will not hesitate to use politics and courts to impose its point of view on the entire country. Whatever actual threat either side poses rarely deserves the hyperbolic rhetoric and policy overreactions to which their opponents so often resort.

If the Establishment Clause were properly understood and comprehensively implemented, its very existence would dampen the fever of our extreme polarization, because it would guarantee that neither side can use its momentary political power to impose an orthodoxy and suppress disagreement. Each of us then could focus on living our own lives in accordance with conscience, expressing our beliefs to our children and to willing listeners, and evaluating public policies on their merits rather than on whether their adoption will empower "the other side."

It is impossible to know how long our current state of toxic polarization will last and how religious diversity and difference will play into it. America has always been home to religiously inspired culture warriors, from the Puritans to the abolitionists to the civil rights and pro-life movements—often with religious voices on both sides of the controversy. Even now, despite the narrative that divides the camps into religious traditionalists and the secular left, there are many left-leaning and progressive Americans—most notably in the Black church—who are motivated both politically and personally by religious convictions.[3] Religion can be a bridge as well as a divide. Who knows what America's fighting faiths will be in one hundred years? What is certain, though, is that the Establishment Clause, if properly understood and enforced, would help to ensure that the people decide that answer for themselves, through personal and collective persuasion and not in legislatures or courts.

The Establishment Clause itself is solely about religion, but establishments can come in many different flavors—secular and ideological as well as religious. Perhaps America's experience with the Establishment Clause can provide a model for handling analogous disputes of other kinds. Modern ideologies—Marxism, environmentalism, identitarianism, nationalism, populism, anti-racism, and numerous other "isms"—entail deep commitments to certain understandings of reality and sometimes resemble religion in their intensity, their seeming imperviousness to evidentiary challenge, and their thirst to enforce their own brand of virtue. To the extent the political parties comprise coalitions of communities united by interests and passions divergent from their fellow citizens—what Madison called "factions"—there is danger that whichever party has the command of government, state or federal, may use that power not only to enact policies consistent with their views but also to entrench themselves in ways that threaten the future prospects of dissenting points of view. The same tools religious establishments employed to promote religious uniformity are at hand to promote uniformity of sentiment on nonreligious matters: compulsory instruction of state-approved values in public education; the use of taxes to support private organizations devoted only to the dissemination of those values; the enforcement of ideological screens for public and private office; and the restriction, directly or indirectly through the deprivation of otherwise available government subsidies, of the ability of dissenting groups to speak, publish, associate, and participate in public life.

The Supreme Court has interpreted other provisions of the First Amendment—the Speech Clause, Press Clause, and Assembly Clause—to require governmental neutrality with respect to private communication. It generally cannot restrict private speech or associations because of the content or viewpoint of the idea communicated. These are important limits on the government's power to throw its considerable weight behind one side in a battle over values, and, like the Establishment Clause's requirement of religious neutrality, they help to protect cultural pluralism.

But the Establishment Clause goes beyond these protections for individual expressive freedom. It has an institutional dimension. The government cannot set up a church; it cannot control a church; it cannot create a monopoly in support of its favored church or churches; it is not itself a participant in debates about religious truth. In this, the provision of the Bill of Rights most similar to the Establishment Clause is the Free Press Clause, which bars creation of a state press, forbids the government from controlling editorial decision-making, and prohibits any licensing of the press. Britain has both a C of E and a BBC. We have neither—though NPR comes close. The principal institutions for the formation and propagation of opinion must be in hands independent of government. It is no wonder that education, which, like religion and the press, is an institution for the propagation of opinion but which is not in private hands, has been so fertile a field for Establishment Clause contestation. As Justice Robert Jackson, one of our wisest Supreme Court justices, wrote in *West Virginia Board of Education v. Barnette* (1943), "Probably no deeper division of our people could proceed from any provocation than from finding it necessary to choose what doctrine and whose program public educational officials shall compel youth to unite in embracing." That is why so many Establishment Clause cases have involved either the content of public education or the creation of alternatives to it.

Of course, the government cannot be neutral with respect to all matters of contention. Laws and policies are necessarily based on values. But the experience of the Establishment Clause could serve as a caution against the use of government power to create uniformity in matters of opinion. As Madison said on the floor of Congress, "The censorial power is in the people over the Government, and not the Government over the people."[4] When governmental power is used to mold the minds of the people in conformity to political strength, the odor of establishment is in the air. The authors of the Bill of Rights blocked such attempts as they relate to religion. A broader spirit of disestablishment is needed to block such attempts as they relate to other ideologies. An understanding of the nature and purpose of establishment, and the reasons for disestablishment, may be the first step.

Notes

. . .

INTRODUCTION

1. *See* Everson v. Board of Education of Ewing Township, 330 U.S. 1, 16 (1947); Leonard Levy, THE ESTABLISHMENT CLAUSE: RELIGION AND THE FIRST AMENDMENT 163 (Univ. North Carolina Press 1986); Lemon v. Kurtzman, 403 U.S. 602 (1971).

2. Thomas Jefferson, *A Bill for Establishing Religious Freedom* (1786), *reprinted in* Michael W. McConnell et al., RELIGION AND THE CONSTITUTION 48–49 (4th ed., New York, Wolters Kluwer 2016).

3. The Court first used the phrase "in tension" in *Tilton v. Richardson*, 403 U.S. 672, 677 (1971), and has used it many times since.

4. School District of Abington Township v. Schempp, 374 U.S. 203, 294 (1963) (Brennan, J., concurring).

5. Mark David Hall, *Jeffersonian Walls and Madisonian Lines: The Supreme Court's Use of History in Religion Clause Cases*, 85 OR. L. REV. 563 (2006); Mark DeWolfe Howe, THE GARDEN AND THE WILDERNESS: RELIGION AND GOVERNMENT IN AMERICAN CONSTITUTIONAL HISTORY 1–31, 149–76 (Univ. Chicago Press 1965); Edward S. Corwin, *The Supreme Court as National School Board*, 14 L. & CONTEMP. PROBS. 3 (1949); John Phillip Reid, *Law and History*, 27 LOY. L.A. L. REV. 193, 220 (1993) (describing the Court's Religion Clause cases as "violations of the canons of historical interpretation"); Daniel L. Dreisbach, *Everson and the Command of History: The*

Supreme Court, Lessons in History, and the Church-State Debate in America, in EVERSON REVISITED: RELIGION, EDUCATION, AND LAW AT THE CROSSROADS 23–58 (Jo Renée Formicola & Hubert Morken eds., Lanham, Md., Rowman & Littlefield 1997).

CHAPTER I

1. Much of this chapter is adapted from Michael W. McConnell, *Establishment and Disestablishment at the Founding, Part I: Establishment of Religion*, 44 WM. & MARY L. REV. 2105 (2003). Readers seeking more copious citations of authority should consult that source. The William & Mary Law Review article was published just as the author assumed the position of Circuit Judge on the United States Court of Appeals for the Tenth Circuit. As a result of his new responsibilities, he did not complete *Part II: Disestablishment.* Chapter 3 of this book covers what Part II would have covered.

2. School District of Abington Township v. Schempp, 374 U.S. 203, 241 (1963) (Brennan, J., concurring).

3. *See* Everson v. Board of Education, 330 U.S. 1, 13 (1947).

4. *See* Everson, 330 U.S. at 8–13.

5. Supremacy Act 1534, 26 Hen. 8 c. 1 (Eng.), *reprinted in* 1 SOURCES OF ENGLISH CONSTITUTIONAL HISTORY (Carl Stephenson & Frederick Marcham eds., Harper & Row rev. ed. 1937).

6. Act of Uniformity 1662, 14 Car. 2 c. 4 (Eng.), *reprinted in* 2 SOURCES OF ENGLISH CONSTITUTIONAL HISTORY, *supra* note 5, at 543–46.

7. *See* First Test Act 1673 25 Car. 2 c. 1 (Eng.), *reprinted in* 2 SOURCES OF ENGLISH CONSTITUTIONAL HISTORY, *supra* note 5, at 555–56; Second Test Act 1678, 30 Car. 2 c. 1 (Eng.), *reprinted in* 2 SOURCES OF ENGLISH CONSTITUTIONAL HISTORY, *supra* note 5, at 556–57; Corporation Act 1661, 13 Car. 2, c. 1 (Eng.), *reprinted in* 2 SOURCES OF ENGLISH CONSTITUTIONAL HISTORY, *supra* note 5, at 542–43; Jefferson, Bill for Establishing Religious Freedom (1779, enacted 1786), *reprinted in* Michael W. McConnell et al., RELIGION AND THE CONSTITUTION 48, 48 (4th ed. 2016).

8. Act against Papists 1593, 35 Eliz. c. 2 (Eng.), *reprinted in* 1 SOURCES OF ENGLISH CONSTITUTIONAL HISTORY, *supra* note 5, at 355–56; Conventicle Act 1664, 16 Carl. 2 c. 4 (Eng.), *reprinted in* 1 SOURCES OF

ENGLISH CONSTITUTIONAL HISTORY, *supra* note 5, at 553; An Act to Prevent and avoid dangers which may grow up by Popish Recusants 1605–6, 3 Jam. 1, c. 5 (Eng.), *reprinted in* 4 STATUTES OF THE REALM 1077 (1963); "Act against Sectaries" 1581, 35 Eliz., c. 1 (Eng.), *reprinted in* 1 SOURCES OF ENGLISH CONSTITUTIONAL HISTORY, *supra* note 5, at 354.

9. *See* Nancy L. Rhoden, REVOLUTIONARY ANGLICANISM: THE COLONIAL CHURCH OF ENGLAND CLERGY DURING THE AMERICAN REVOLUTION (NYU Press 1999).

10. 1 PAPERS OF THOMAS JEFFERSON 539–44 (Julian P. Boyd ed., 1950).

11. Citations to the Diocesan Canons and other Virginia laws summarized in this paragraph may be found in McConnell, *Establishment and Disestablishment at the Founding, supra* note 1, at 2118–19.

12. 1 William Waller Hening, THE STATUTES AT LARGE: BEING A COLLECTION OF ALL THE LAWS IN VIRGINIA 123 (New York, R. & W. & G. Bartow 1823).

13. H. J. Eckenrode, SEPARATION OF CHURCH AND STATE IN VIRGINIA 13–14 (Richmond, Virginia, Dept. of Archives and History 1910).

14. Elisha Williams, THE ESSENTIAL RIGHTS AND LIBERTIES OF PROTESTANTS (Boston, 1744), *reprinted in* Michael W. McConnell et al., RELIGION AND THE CONSTITUTION 27–28 (4th ed., New York, Wolters Kluwer 2016).

15. Isaac Backus, GOVERNMENT AND LIBERTY DESCRIBED (1778), *reprinted in* ISAAC BACKUS ON CHURCH, STATE, AND CALVINISM: PAMPHLETS 1754–1789, at 351 (William G. McLoughlin ed., Harvard Univ. Press 1968).

16. 4 William Blackstone, COMMENTARIES ON THE LAWS OF ENGLAND *51–52 (1765).

17. MASS. CONST. of 1780, art. III, *amended by* MASS. CONST. art. XI (1833).

18. A. G. Roeber, FAITHFUL MAGISTRATES AND REPUBLICAN LAWYERS: CREATORS OF VIRGINIA LEGAL CULTURE, 1680–1810, at 141–42 (Univ. of N.C. Press 1980). Another study, based on records from Caroline County between 1740 and 1749, concluded that grand jury presentments for church nonattendance were "clearly routine," but not as common as those for some other crimes, such as charges of neglect against road surveyors. Rhys Isaac, *Religion and Authority: Problems of the Anglican Establishment in Virginia in the Era of the Great Awakening and the Parsons' Cause*, 30 WM. & MARY Q., no. 1 (Jan. 1973), at 4 n.2.

19. 1 William G. McLoughlin, NEW ENGLAND DISSENT 1630–1833: THE BAPTISTS AND THE SEPARATION OF CHURCH AND STATE 15–17 (Harvard Univ. Press 1971).

20. *See* John Witte, THE REFORMATION OF RIGHTS (2007); 1 McLoughlin, *supra* note 20, at 560 (Adams quote); 12 JOURNALS OF THE CONTINENTAL CONGRESS, 1774–1789, at 1001–2 (1908).

21. *See* Sanford H. Cobb, THE RISE OF RELIGIOUS LIBERTY IN AMERICA: A HISTORY 123, 276, 420, 437 (New York, MacMillan 1902).

22. *See* McConnell, *Establishment and Disestablishment*, 44 WM. & M. L. REV. at 2167–69.

23. Letter from James Madison to William Bradford (Jan. 24, 1774), in 1 PAPERS OF JAMES MADISON (W. Hutchinson & W. M. E. Rachal eds., 1962).

24. Marcus Wilson Jernegan, *The Development of Poor Relief in Colonial New England*, 5 SOC. SERV. REV. 175, 183–85 (1931).

25. Arthur P. Middleton, *The Colonial Virginia Parish*, 40 HIST. MAG. PROTESTANT EPISCOPAL CHURCH 435 (1971).

26. *See supra* note 7 for citations to the First Test Act (1675), Second Test Act (1678), and Corporation Act (1661).

27. 6 Ann. c. 23 (1707) (Eng.), *reprinted in* 2 Danby Pickering, THE STATUTES AT LARGE, FROM THE SECOND TO EIGHTH YEAR OF QUEEN ANNE 375–78 (London, Joseph Bentham 1764).

28. John Wesley Brinsfield, RELIGION AND POLITICS IN COLONIAL SOUTH CAROLINA 23 (Easley, S.C., Southern Historical Press 1983).

29. *See* Torcaso v. Watkins 367 U.S. 488 (1961).

30. *See* William Hogue, *The Civil Disability of Ministers of Religion in State Constitutions*, 36 J. OF CHURCH & STATE 329, 330–32, 338–42 (1994); 1 Blackstone, COMMENTARIES *364; John Witte Jr., THE REFORMATION OF RIGHTS: LAW, RELIGION, AND HUMAN RIGHTS IN EARLY MODERN CALVINISM 309 (Cambridge Univ. Press 2007); McDaniel v. Paty 435 U.S. 618, 624 (1978) (noting that "one way to assure disestablishment was to keep clergymen out of public office.").

31. *See* Albert E. McKinley, THE SUFFRAGE FRANCHISE IN THE THIRTEEN ENGLISH COLONIES IN AMERICA 475–77 (Philadelphia, Univ. of Penn. Press 1905).

32. Niccolò Machiavelli, THE DISCOURSES 139, 143 (Bernard R. Crick ed., Leslie J. Walker trans., New York, Penguin Books 1970) [1531].

33. Edmund Burke, Speech on Unitarians' Petition for Relief (May 11, 1792), *in* 4 THE WRITINGS AND SPEECHES OF EDMUND BURKE 491 (P. J. Marshall & Donald Bryant eds., Oxford Univ. Press 2015) (emphasis omitted).

34. Isaac Backus, *An Appeal to the Public for Religious Liberty* (1773), *in* ISAAC BACKUS ON CHURCH, STATE, AND CALVINISM, *supra* note 16, at 324.

35. *See* Weldon S. Crowley, *Erastianism in England to 1640*, 32 J. CHURCH & STATE 549 (1990); Weldon S. Crowley, *Erastianism in the Long Parliament, 1640–1646*, 21 J. CHURCH & STATE 451 (1979); Weldon S. Crowley, *Erastianism in the Westminster Assembly*, 15 J. CHURCH & STATE 49 (1973).

36. *See* William Warburton, THE ALLIANCE BETWEEN CHURCH AND STATE (London, Fletcher Gyles 1736); Mary Elizabeth Quinlivan, IDEOLOGICAL CONTROVERSY OVER RELIGIOUS ESTABLISHMENT IN REVOLUTIONARY VIRGINIA 10–11, 37–39 (1971) (unpublished PhD dissertation, Univ. of Wisconsin) (on file with author).

37. Alexis de Tocqueville, DEMOCRACY IN AMERICA 265 (J. P. Meyer & Max Lerner eds., George Lawrence trans., Harper & Row 1966) (1835).

38. Articles of Religion, No. 37, *in* THE 1662 BOOK OF COMMMON PRAYER 644 (Downers Grove, Il., InterVarsity Press 2021).

39. *See* Canon I, CONSTITUTIONS AND CANONS ECCLESIASTICAL, folio 12r (London, Robert Baker 1603).

40. *See* Rhoden, *supra* note 10 at 68, 71.

41. For an account of James I's thoughts on episcopacy and the circumstances of his famous quip, *see* Maurice Lee Jr., *James VI and the Revival of Episcopacy in Scotland: 1596–1600*, 43 CHURCH HISTORY 50 (1974); Richard Gardiner, THE PRESBYTERIAN REBELLION: AN ANALYSIS OF THE PERCEPTION THAT THE AMERICAN REVOLUTION WAS A PRESBYTERIAN WAR, at ix (May 2005) (PhD dissertation, Marquette University) (ProQuest) (https://www-proquest-com.stanford.idm.oclc.org/dissertations-theses/presbyterian-rebellion-analysis-perception-that/docview/304991131/se-2?accoun tid=14026); Edmund Burke, *Speech on Moving His Resolutions for Conciliation with the Colonies* (March 22, 1775), *in* EDMUND BURKE: SELECTED WRITINGS AND SPEECHES 159–60 (Peter J. Stanlis ed., Garden City, N.Y., Anchor Books 1963).

42. William Henry Foote, SKETCHES OF VIRGINIA: HISTORICAL AND BIOGRAPHICAL, FIRST SERIES 338 (Richmond, Va., John Knox Press 1966).

CHAPTER 2

1. *See* Jonathan Sarna, *American Jews and Church-State Relations: The Search for "Equal Footing"* (American Jewish Committee 1989).

2. The Records of the Federal Convention of 1787, Vol. 2, at 335 (Aug. 20, 1787) (M. Farrand ed. 1911); *id.* at 587–88 (Sept. 12, 1787); RELIGION AND THE CONSTITUTION 50 (McConnell et al. eds. 4th ed., N.Y., Wolters Kluwer 2016); Robert B. Semple, A HISTORY OF THE RISE AND PROGRESS OF THE BAPTISTS IN VIRGINIA 102 (G.W. Beale rev., Richmond, Va., Pitt & Dickinson 1894).

3. 10 THE DOCUMENTARY HISTORY OF THE RATIFICATION OF THE CONSTITUTION 1223–24 (J. Kaminski et al. eds. 1976).

4. Letter to Rev. George Eve (Jan. 2, 1789), *in* 11 PAPERS OF JAMES MADISON 404–5 (William T. Hutchinson et al. eds., Univ. of Virginia Press 1977); *see* Mark S. Scarberry, *John Leland and James Madison: Religious Influence on the Ratification of the Constitution and the Proposal of the Bill of Rights*, 113 PENN. ST. L. REV. 733 (2009); Paul Finkelman, *James Madison and the Bill of Rights: A Reluctant Paternity*, 1990 SUP. CT. REV. 301.

5. 1 ANNALS OF CONGRESS 451–52 (1789).

6. All quotations from the debates are from *id.* at 757–59. It should be noted that the Annals were not an official verbatim record of the debates, but notes taken by a private journalist for newspaper publication. We do not know how complete or accurate they are. *Cf.* Mary Sarah Bilder, MADISON'S HAND: REVISING THE CONSTITUTIONAL CONVENTION (Harvard Univ. Press 2015) (documenting the gaps and inaccuracies in Madison's Notes of the Constitutional Convention).

7. For a detailed description of the Connecticut system, see Robert J. Imholt, *Connecticut: A Land of Steady Habits*, in Carl H. Esbeck & Jonathan J. Den Hartog, DISESTABLISHMENT AND RELIGIOUS DISSENT: CHURCH-STATE RELATIONS IN THE NEW AMERICAN STATES 1776–1833 (Univ. of Missouri Press 2019), at 327, 334.

8. Wallace v. Jaffree, 472 U.S. 38, 113 (1985) (Rehnquist, J., dissenting); Douglas Laycock, *"Noncoercive" Support for Religion: Another False Claim About the Establishment Clause*, 26 VAL. U. L. REV. 37 (1991).

9. *See, e.g.*, Akhil Amar, THE BILL OF RIGHTS 33, 247 (Yale Univ. Press 1998); Vincent Phillip Muñoz, RELIGIOUS LIBERTY AND THE AMERICAN FOUNDING 175 (Univ. Chicago Press 2022). Some conclude that the

Establishment Clause only prohibited a national church. *See* Donald L. Drakeman, Church, State, and Original Intent 330 (Cambridge Univ. Press 2010).

10. *Compare* Michael W. McConnell, *The Origins and Historical Understanding of Free Exercise of Religion*, 103 Harv. L. Rev. 1409 (1990) (arguing that the history supports accommodations) *with* Philip A. Hamburger, *A Constitutional Right of Religious Exemption: An Historical Perspective*, 60 Geo. Wash. L. Rev. 915 (1992) (arguing the opposite) *and* Vincent Phillip Muñoz, *Two Concepts of Religious Liberty: The Natural Rights and Moral Autonomy Approaches to the Free Exercise of Religion*, 110 Am. Pol. Sci. Rev. 369 (2016).

CHAPTER 3

1. *See* Nancy Rhoden, Revolutionary Anglicanism: The Colonial Church of England Clergy During the American Revolution (NYU Press 1999).

2. George Washington, *Washington's Farewell Address to the People of the United States*, S. Doc. No. 106-21, at 20 (2nd Sess. 2000) (1796) (emphasis added); Gordon Wood, The Creation of the American Republic, 1776–1787, at 68 (Univ. North Carolina Press 1969) (quoting Samuel Williams, *A Discourse on the Love of Our Country* 13 (Salem, 1775)); Alexis de Tocqueville, Democracy in America 271 (J. P. Meyer & Max Lerner eds., George Lawrence trans., Harper & Row 1966) (1835); *see* Herbert Storing, What the Anti-Federalists Were For 22–23 (Univ. Chicago Press 1981) (quoting many other sources on religion and republican virtue to similar effect).

3. Sidney Mead, The Old Religion in the Brave New World: Reflections on the Relation between Christendom and the Republic 2 (Univ. California Press 1977).

4. H. J. Eckenrode, Separation of Church and State in Virginia 86 (Richmond, Virginia, Dept. of Archives and History 1910) (quoting Madison's floor debate with Patrick Henry in 1784).

5. Letter from James Madison to Thomas Jefferson (Oct. 24, 1787), *in* 5 The Writings of James Madison 17, 30–31 (Gaillard Hunt ed., New York,

G.P. Putnam's Sons 1904); THE FEDERALIST, No. 51, at 322 (James Madison) (Clinton Rossiter ed., Signet 1961); *id.* No. 10, at 81 (Madison).

6. Everson v. Board of Education of Ewing Township, 330 U.S. 1, 13 (1947).

7. Mark David Hall, *Madison's Remonstrance, Jefferson's Statute for Religious Liberty, and the Creation of the First Amendment*, 3 AMERICAN POL. THOUGHT 32, 40 (2014).

8. Isaac Backus, *Address to the Honorable Congress of the Massachusetts Province* (Nov. 22, 1774), *quoted in* Mark Storslee, *Church Taxes and the Original Understanding of the Establishment Clause*, 160 U. PENN. L. REV. 111, 127 (2020); James Madison, *Memorial and Remonstrance Against Religious Assessments* (1785), ¶ 1, *reprinted in* Michael W. McConnell et al., RELIGION AND THE CONSTITUTION 43, 43–44 (4th ed., New York, Wolters Kluwer 2016).

9. 3 Thomas Hobbes, LEVIATHAN 1112 (Noel Malcolm ed., Oxford Univ. Press 2012) (1651).

10. *See* Madison, *Memorial and Remonstrance*, *supra* note 7, at 43; *see* Eckenrode, *supra* note 4, at 74–115; Thomas Buckley, CHURCH AND STATE IN REVOLUTIONARY VIRGINIA (Univ. Virginia Press 1977)

11. *See* Vincent Phillip Muñoz, RELIGIOUS LIBERTY AND THE AMERICAN FOUNDING 69-82 (Univ. Chicago Press 2022) for an insightful discussion of the differences between Madison and Jefferson.

12. Letter from Jefferson to Benjamin Waterhouse (June 26, 1822), 15 THE WRITINGS OF THOMAS JEFFERSON 383, 384–85 (Andrew A. Lipscombe ed., Washington 1903); Letter from James Madison to Robert Walsh Jr. (Mar. 2, 1819), 1 THE PAPERS OF JAMES MADISON: RETIREMENT SERIES 427, 427–32 (David B. Mattern ed., Univ. of Virginia Press 2009). Jack Rakove, BEYOND BELIEF, BEYOND CONSCIENCE: THE RADICAL SIGNIFICANCE OF THE FREE EXERCISE OF RELIGION 98 (Oxford Univ. Press 2020).

13. Delaware had establishments under the Swedes and the Dutch, but these were eliminated by 1682, when it was incorporated into Pennsylvania.

14. Unless otherwise cited, the original sources quoted in connection with state-by-state constitutional developments can be found in DISESTABLISHMENT AND RELIGIOUS DISSENT: CHURCH-STATE RELATIONS IN THE NEW AMERICAN STATES 1776–1833 (Carl H. Esbeck & Jonathan J. Den Hartog eds., Univ. Missouri Press 2019) (hereinafter Esbeck & Den Hartog, Disestablishment).

15. *See* John Fea, *Disestablishment in New Jersey, in* Esbeck & Den Hartog, DISESTABLISHMENT, *supra* note 14, at 25, 25–26.

16. *See* Nicholas P. Miller, *North Carolina: Early Toleration and Disestablishment, in* Esbeck & Den Hartog, DISESTABLISHMENT, *supra* note 14, at 97, 106–7.

17. *See* David Little, *The Pennsylvania Experiment with Freedom of Conscience and Church-State Relations, in* Esbeck & Den Hartog, DISESTABLISHMENT, *supra* note 14, at 71, 86–89.

18. *See* Del. Const. of 1776, art. XXIX; Evan Haefeli, *Delaware: Religious Borderland, in* Esbeck & Den Hartog, DISESTABLISHMENT, *supra* note 14, at 37, 41, 44, 49; William M. Hogue, *The Civil Disability of Ministers of Religion in State Constitutions*, 36 J. CHURCH & STATE 329, 341 (1994).

19. *See* Kyle T. Bulthuis, *Religious Disestablishment in the State of New York, in* Esbeck & Den Hartog, DISESTABLISHMENT, *supra* note 14, at 115, 121, 128. On the property holdings of Trinity Church, *see* Elizabeth Mensch, *Religion, Revival, and the Ruling Class: A Critical History of Trinity Church*, 36 BUFF. L. REV. 427, 429, 549 (1987).

20. *See* Miles Smith IV, South Carolina, *in* Esbeck & Den Hartog, DISESTABLISHMENT, *supra* note 14, at 181, 189–90, 197.

21. *See* Carl Esbeck, *Disestablishment in Virginia*, 1776–1802, *in* Esbeck & Den Hartog, DISESTABLISHMENT, *supra* note 14, at 139–40, 144–45, 161–63.

22. *See* Michael D. Breidenbach, *Church and State in Maryland, in* Esbeck & Den Hartog, DISESTABLISHMENT, *supra* note 14, at 309, 314–21.

23. *See* Joel A. Nichols, *Georgia: The Thirteenth Colony, in* Esbeck & Den Hartog, DISESTABLISHMENT, *supra* note 14, at 225, 226–27, 234–37.

24. *See* Shelby M. Balik, *In the Interests of True Religion: Disestablishment in Vermont, in* Esbeck & Den Hartog, DISESTABLISHMENT, *supra* note 14, at 293, 296–99.

25. *See* Robert J. Imholt, *Connecticut: A Land of Steady Habits, in* Esbeck & Den Hartog, DISESTABLISHMENT, *supra* note 14, at 327, 342–44 (emphasis added); Brian Franklin, *Towns and Toleration: Disestablishment in New Hampshire, in* Esbeck & Den Hartog, DISESTABLISHMENT, *supra* note 14, at 351, 352; Marc M. Arkin, *Maine, in* Esbeck & Den Hartog, DISESTABLISHMENT, *supra* note 14, at 373; John Witte Jr. & Justin Latterell, *The Last American Establishment: Massachusetts, 1780–1833, in* Esbeck & Den Hartog, Disestablishment, *supra* note 14, at 399.

26. Thomas Buckley, Church and State in Revolutionary Virginia 84, 80 (Univ. Virginia Press 1977) (quoting Anglican Reverend David Griffith, and a Presbyterian petition to the Virginia House of Delegates, respectively).

27. Kellen Funk, *Church Corporations and the Conflict of Laws in Antebellum America*, 32 J. L. & Rel. 263, 267–68 (2017).

28. Carl Esbeck, *Disestablishment in Virginia, 1776–1802, in* Esbeck & Den Hartog, Disestablishment, *supra* note 14, at 163–65, 171; Sarah Barringer Gordon, *Religious Corporations and Disestablishment, 1780–1840, in* The Rise of Corporate Religious Liberty 63 (M. Schwartzman, C. Flanders, & Z. Robinson eds., Oxford Univ. Press 2016).

29. 22 Annals of Congress, 982–83 (1811), *reprinted in* Michael W. McConnell et al., Religion and the Constitution 261, 262 (4th ed., New York, Wolters Kluwer 2016).

30. Joseph Chisholm, *Civil Incorporation of Church Property, in* 7 Catholic Encyclopedia (1910), http://www.newadvent.org/cathen/07719b.htm; Gordon, *supra* note 28, at 71–74.

31. Terrett v. Taylor, 13 U.S. (9 Cranch) 43, 51–52 (1815); Town of Pawlet v. Clark, 13 U.S. 292 (1815); *see also* Trustees of Dartmouth College v. Woodward, 17 U.S. (4 Wheat.) 518 (1819); Fletcher v. Peck, 10 U.S. (6 Cranch) 87 (1810).

32. *See* Michael W. McConnell, *The Supreme Court's Earliest Church-State Cases: Windows on Religious-Cultural-Political Conflict in the Early Republic*, 37 Tulsa L. Rev. 6, 8–20 (2001). On the situation in Vermont, *see* Balik, *supra* note 20, at 300–301.

33. *See* George M. Marsden, The Soul of the American University: From Protestant Establishment to Established Nonbelief 33–100 (Oxford Univ. Press 1996); Mark Douglas MacGarvie, One Nation Under Law: America's Early National Struggles to Separate Church and State 156–58 (Northern Illinois Univ. Press 2004).

34. MacGarvie, *supra* note 33 at 165–78.

35. *See* William M. Hogue, *The Civil Disability of Ministers of Religion in State Constitutions*, 36 J. Church & St. 329, 330–31 (1994); McDaniel v. Paty, 435 U.S. 618 (1978); Nichols, Georgia, in Esbeck & Den Hartog, Disestablishment, *supra* note 14, at 235, 239.

36. This section is adapted from Michael W. McConnell, *Establishment and Disestablishment at the Founding, Part I: Establishment of Religion*, 44 W. &

M. L. Rev. 2105 (2003). Unless specified, all citations in this section can be found in that source. Further details on each state can be found in Esbeck & Den Hartog, DISESTABLISHMENT, *supra* note 14.

37. *See* Buckley, *supra* note 25, at 81–83, 92.

38. Esbeck, *supra* note 17, at 152; Letter from Richard Henry Lee to James Madison (Nov. 26, 1784), *in* 8 THE PAPERS OF JAMES MADISON 149–52 (R. Rutland & W. Rachal eds., Univ. of Chicago Press 1973).

39. *See* Michael S. Ariens, *Church and State in Ohio, 1785–1833*, *in* Esbeck & Den Hartog, DISESTABLISHMENT, *supra* note 14, at 249, 262.

40. *See* Brian Franklin, *Towns and Toleration: Disestablishment in New Hampshire*, *in* Esbeck & Den Hartog, DISESTABLISHMENT, *supra* note 14, at 351; Cong. Rec.—Senate 5581 (1976) (discussion of the New Hampshire provision).

41. The classic account is William G. McLoughlin's two-volume NEW ENGLAND DISSENT 1630–1833: THE BAPTISTS AND THE SEPARATION OF CHURCH AND STATE (Harvard Univ. Press 1971). *See also* Storslee, *supra* note 8.

42. Isaac Backus's Draft for a Bill of Rights for the Massachusetts Constitution (1779), *reprinted in* ISAAC BACKUS ON CHURCH, STATE, AND CALVINISM: PAMPHLETS 1754–1789, at 487 (William G. McLoughlin ed., Harvard Univ. Press 1968).

43. Petition to the House of Delegates from Sundry Inhabitants of Amelia County (November 8, 1784); Phillips Payson, *Election Sermon of 1778*, *in* AMERICAN POLITICAL WRITING DURING THE FOUNDING ERA, 1760–1805, at 528–30 (Charles S. Hyneman & Donald S. Lutz, eds., Liberty Fund 1983); Barnes v. First Parish in Falmouth, 6 Mass. 400 (1810).

44. Locke v. Davey, 540 US. 712, 721–23 & n.5 (2004) (distinguishing between the training of clergy and other education); Espinoza v. Montana Department of Revenue, 140 S. Ct. 2246, 2257–58 (2020) (repeating the claim and citing cases).

45. McGarvie, *supra* note 33, at 156–68; Storslee, *supra* note 8; Mass. Const. of 1780, pt. 2, ch. V, art. I.

46. Mark Storslee, *supra* note 8 at 149, 150–52; Mass. Constitution of 1780, pt. 2, ch. V, art. I.

47. Petition Presented to the General Assembly by the Hanover Presbytery (Oct. 24, 1776), *in* Charles F. James, DOCUMENTARY HISTORY OF THE STRUGGLE FOR RELIGIOUS LIBERTY IN VIRGINIA 227 (Charles F. James

ed., Lynchburg, Va., J.P. Bell Co. 1900); Petition from Rockbridge County (Dec. 1, 1785), *quoted in* Eckenrode, *supra* note 4, at 97; Petitions for the Repeal of an Act Supporting Ministers of the Gospel (Oct. 1794), *in* 10 STATE PAPERS OF VERMONT 90–96 (Allen Soule ed., 1958), *quoted in* Balik, *supra* note 20, at 298; Madison, *Memorial and Remonstrance* ¶ 12, *reprinted in* McConnell et al., RELIGION AND THE CONSTITUTION, *supra* note 24, at 43, 46.

48. Hanover Petition of 1778, *partially reproduced in* Robert Baird, RELIGION IN THE UNITED STATES OF AMERICA 237, *quoted in* Esbeck, *supra* note 17, at 177 n.62.

49. *See* Madison, *Memorial and Remonstrance* ¶ 6, and Jefferson, *Bill for Establishing Religious Freedom* (1779), both *reproduced in* McConnell et al., RELIGION AND THE CONSTITUTION, *supra* note 24, at 45, 49, respectively. For David Hume's support of "a public establishment of religion in every civilized community" to restrain clerics by "brib[ing] their indolence," *see* 3 THE HISTORY OF ENGLAND FROM THE INVASION OF JULIUS CAESAR TO THE REVOLUTION IN 1688, at 134–37 (1778) (Liberty Fund ed., 1983). For an account of how the French revolutionary regime attempted to co-opt the clergy, *see* Emmet Kennedy, A CULTURAL HISTORY OF THE FRENCH REVOLUTION 145–55 (Yale Univ. Press 1989).

CHAPTER 4

1. The first word of the Amendment raises interesting questions about application to the executive and judicial branches, which we do not have space here to address. *See* Shrum v. City of Coweto, 449 F.3d 1132, 1140–43 (10th Cir. 2006); Mark. P. Denbeaux, *The First Word of the First Amendment*, 80 NW. U. L. REV. 1156, 1169–70 (1986).

2. Elk Grove Unified Sch. Dist. v. Newdow, 542 U.S. 1, 51 (2004) (Thomas, J., concurring).

3. Permoli v. Municipality No. 1 of New Orleans, 44. U.S. (3 How.) 589, 606 (1845).

4. *See, e.g.*, Michael Kent Curtis, *The Fourteenth Amendment and the Bill of Rights*, 14 CONN. L. REV. 237, 243–44 (1982).

5. Cong. Globe, 39th Cong., 1st Sess. 474 (1866); Cong. Globe, 38th Cong., 1st Sess. 1202 (1864).

6. United States v. Cruikshank, 92 U.S. 542, 554–55 (1875); Slaughter-House Cases, 83 U.S. (16 Wall.) 36, 47 (1972).

7. *See, e.g.,* West Virginia State Board of Education v. Barnette, 319 U.S. 624, 638 (1943); Palko v. Connecticut, 302 U.S. 319, 325 (1937).

8. Twining v. State of New Jersey, 211 U.S. 78, 99 (1908).

9. Nathan S. Chapman & Michael W. McConnell, *Due Process as Separation of Powers*, 121 YALE L.J. 1672, 1727 (2012).

10. Cong. Globe, 39th Cong., 1st Sess. 2764–67 (1866); Cong. Globe, 39th Cong., 1st Sess. 1033–34 (1865).

11. One substantive complication is that the Privileges or Immunities Clause may not extend to noncitizens, while the Due Process Clause protects all "persons." It seems likely, however, that the Equal Protection Clause would prohibit any state from discriminating against noncitizens with respect to the rights of the Bill of Rights.

12. Sch. Dist. of Abington v. Schempp, 374 U.S. 203, 310 (1963) (Stewart, J., dissenting).

13. *See* Vincent Phillip Muñoz, *The Original Meaning of the Establishment Clause and the Impossibility of Its Incorporation*, 8 U. PA. J. CONST. L. 585 (2006); Steven D. Smith, FOREORDAINED FAILURE: THE QUEST FOR A CONSTITUTIONAL PRINCIPLE OF RELIGIOUS FREEDOM (Oxford Univ. Press 1995). *But see* Kurt Lash, *The Second Adoption of the Establishment Clause: The Rise of the Nonestablishment Principle*, 27 ARIZ. S. L.J. 1085 (1995).

14. *See, e.g.,* Steven K. Green, THE BIBLE, THE SCHOOL, AND THE CONSTITUTION: THE CLASH THAT SHAPED MODERN CHURCH-STATE DOCTRINE (Oxford Univ. Press 2014); Philip Hamburger, SEPARATION OF CHURCH AND STATE (Harvard Univ. Press 2002).

15. Michael W. McConnell, et al., RELIGION AND THE CONSTITUTION 325 (4th ed., New York, Wolters Kluwer 2016).

16. Steven K. Green, *The Blaine Amendment Reconsidered*, 36 AM. J.L. HIST. 38, 59, 67 (1992).

17. *See* Ronald E. Butchart, NORTHERN SCHOOLS, SOUTHERN BLACKS, AND RECONSTRUCTION: FREEDMEN'S EDUCATION, 1862–1875 4–9, 33–52 (Westport, Connecticut, Greenwood Press 1980).

18. *See* Commonwealth v. Cooke, 7 Am. L. Reg. 417 (Police Ct. Bos. Mass. 1859) (rejecting constitutional challenge to beating a student for refusing to recite the Ten Commandments and Lord's Prayer in their Protestant version); Green, *supra* note 14 at 80–84 .

CHAPTER 5

1. The only exception is *Bradfield v. Roberts*, 175 U.S. 291, 299–300 (1899), which held that it does not violate the Establishment Clause for the government to fund religious hospitals. The decision had little influence on subsequent Establishment Clause doctrine.

2. Committee for Public Education v. Nyquist, 413 U.S. 756, 783 n.39 (1973).

3. Lamb's Chapel v. Center Moriches Union Free School District, 508 U.S. 384, 398–99 (1993) (Scalia, J., concurring).

4. American Legion v. American Humanist Ass'n, 139 S. Ct. 2067 (2019); *see especially id.* at 2080–82 (the critique of Lemon), *id.* at 2095 (Kagan, J., concurring); Kennedy v. Bremerton School Dist., 142 S. Ct. 2407, 2428–29 (2022); Rodriguez de Quijas v. Shearson/American Express, Inc., 490 U.S. 477, 484 (1989).

5. "Originalism" is the idea that the words of the Constitution should be given the meaning they most likely would have had at the time the relevant provision was adopted. "Liquidation" is the idea that ambiguous terms should be interpreted in accordance with long-standing practice and precedent, rather than the normative opinions of current judges.

CHAPTER 6

1. McDaniel v. Paty, 435 U.S. 618, 639 (1978) (Brennan, J., concurring).

2. Madison, *Memorial and Remonstrance*; *see* Chapter 3.

3. *See* Michael W. McConnell, *The Origins and Original Understanding of Free Exercise of Religion*, 103 Harv. L. Rev. 1409, 1503–11 (1990).

4. Letter from George Washington to the Religious Society Called Quakers (c.13 Oct. 1789).

5. *See, e.g.*, Simon's Executors v. Gratz, 2 Pen. & W. 412, 414 (Pa. 1831).

6. Douglas Laycock, *Regulatory Exemptions of Religious Behavior and the Original Understanding of the Establishment Clause*, 81 Notre Dame L. Rev. 1793, 1796 (2006).

7. The Selective Draft Law Cases, 245 U.S. 366, 389–90 (1918).

8. 1 Annals of Cong. 778–80, 796 (Aug. 17, 20, 1789) (J. Gales ed. 1834).

9. Katcoff v. Marsh, 755 F.2d 223, 225 (2d Cir. 1985).

10. Marsh v. Chambers, 463 U.S. 783, 786, 790 (1983).

11. James E. Ryan, *Smith and the Religious Freedom Restoration Action: An Iconoclastic Assessment*, 78 Va. L. Rev. 1407, 1446 (1992).

12. One of the authors of this book, McConnell, was the principal author of these briefs in his capacity as a lawyer in the Office of the Solicitor General.

13. Wallace v. Jaffree, 472 U.S. 38, 83 (1985) (O'Connor, J., concurring).

14. 483 U.S. 327 (1987).

15. 544 U.S. 709 (2005).

16. Prior decisions described the necessary burden as "substantial" or "potentially serious." *See, e.g.*, Texas Monthly, Inc. v. Bullock, 489 U.S. 1, 18 n.8 (1989).

17. Welsh v. United States, 398 U.S. 333 (1970); United States v. Seeger, 380 U.S. 163 (1965); Washington Ethical Society v. District of Columbia, 249 F.2d 127 (D.C. Cir. 1957); EEOC Compliance Manual, Section 12 (Religious Discrimination); Hernandez v. Commissioner of Internal Revenue, 490 U.S. 680 (1989); United States v. Lee, 455 U.S. 252 (1982).

18. 512 U.S. 687 (1994).

19. 139 S. Ct. 661 (2019).

20. Frederick Mark Gedicks & Andrew Koppelman, *Invisible Women: Why an Exemption for Hobby Lobby Would Violate the Establishment Clause*, 67 Vand. L. Rev. En Banc 51, 51 (2014).

21. Texas Monthly, 489 U.S. at 18 n.8.

22. James W. Tollefson, The Strength Not to Fight 7 (1993).

23. 472 U.S. 703, 709 (1985).

24. ACLU v. Tarek ibn Ziyad Academy, 643 F.3d 1088 (8th Cir. 2011). One of the authors of this book, McConnell, represented the parents of the Muslim children in their unsuccessful attempt to intervene in support of the school.

25. Zorach v. Clauson, 343 U.S. 306, 309, 313–14 (1952).

26. Bear Lodge Multiple Use Ass'n v. Babbitt, 175 F.3d 814 (10th Cir. 1999); Lyng v. Northwest Indian Cemetery Protective Ass'n, 485 U.S. 439 (1988).

CHAPTER 7

1. West Virginia Bd. of Educ. v. Barnette, 319 U.S. 624 (1943).

2. *See* Beverly McAnera, *The Raising of Funds by the Colonial Colleges*, 38 MISS. VALLEY HIST. REV. 591 (Oxford Univ. Press 1952); George M. Marsden, THE SOUL THE AMERICAN UNIVERSITY 33–100 (Oxford Univ. Press 1994); Mark Douglas MacGarvie, ONE NATION UNDER LAW: AMERICA'S EARLY NATIONAL STRUGGLES TO SEPARATE CHURCH AND STATE 156–158 (Northern Illinois Univ. Press 2004); Mark Storslee, *Church Taxes and the Original Understanding of the Establishment Clause*, 169 U. PA. L. REV. 112 (2020).

3. For descriptions of the pluralistic educational system of this period, *see* Carl F. Kaestle, PILLARS OF THE REPUBLIC: COMMON SCHOOLS AND AMERICAN SOCIETY, 1780–1860, at 57, 166–67 (New York, Hill & Wang 1983); Lloyd P. Jorgenson, THE STATE AND THE NON-PUBLIC SCHOOL, 1825–1925, at 1–19 (Univ. Missouri Press 1987); Diane Ravitch, THE GREAT SCHOOL WARS, NEW YORK CITY, 1805–1973: A HISTORY OF THE PUBLIC SCHOOLS AS BATTLEFIELD OF SOCIAL CHANGE 6–7 (Johns Hopkins Univ. Press 1974); Richard J. Gabel, PUBLIC FUNDS FOR CHURCH AND PRIVATE SCHOOLS 147–470 (Catholic Univ. America 1937).

4. Vidal v. Girard's Executors, 43 U.S. 127 (1844); for a discussion of the case, *see* Michael W. McConnell, *The Supreme Court's Earliest Church-State Cases: Windows on Religious-Cultural-Political Conflict in the Early Republic*, 37 TULSA L. REV. 7, 20–30 (2001).

5. Northwest Ordinance, Act of Aug. 7, 1789, ch. 8, 1 Stat. 50-53 (readoption of the Northwest Ordinance of July 13, 1787).

6. *See* Nathan S. Chapman, *Forgotten Federal-Missionary Partnerships: New Light on the Establishment Clause*, 96 NOTRE DAME L. REV. 677 (2020).

7. *See, e.g.*, David B. Tyack, *Onward Christian Soldiers: Religion in the American Common School*, *in* HISTORY AND EDUCATION: THE EDUCATIONAL USES OF THE PAST 217 (Paul Nash ed., New York, Random House 1970); Charles Leslie Glenn, THE MYTH OF THE COMMON SCHOOL (Univ. Massachusetts Press 1988).

8. Steven K. Green, THE SECOND DISESTABLISHMENT: CHURCH AND STATE IN NINETEENTH-CENTURY AMERICA 257 (Oxford Univ. Press 2010); Ravitch, *supra* note 3.

9. 100 MICH. L. REV. 279 (2001).

10. *See, e.g.,* John Tracy Ellis, AMERICAN CATHOLICISM 151 (2d rev. ed. Univ. Chicago Press 1969) (quoting Professor Arthur M. Schlesinger Sr.).

11. The quote is from Horace Bushnell, quoted in GLENN, *supra* note 7, at 227–29. Bushnell, a theologian, is regarded as the father of liberal Protestantism.

12. For conflicting views about the relative role of anti-Catholic animus and republican ideology in the common school movement, compare Philip Hamburger, SEPARATION OF CHURCH AND STATE ch. 8 (Harvard Univ. Press 2002), with Stephen K. Green, THE BIBLE, THE SCHOOL, AND THE CONSTITUTION: THE CLASH THAT SHAPED MODERN CHURCH-STATE DOCTRINE ch. 2 (Oxford Univ. Press 2012).

13. "Petition of the Catholics of New York" (1840), quoted in James W. Fraser, BETWEEN CHURCH AND STATE: RELIGION AND PUBLIC EDUCATION IN A MULTICULTURAL AMERICA 55 (Johns Hopkins Univ. Press 1999).

14. Quoted in Jeffries & Ryan, *supra* note 9, at 301.

15. *See* Jeffries & Ryan, *supra* note 9, at 279.

16. Freedmen's Bureau Act, Act of July 16, 1866, §13. *See* Ronald E. Butchart, NORTHERN SCHOOLS, SOUTHERN BLACKS, AND RECONSTRUCTION: FREEDMEN'S EDUCATION, 1862–1875, at 4–9, 33–52 (Westport, Connecticut, Greenwood Press 1980); Ward M. McAfee, RELIGION, RACE, AND RECONSTRUCTION: THE PUBLIC SCHOOLS IN THE POLITICS OF THE 1870s (State Univ. New York Press 1998).

17. Quoted in Anson Phelps Stokes & Leo Pfeffer, CHURCH AND STATE IN THE UNITED STATES 272 (rev. one-vol. ed., New York, Harper & Row 1964).

18. 4 Cong. Rec. 5453 (1876).

19. *Id.* at 5587–88, 5591.

20. *Id.* at 5588 (1876) (Sen. Edmunds), 5590 (Sen. Bogy), 5584 (Sen. Kernan).

21. 268 U.S. 510 (1925).

22. Will Herberg, PROTESTANT, CATHOLIC, JEW (Univ. Chicago Press 1955).

23. Technically, the first federal constitutional challenge to reach the Supreme Court was Cochran v. Louisiana Bd. of Education, 281 U.S. 370 (1930). The Cochran plaintiffs did not frame their challenge under the First Amendment but the Due Process Clause, on the theory that it violated due process to tax people for support of a private activity.

24. 330 U.S. 1 (1947).

25. *See* Storslee, *supra* note 2; Carl H. Esbeck, *Disestablishment in Virginia, 1776–1802, in* DISESTABLISHMENT AND RELIGIOUS DISSENT: CHURCH-STATE RELATIONS IN THE NEW AMERICAN STATES 139 (Carl H. Esbeck & Jonathan J. Den Hartog eds., Univ. Missouri Press 2019); Thomas E. Buckley, ESTABLISHING RELIGIOUS FREEDOM: JEFFERSON'S STATUTE IN VIRGINIA ch. 3 (Univ. Virginia Press 2013); Madison, *Memorial and Remonstrance* (quoted in Chapter 3).

26. All quotations are from *Everson, supra.*

27. JOHN DEWEY, 15 THE LATER WORKS, 1925–53, at 284–85 (Jo Ann Boydston ed., Southern Illinois Univ. Press 1989).

28. Board of Education v. Allen, 302 U.S. 226 (1968); *id.* at 251–52 (Black, J., dissenting).

29. 403 U.S. 602 (1971).

30. Bowen v. Kendrick, 487 U.S. 589, 615 (1988).

31. All quotations in this paragraph are from *Nyquist*, 413 U.S. 756 (1973).

32. Meek v. Pittenger, 421 U.S. 349 (1975); Wolman v. Walter, 433 U.S. 229 (1977); Aguilar v. Felton, 473 U.S. 402 (1985). One of the authors of this book was principal writer of the unsuccessful brief defending the program in *Aguilar.*

33. All quotations in this paragraph come from *Witters*, 474 U.S. 481 (1986).

34. Zobrest v. Catalina Foothills School Dist., 509 U.S. 1 (1993); Rosenberger v. Rector & Visitors of the University of Virginia, 536 U.S. 639 (2002). One of the authors, McConnell, represented the student group in *Rosenberger.*

35. Agostini v. Felton, 536 U.S. 639 (2002), overruling Aguilar v. Felton, 473 U.S. 402 (1985) and partially overruling Grand Rapids v. Ball, 473 U.S. 373 (1985); Mitchell v. Helms, 530 U.S. 793, 808 (2000), overruling Meek v. Pittenger, 421 U.S. 349 (1975), and Wolman v. Walter, 423 U.S. 229 (1977); Zelman v. Simmons-Harris, 536 U.S. 639, 662 (2002). One of the authors, McConnell, was counsel in *Aguilar*, *Grand Rapids*, and *Mitchell* and filed amicus briefs in *Agostini*, *Witters*, *Zobrest*, and *Zelman.*

36. 540 U.S. 712 (2004).

37. 137 S.Ct. 2012 (2017).

38. 140 S.Ct. 2246 (2020).

CHAPTER 8

1. *See* Bruce J. Dierenfield, THE BATTLE OVER SCHOOL PRAYER: HOW *ENGEL V. VITALE* CHANGED AMERICA, Table 1 (Univ. Press Kansas 2007).

2. Engel v. Vitale, 370 U.S. 421 (1962); Abington School Dist. V. Schempp, 374 U.S. 203 (1963). Quotes from the decisions will not be separately footnoted.

3. *See* Carl F. Kaestle, PILLARS OF THE REPUBLIC: COMMON SCHOOLS AND AMERICAN SOCIETY, 1780–1860 (New York, Hill & Wang 1983).

4. Cantwell v. Connecticut, 310 U.S. 296, 303 (1940) (emphasis added); *see* McCollum v. Bd. of Educ., 333 U.S. 203 (1948); Zorach v. Clauson, 343 U.S. 306 (1952); McGowan v. Maryland, 366 U.S. 420, 451–52 (1961).

5. The first non-Christian chaplain, a Jew, was selected during the Civil War.

6. 140 S. Ct. 2246 (2020).

7. Abington Township v. Schempp, cite (Goldberg, J., concurring).

8. 1 Adams Family Correspondence 156 (Sara Martin, ed. 2008).

9. *Letter from John Adams to Abigail Adams*, 16 September 1774, *in* 1 THE ADAMS PAPERS: ADAMS FAMILY CORRESPONDENCE, December 1761–May 1776, 156–57 (Butterfield ed., Harvard Univ. Press 1963); Joel A. Nichols, *Georgia: The Thirteenth Colony*, *in* DISESTABLISHMENT AND RELIGIOUS DISSENT: CHURCH-STATE RELATIONS IN THE NEW AMERICAN STATES, 1776-1833, at 238 (Carl H. Esbeck & Jonathan J. Den Hartog, Univ. Missouri Press 2019).

10. James Madison, *Detached Memorandum*, *reprinted in* McConnell et al., RELIGION AND THE CONSTITUTION 61 (4th ed., New York, Wolters Kluwer 2016).

11. Town of Greece v. Galloway, 572 U.S. 565, cite (2014).

12. Bender v. Williamsport Area Sch. Dist., 741 U.S. 548, 555 (3d Cir. 1984).

13. *See* Walz v. Egg Harbor Twp. Bd. of Educ., 342 F.3d 271 (3d Cir. 2003) (student distributing pencils saying "Jesus loves the little children"); Westfield High Sch. L.I.F.E. Club v. City of Westfield, 249 F.Supp.2d 98 (Mass. D. Ct. 2003) (student club distributing candy canes); Settle v. Dickson Cnty. Sch. Bd., 53 F.3d 152 (6th Cir. 1995) (research paper about Jesus); Bishop v. Aranov, 962 F.2d 1066 (1991) (college professor); Roberts v. Madigan, 921 F.2d 1047 (10th Cir. 1990) (teacher reading Bible).

14. Kennedy v. Bremerton School Dist., 142 S. Ct. 2407 (2022).

CHAPTER 9

1. Stephanie H. Barclay, Brady Earley, & Annika Boone, *Original Meaning and the Establishment Clause: A Corpus Linguistic Analysis*, 61 ARIZ. L. REV. 505, 543 (2019).

2. James H. Hutson, RELIGION AND THE FOUNDING OF THE AMERICAN REPUBLIC 50–51 (Washington, D.C., Library of Congress 1998).

3. Michael W. McConnell, *No More (Old) Symbol Cases*, 2018–2019 CATO SUP. CT. REV. 91, 107.

4. Thomas Jefferson to Samuel Miller, 23 January 1808, National Archives, Library of Congress, Founders Online (unpublished "Early Access Document"); James Madison, Detached Memoranda (ca. 1820), reprinted in McConnell, et al., RELIGION AND THE CONSTITUTION (4th ed., New York, Wolters Kluwer 2016).

5. 559 U.S. 700 (2010).

6. 465 U.S. 668 (1984).

7. Allegheny, *supra*, at 593, quoting Wallace v. Jaffree, 472 U.S. 38, 70 (1985) (O'Connor, J., concurring in judgment).

8. 139 S. Ct. 2067, 2084–85 (2019).

9. For a recent example, *see* an earlier volume in this series, Erwin Chemerinsky & Howard Gilman, THE RELIGION CLAUSES: THE CASE FOR SEPARATING CHURCH AND STATE 77 (Oxford Univ. Press 2020) ("religious symbols do not belong on public property").

CHAPTER 10

1. Letter from Thomas Jefferson to the Reverend Samuel Miller (Jan. 23, 1808), *in* Daniel L. Dreisbach, THOMAS JEFFERSON AND THE WALL OF SEPARATION BETWEEN CHURCH AND STATE 63 (New York Univ. Press 2002).

2. *See* Kedroff v. St. Nicholas Cathedral, 344 U.S. 94, 116 (1952); *see also* EEOC v. Catholic Univ. of Am., 83 F.3d 455, 460 (D.C. Cir. 1996) (observing

that, under *Kedroff,* government may not "encroach[] on the ability of a church to manage its internal affairs").

3. Stanley Grenz, ISAAC BACKUS—PURITAN AND BAPTIST: HIS PLACE IN HISTORY, HIS THOUGHT AND THEIR IMPLICATIONS FOR MODERN BAPTIST THEOLOGY 172 (Mercer Univ. Press 1983).

4. *See, e.g.,* CONN. CONST. of 1818, art. VII, § 1 ("Each and every [religious] society or denomination" has the "power and authority to support and maintain the ministers or teachers of their respective denominations . . . ."); ME. CONST. of 1820, art. I, § 3 ("All religious societies . . . shall at all times have the exclusive right of electing their public teachers, and contracting with them for their support and maintenance."); MASS CONST. of 1780, amend. XI (1833) ("The several religious societies of this commonwealth . . . shall ever have the right to elect their pastors or religious teachers . . . ."); N.H. CONST. of 1784, pt. I, art. VI ("Religious societies, shall at all times have the exclusive right of electing their own public teachers . . . .").

5. S.C. CONST. of 1778, art. XXXVIII.

6. N.H. CONST. of 1784, pt. I, art. VI.

7. From James Madison to John Carroll, 20 November 1806, *Founders Online,* National Archives, https://founders.artchives.gov/documents/Madison/99-01-02-1094.

8. The public accommodation provisions of the Civil Rights Act of 1875, which applied to private conduct, were invalidated in the *Civil Rights Cases,* 109 U.S. 3, 11 (1883), as beyond the scope of the enforcement power granted to Congress by section 5 of the Fourteenth Amendment.

9. Cong. Globe, 41st Cong., 2d Sess. 3434 (May 13, 1870). Citations to the debates over this measure can be found at Cong. Globe, 42d Cong., 2d Sess., at 759 (Carpenter), 847–48 (Frelinghuysen), 898 (Morton), 899 (recording vote of 29–24 to drop application to churches), App. 5 (Morrill).

10. Not to be confused with his uncle and adoptive father, Theodore Frelinghuysen, Henry Clay's running mate, immortalized in the campaign slogan: "Hurrah, hurrah, the nation's risin'. Vote for Clay and Frelinghuysen!"

11. To be sure, some senators, including Senator Charles Sumner, who had drafted the bill, argued that application of the Act to churches did not violate the Constitution; *see id.* at 823–26, 896 (Sumner), 843 (Sherman). Their views, however, did not prevail, and even Sherman voted to drop the reference to churches in deference to the arguments of colleagues and to strengthen support for the remainder of the bill. *See id.* at 897.

12. 565 U.S. 171 (2012).

13. *See* Hosanna-Tabor, *supra*; Our Lady of Guadalupe School v. Morrissey-Berru, 140 S.Ct. 2049 (2020).

14. See Patrick J. Dignan, A HISTORY OF THE LEGAL INCORPORATION OF CATHOLIC CHURCH PROPERTY IN THE UNITED STATES (Catholic Univ. America 1784–1932) ch. 6 (1933). For a dramatic episode of conflict between bishop and lay trustees, *see* Michael W. McConnell, *Schism, Plague, and Last Rites in the French Quarter: The Strange Story Behind the Supreme Court's First Free Exercise Case, in* FIRST AMENDMENT STORIES (Richard Garnett & Andrew Koppelman eds., New York, Foundation Press 2011) (New Orleans).

15. All citations in the remaining portion of this chapter may be found in Michael W. McConnell & Luke W. Goodrich, *On Resolving Church Property Disputes*, 58 ARIZ. L. REV. 307 (2016), and will not be individually footnoted.

16. *Memorial and Remonstrance*, ch. 3.

17. 80 U.S. 679, 728–29 (1871).

18. Maryland and Virginia Eldership of Churches of God v. Church of God at Sharpsburg, Inc., 396 U.S. 367, 370 (1970) (Brennan, J., concurring).

19. Jones v. Wolf, 443 U.S. 595, 603 (1979).

CHAPTER 11

1. Jefferson to John Adams (May 5, 1817), ADAMS-JEFFERSON LETTERS, 2:512.

2. *See, e.g.*, William Galston, LIBERAL PLURALISM: IMPLICATIONS OF VALUE PLURALISM FOR POLITICAL THEORY AND PRACTICE (Cambridge Univ. Press 2002); John Inazu, CONFIDENT PLURALISM: SURVIVING AND THRIVING THROUGH DEEP DIFFERENCE (Univ. Chicago Press 2016).

3. See James Davison Hunter, Carl Desportes Bowman, & Kyle Puetz, DEMOCRACY IN DARK TIMES: THE 2020 IASC SURVEY OF AMERICAN POLITICAL CULTURE (Charlottesville, Virginia, Finstock & Tew 2020).

4. 1 Annals of Congress 934 (1794).

Index

. . .

For the benefit of digital users, indexed terms that span two pages (e.g., 52–53) may, on occasion, appear on only one of those pages.

Abington Township v. Schempp, 145
abortion, 94–95, 109–11
accommodations for religious exercise
    alleviation of burdens on private religious
        exercise and, 105–6
    antidiscrimination laws and, 100, 102–4,
        169, 175–78
    charter schools and, 114
    denominational neutrality standard and,
        105, 107–8
    drug laws and, 4, 100
    Establishment Clause arguments
        regarding, 94–95, 101–2, 103, 104–5,
        109–12, 114–16
    food inspection laws and, 100
    Free Exercise Clause and, 5–6, 100–1,
        103–4, 110–11, 116
    gambling laws and, 100
    impact on nonbeneficiaries standard and,
        105, 109
    legal concerns regarding endorsement of
        religion via, 106–7
    Lemon v. Kurtzman and, 89–90, 96–
        105, 113–16
    military chaplains and, 98–99, 114
    military conscription exemptions and, 95,
        97–98, 100, 107–8
    Native Americans and, 100–1, 109, 115–16

prisoners and, 100–1, 105, 108, 109, 111–12
religious clothing during military duty
    and, 100, 106–7
Religious Freedom Restoration Act
    and, 100–1
Religious Land Use and Institutionalized
    Persons Act and, 100–1, 105
sabbath observation and, 96–97, 107–8,
    110, 113
state laws and, 96
tax exemptions and, 100, 106, 107–8
third-party harm principle and, 109–13
Washington on, 96–97
zoning regulations and, 109
Act Against Papists (England, 1593), 14
Act of Supremacy (England, 1534), 12, 15–16
Acts of Uniformity (England, 1549, 1559, and
    1662), 10–11, 13, 15–16, 19
Adams, John, 17, 22
Adams, Sam, 152
Agostini v. Felton, 138–39
Alito, Samuel, 171
Allen case *(Board of Education v. Allen)*,
    132–35, 136–37
"Americanization" of immigrants, 117–18,
    127–28, 146–47
American Legion v. American Humanist Ass'n,
    168–69, 170–71

American Party (Know-Nothing Party), 123–24
American Revolution
 Church of England and, 15–16, 19, 22,
  30–31, 42, 52
 disestablishment of state churches
  during, 42–43
 Loyalist Tories in American colonies
  during, 19, 22, 52
 military chaplains and, 98–99
 military conscription during, 97
 Puritans and, 22, 31, 42–43, 67
 Stamp Act (1765) and, 30–31
Ames, Fisher, 39–40
Amos case *(Corporation of Presiding Bishop v.*
 Amos), 102–5, 111–12
Anglican Church. *See* Church of England
anti-Catholicism. *See also* Catholic Church
 Blaine Amendment and, 82–83,
  126, 141–42
 in colonial America, 23, 27, 55
 common schools and, 122–23
 decline after World War II of, 128, 142–43
 in early American republic, 52
 in England, 13–14, 25
 Know-Nothing Party and, 123–24
 Ku Klux Klan, 127–28
 nineteenth-century immigration and,
  81–83, 117–18, 179–80
 religious tests for state offices and,
  51, 52–53
 school bible reading and, 83–84
 violence and, 123–24
Anti-Federalists, 33–34
Assessment Bill (Virginia, 1785), 10, 32,
 46–47, 65–66, 72
atheism, 106–7, 145, 164

Backus, Isaac, 28–29, 46–47
Baptists
 Bill of Rights and, 35
 clergy licensing laws in colonial America
  and, 174
 colonial era restrictions against, 23–24
 Constitutional Convention (1787)
  and, 33–34
 decentralized leadership structure
  and, 183–84
 disestablishment of state church in
  Virginia and, 58–60
 establishment of state churches opposed
  by, 20–21, 23–24, 28–29, 45, 46–47,
  54–55, 68–69

First Great Awakening and, 23–24
 in Massachusetts, 20, 24, 46–47, 56–
  57, 68–69
 schools run by, 119–21, 124–25
 slavery and, 23–24
 state funding for clerical education and,
  71, 118–19
 Toleration Act (1688) and, 13, 23–24
Bear Lodge v. Babbitt, 115–16
Benson, Egbert, 97–98
Bible reading at schools
 Blaine Amendment and, 83–84, 125–26
 common schools and, 121–24, 126–
  27, 146–47
 Douay translation and, 83–84
 Establishment Clause and, 154
 government funding for public schools
  and, 125
 King James Bible and, 81–82, 83–84, 121,
  123–24, 146–47
Biden, Joe, 152–53
Bill for Establishing Religion Freedom
 (Virginia)
 adoption (1786) of, 3, 65–66
 disestablishment of Episcopal Church
  and, 46–47, 54–55, 130
 Establishment Clause and, 10
 Everson v. Board of Education and, 129–30
 rights of conscience and, 54, 130, 149
Bill of Rights. *See also specific amendments*
 Congressional debates (1789–91) regarding
  religious freedoms and, 36–41, 67
 Constitutional Convention (1787)
  and, 33–34
 Constitutional ratification debates (1787–
  89) and, 34–35
 incorporation against state laws of,
  76–80, 129
 Madison and, 35–36, 37–39, 40–41, 76
 slavery and, 77
Bingham, John, 78–79
Black, Hugo, 78–79, 132–33
Blackmun, Harry, 163, 165–66
Blackstone, William, 26–27
Blaine Amendment
 anti-Catholicism and, 126, 141–42
 Bible reading at schools and, 83–
  84, 125–26
 Congress's failure to pass (1875), 82–
  84, 127
 government funding for religious schools
  barred under, 82–84, 125–27

religious tests for state offices barred under, 125–26
state constitutional amendments modeled after, 127, 140–41
states' establishment of religions prohibited under, 82
states' interference with free exercise of religion barred under, 82
text of, 82
Board of Education v. Allen, 132–35, 136–37
Book of Common Prayer, 12–13, 52
Bremerton case *(Kennedy v. Bremerton School District)*, 92–93, 155–56
Brennan, William
on accommodations for religious exercise, 94–95
Corporation of Presiding Bishop v. Amos and, 104
on the Establishment Clause's origins, 10
formal title doctrine and, 183
Lynch v. Donnelly and, 163–64, 166
on Religion Clauses and Founding Fathers, 5–6
Texas Monthly, Inc. v. Bullock, 110
Breyer, Stephen, 166–67, 171
Burger, Warren, 109, 133–34, 163
Burke, Edmund, 28, 31

Caldor case *(Estate of Thornton v. Caldor, Inc.)* and, 113
Calvin, John, 11–12
Carpenter, Matthew, 176–77
Carroll, Daniel, 37
Carroll, John, 175
Carson v. Makin, 141–42
Catholic Church. *See also* anti-Catholicism
church incorporation laws and, 60–61, 179–80
Church of England's break (1533) with, 12
common schools and, 121
hierarchical leadership structure of, 60–61, 183–84
missionary schools in United States run by, 120–21
pope's leadership of, 12, 23, 52, 126, 183–84
school bible reading and, 83–84
schools run by, 81–82, 83–84, 122–25, 127–28, 129, 132, 133
transubstantiation doctrine and, 25, 52
Chaplain Corps (US military), 98–99
Cheyenne River Sioux, 115–16

Christmas displays in public spaces, 157–58, 163–66
church autonomy
church doctrine and, 57, 58–59, 73–74, 173–75, 179, 182–85
church incorporation laws and, 58–61, 179–80, 184–85
church property disputes and, 179–85
clergy selection and, 174–75, 178–79
deferential approach *versus* neutral principles approach to, 183–84–
employment law and, 175–79
Establishment Clause and, 182, 191
Jefferson on, 173
Church of England. *See also* Episcopal Church
Act of Supremacy (1534) and, 12, 15–16
American Revolution and, 15–16, 19, 22, 30–31, 42, 52
bishops and, 12, 15–16, 29
Book of Common Prayer and, 12–13, 52
break from Catholic Church (1533) by, 12
Canons (1603) of, 30
clergy licensing laws in colonial America and, 174
compulsory church attendance laws and, 20
Corporation Act (1661) and, 13–14, 25
as established state church in American colonies, 9, 11–12, 15–17, 19–20, 22, 24–25, 26, 55, 64–65, 174
as established state church in England, 9, 11–16, 141–42
King James Bible and, 12–13
marriages and, 17, 25
monarch's leadership of, 11–12, 13–14, 15–16, 19, 29–30, 42–43
obedience to political authority and, 30–31
ordination of ministers and, 19
Parliament of Great Britain and, 11–13, 29
slavery and, 17
Test Acts (1670s) and, 13–14, 25
Thirty-nine Articles of Faith and, 12–13
tithes and public state support for, 21–22, 73
vestry leadership in American colonies and, 15–16, 22
City of Boerne v. Flores, 103–4
Civilization Funds Act of 1820, 120–21
Civil Rights Act of 1866, 77
Civil Rights Act of 1875, 175–76

Civil Rights Act of 1964, 100–1, 102–4, 175–78
Civil War, 77
Clinton, DeWitt, 122
College of Philadelphia, 62–63
Committee on Public Education v. Nyquist, 134–39
common schools. *See also* public schools
    "Americanization" of immigrants and, 117–18, 146–47
    anti-Catholicism and, 122–23
    Bible reading at, 81–82, 83–84, 121–24, 126–27, 146–47
    compulsory attendance and, 117–18, 146–47
    compulsory public financial support for, 117–18, 123, 146–47
    in New York City, 122
    patriotism and, 117–18
    Protestant ideology of, 117–18, 122–24, 146–47
    religious education at, 121–23, 126–27
Congregationalists. *See also* Puritans
    disestablishment of state churches during American republic and, 61–62
    schools run by, 124–25
    Toleration Act (1688) and, 13
Congress of the United States
    accommodations for religious exercise provided through laws passed by, 100–1, 115–16
    Blaine Amendment and, 82–84, 127
    Establishment Clause and, 4–5
    first session (1789–91) of, 33, 34–41, 97–99
    legislative chaplains and, 99
    military chaplains and, 98–99
    Necessary and Proper Clause and, 34, 37–38
    prayers at beginning of proceedings at, 153
    religious symbols in public spaces and, 162
    student religious groups at public schools protected under law by, 154–55
Connecticut
    compulsory church attendance law in, 56
    disestablishment of state church in, 56–57, 174–75
    Puritanism as established church before 1818 in, 11–12, 38, 56, 67, 76
    sabbath laws and, 113
Constitution of the United States. *See also* *specific amendments*
    Article I of, 35–36, 76

Article VI of, 15–16, 26, 125–26
Article V of, 34–35
    Constitutional Convention and, 33–34
    ratification (1787–89) of, 34–35
Continental Congress, 22, 52, 66–67, 97–99, 152
contraception, 109
Conventicle Act (England, 1664), 14
Corporation Act (England, 1661), 13–14, 25–26
Corporation of Presiding Bishop v. Amos, 102–5, 111–12
crosses in public spaces, 155–56, 157–58, 162, 168–69, 170–71
Cutter v. Wilkinson
    alleviation of burdens on religious exercise standard and, 105–6
    denominational neutrality standard and, 105, 107–8
    impact on nonbeneficiaries standard and, 105, 109
    prisoners' religious rights and, 111–12

Dartmouth College, 63–64, 70–71
Davey, Joshua, 139–40
Delaware, 49–50, 51–52, 66–67
Devils Tower National Monument (Wyoming), 115–16
Dewey, John, 131–32
disestablishment of state churches
    bans on clergy holding political office and, 64
    Baptists' role in promoting, 20–21, 23–24, 28–29, 45, 46–47, 54–55, 68–69
    church autonomy and, 57, 58–59, 73–74, 173–75
    church incorporation laws and, 58–61, 179
    church properties and, 61–62
    colleges and, 62–64, 118–19
    compulsory church attendance requirements repealed via, 54–55, 57, 73–74, 145
    denominational equality provisions and, 57, 107–8, 154–55
    elimination of religious tests for political participation and, 57, 73–74
    Establishment Clause and, 80
    Jefferson and, 31–32, 45–47, 48–49
    Madison and, 33, 44–49, 64–66, 80
    religious institutions' civic functions and, 57, 80–81

religious taxation issues and, 52–57, 64–73
rights of conscience arguments regarding,
46–48, 54–55, 57, 72, 145
secularization and, 44
state constitutions and, 49–53, 56–
57, 174–75
District of Columbia, 60, 120–21, 153, 179
drug laws, 4, 100
Dunn v. Ray, 108
Dutch Reformed Church, 21–22, 52, 119

Edward VI (king of England), 12
Eisenhower, Dwight, 128
Elizabeth I (queen of England), 13
Employment Division v. Smith, 100–1,
104–5, 150
endorsement test
baseline establishment question
and, 169–70
construction-removal distinction
and, 168–69
endorsement-preference distinction
and, 167–68
Kennedy v. Bremerton School District
and, 92–93
Lynch v. Donnelly and, 164–66
reasonable observer test and, 164–65, 169
Engel v. Vitale
coercion standard and, 145, 147–51
concurring opinion in, 150–51
Establishment Clause and, 148–51
Free Exercise Clause and, 148, 149–51
noncoercive official prayers and, 151
The Enlightenment, 47–48
Episcopal Church. *See also* Church of
England
creation after American Revolution of,
42–43, 58
disestablishment of state churches
during early American republic and,
54–55, 61–62
as established church in states of early
American republic, 52–53
property ownership issues and, 61–62
schools run by, 119
vestry leaders of, 58–59
Equal Access Act, 154–55
Equal Employment Opportunity
Commission (EEOC), 106–7, 178–79
Erastianism, 29
Espinoza v. Montana Department of Revenue,
141–42, 149–50

Establishment Clause
accommodations for religious exercise
and, 94–95, 101–2, 103, 104–5, 109–
12, 114–16
Bible reading at schools and, 154
Bill for Establishing Religion Freedom
(Virginia) and, 10
church autonomy and, 182, 191
Congressional debates (1789–91)
regarding creation of, 5–6, 36–41
conscientious objectors to military service
and, 41
endorsement test and, 92–93, 164–
66, 167–70
Fourteenth Amendment and, 4–5,
124–25, 187
Free Exercise Clause and, 3–5, 111, 139–
40, 147–48, 150–51
incorporation against state laws of, 75,
77–78, 79–81, 82–83, 87–88, 124–26,
175–76, 187
individual states' established religions
and, 40, 42, 45–46, 75–76, 79–80
legal standing questions and, 81, 115–16
legislative chaplains and, 99
military chaplains and, 98–99, 148–49
military conscription and, 4, 97–98
neutrality principle and, 108, 139–41,
148–49, 170, 184–85, 186–88, 190–91
no-aid separationism and, 130–31,
139, 142–43
polarized nature of contemporary
American political culture and, 188–89
prayer at public events and, 151–52, 153
prayer in public schools and, 88, 144–45,
147–49, 154, 155
religion-only subsidies and, 106
religious coercion prohibited by, 5–6, 10,
14–15, 42, 73–74, 80, 137, 148–49, 153,
187, 191
religious institutions' civic functions
and, 80–81
religious schools and, 4, 127–28, 130–31,
134–35, 137–38, 139–40, 169
religious symbols and, 158, 159, 161–64,
166, 169, 187–88
secularism and, 3–4, 5–6
separation of church and state standard
and, 10, 87–88, 90, 98–99
student religious groups at public schools
and, 154–55
text of, 1, 3

establishment of state churches
  Church of England in American colonies
    and, 9, 11–12, 15–17, 19–20, 22, 24–25,
    26, 55, 64–65, 174
  colleges and, 62–63
  compulsory church attendance and, 20–21,
    42, 187
  government control over church doctrine
    and, 19–20, 29, 42, 187
  land grants and, 21–22
  multiple establishment concept
    and, 43–44
  political participation linked to state
    church membership and, 25–27, 42, 187
  prohibition of worship by other
    denominations and, 23–24, 42, 187
  public financial support for churches and,
    21–22, 42, 187
  public virtue arguments regarding, 31–32,
    43–44, 46–47
  Puritan Church in New England colonies
    and, 2, 11–12, 15–16, 17–18, 22, 26,
    28–29, 38, 46–47, 56, 67, 76–77
  state churches' civil functions and, 24–25,
    42, 187
  in states of early American
    Republic, 43–44
  theological *versus* political rationale
    for, 27–29
Estate of Thornton v. Caldor, Inc., 113
Everson v. Board of Education
  Bill for Establishing Religion Freedom
    (Virginia, 1785) and, 129–30
  dissenting opinions in, 87–88, 131–
    32, 133–34
  Establishment Clause and, 130–31
  incorporation of Establishment Clause to
    state laws and, 87–88
  public funding for religious institutions
    restricted under, 87–88, 130–31, 134–
    35, 140–41
  religious discrimination prohibited
    under, 87–88
  specific New Jersey busing program
    upheld in, 130–31
  "wall of separation" between church and
    state and, 2, 87–88, 129
Ewing Township (New Jersey), 129

Federalist No. 10, 40–41
Federalists, 34–35
Fifteenth Amendment, 57

First Amendment. *See also* Establishment
    Clause; Free Exercise Clause
  First Congress's debates regarding, 33
  Free Assembly Clause and, 190
  Free Press Clause and, 190–91
  Free Speech Clause and, 90, 154–
    55, 190–91
  incorporation against state laws of, 77–78
First Great Awakening, 19–20
Fletcher v. Peck, 62
Fourteenth Amendment
  Due Process Clause of, 77–79
  Equal Protection Clause and, 77
  Establishment Clause and, 4–5, 124–
    25, 187
  extension of constitutional protections
    to all US citizens under, 57, 77–80,
    81, 82–83
  incorporation of Religious Clauses against
    state laws and, 4–5, 175–76, 187
  Privileges or Immunities Clause of, 78–79, 81
France, 23, 61, 73
Franklin, Benjamin, 159
Freedmen's Bureau, 82–83, 124–25
Free Exercise Clause
  accommodations for religious exercise
    and, 5–6, 100–1, 103–4, 110–11, 116
  antidiscrimination law and, 106–7, 177–78
  atheism and, 106–7
  church autonomy regarding doctrine
    and, 182
  clergy's right to serve in public office
    and, 26–27
  Congressional debates (1789–91)
    regarding creation of, 37–41
  conscientious objectors to military service
    and, 41
  Establishment Clause and, 3–5, 111,
    139–40, 147–48, 150–51
  incorporation against state laws of, 77–78,
    80, 82–83, 125–26, 175–76
  Lemon v. Kurtzman and, 90, 102
  military conscription exemptions
    and, 97–98
  prayer in public schools and, 147–48,
    149–50, 155–56
  religious accommodations at public
    schools and, 5–6
  religious clothing and, 155–56
  religious coercion and, 148, 149–50
  religious schools and, 139–40, 149–50
  religious symbols and, 5–6

state laws and, 76
tax exemptions and, 106–7
text of, 3
Free School Society, 119, 121–22
Frelinghuysen, Frederick, 176

George III (king of England), 31
Georgia
  anti-Catholic restrictions in, 23
  Church of England as established church
    during colonial era in, 11–12, 17, 55
  Jews and Protestant dissenters during
    colonial era in, 55
  prayer at legislative sessions in, 152
  religious tax debates in, 66
Gerry, Elbridge, 36–37, 39
GI Bill, 136–37
Ginsburg, Ruth Bader, 105, 140–41
Girard, Stephen, 120
Goldberg, Arthur, 150–51
Gorsuch, Neil, 78–79, 171
Grant, Ulysses S., 125–26
Great Awakenings, 19–20, 49, 63–64, 174

Harlan, John Marshall, 150–51
Harvard College, 19–20, 70–71, 118–19
Henry, Patrick, 10, 35, 65–66, 129
Henry VIII (king of England), 12
Herberg, Will, 128
Hobbes, Thomas, 47–48
*Hosanna-Tabor Evangelical Lutheran Church
  & School v. EEOC*, 178–79
House of Lords (Great Britain), 26–27
Howard, Jacob, 78–79
Hume, David, 73
Huntington, Samuel, 38, 67

Jackson, Robert, 117–18, 191
James I (king of England), 31
James II (king of England), 13–14
Jay, John, 23, 52, 152
Jefferson, Thomas
  on churches' independence from
    government, 173
  disestablishment of state churches
    supported by, 31–32, 45–47, 48–49
  on established religion and
    hypocrisy, 13–14
  missionary schools in United States
    and, 120–21
  religious services at government buildings
    approved by, 153, 160–61

religious taxes opposed by, 68–69
Second Great Awakening and, 49
on "sectarian dogmas" and political
  divisions, 186–87
secularism and, 45
slavery and the estate of, 17
Thanksgiving Day prayer proclamations
  and, 152–53, 161
Unitarianism and, 49
University of Virginia and, 71, 153
US government seal and, 159
Virginia's Bill for Establishing Religion
  Freedom and, 3, 10, 46–47, 54–55,
  65–66, 129, 149
"wall of separation" between church and
  state and, 2, 87–88
William & Mary College and, 62–63
Jeffries, John, 122–23
Jews
  in colonial America, 27, 55
  Constitutional Convention (1787) and, 33–34
  in England, 13
  Hasidic community in New York State
    and, 107–8
  menorahs in public displays and, 157–
    58, 165–66
  nineteenth century immigration
    and, 117–18
  schools and, 119, 121, 123–24, 127–28, 145
Jones v. Wolf, 185

Kaestle, Carl F., 146–47
Kagan, Elena, 92–93, 108, 171
Kavanaugh, Brett, 171
Kennedy, John F., 128
Kennedy v. Bremerton School District, 92–
  93, 155–56
King, Jr., Martin Luther, vii
King James Bible, 12–13, 81–82, 83–84, 121,
  123–24, 146–47
Kiryas Joel v. Grumet, 107–8
Know-Nothing Party (American
  Party), 123–24
Ku Klux Klan, 127–28

Laycock, Douglas, 96–97
Lee, Richard Henry, 65–66
Lemon v. Kurtzman ("Lemon Test")
  accommodations for religious exercise
    and, 89–90, 96–105, 113–16
  democratic majorities' religious beliefs
    and, 88–89

Lemon v. Kurtzman ("Lemon Test") (*cont.*)
excessive entanglement standard and,
88, 90–91, 101–2, 104, 114–16, 133–34,
163–64, 187–88
Free Exercise Clause and, 90, 102
government funding for religious schools
and, 88, 91, 133–37, 138–39
prayer in public schools and, 92–93
primary effect standard and, 88, 89–91,
101, 115–16, 133–34, 138–39, 163–
64, 187–88
religious symbols in public spaces and,
92–93, 163–64, 167, 170–71
secular purpose requirement and, 88–89,
90, 101, 102–3, 115–16, 163–64, 187–88
separation between church and state
requirement and, 2, 88–89, 90
Supreme Court's departures from
precedents of, 91–93, 103–5, 187–88
Levy, Leonard, 2
Little Sisters of the Poor, 95
Livermore, Samuel, 39, 67
Locke v. Davey, 139–40
Lutherans, 13, 119, 183–84
Lynch v. Donnelly, 163–66, 169
*Lyng v. Northwest Indian Cemetery Protective
Association*, 115–16

Machiavelli, Niccolò, 28
Madison, James
Bill of Rights and, 35–36, 37–39, 40–41, 76
checks and balances in republican
government supported by, 31–32, 45
on church autonomy regarding doctrine
and clergy selection, 175, 182
church incorporation law for District of
Columbia vetoed by, 60, 179
on conscientious objectors and
compulsory military service, 41, 97–98
Constitution's ratification and, 34
disestablishment of state churches
supported by, 33, 44–49, 64–66, 80
on factions in government, 40–41, 190
on government as "incompetent judge of
religious truth," 90–91
military conscription and, 97
missionary schools in United States
and, 120–21
on people's censorial power over
government, 191–92
religious beliefs of, 49
religious taxes opposed by, 72–73

on rights of conscience, 47–48, 68–69, 95,
130, 149
Thanksgiving Day prayer proclamations
and, 152–53, 161
Virginia Bill Establishing Religious
Freedom and, 65–66, 129
on Virginia's imprisonment of Baptists
during 1770s, 23–24
Maine, 56–57, 174–75
Mann, Horace, 121, 146–47
Marshall, Thurgood, 137–38
Maryland
Catholics in, 37, 55
church incorporation laws in, 179–80
Church of England as established church
in, 11–12, 20
Declaration of Rights and, 66
disestablishment of Episcopal state
church in, 55
religious tax debates in, 66
state support for clerical education during
early republic era in, 71
Mason, George, 33–34
Massachusetts
Baptists in, 20, 24, 46–47, 56–57, 68–69
compulsory church attendance law before
1833 in, 20, 37–38, 56
disestablishment of state church
in, 174–75
Puritanism as established church before
1833 in, 2, 11–12, 22, 26, 46–47,
56, 76–77
religious requirements for officeholding
prior to 1821 in, 26
religious taxes prior to 1833 in, 56–
57, 68–70
McGuffy Reader, 133, 146–47
Mead, Sidney, 44
menorahs in public spaces, 157–58, 165–66
Methodists, 119, 124–25, 183–84
military conscription exemptions
American Revolution and, 97
clergy and, 100
Congressional debates regarding, 97–98
Establishment Clause and, 4, 97–98
Free Exercise Clause and, 97–98
legal concerns about endorsement of
religion via, 106–7
Lemon test and, 89–90
Madison and, 41
nonreligious military exemptions and,
101, 106–7

Pennsylvania's Charter of Privileges (1701)
and, 51
Quakers and, 34, 95
Second Amendment and, 97–98
Vietnam War and, 106–7, 111–12
Missouri, 140–41
Mitchell v. Helms, 138–39
Monroe, James, 35, 120–21
Montana, 127, 141
Moore, Roy, 168–69
Morris, Gouverneur, 52
Morton, Oliver, 177
Moynihan, Daniel Patrick, 136–37

National Day of Prayer, 161
National Environmental Protection
Act, 100–1
National Historic Preservation Act, 100–1
National Teachers Association, 123–24
Native American Graves Protection and
Repatriation Act, 100–1
Native Americans, 100–1, 109, 115–16, 120–21
nativity scenes in public spaces, 157–
58, 163–66
Necessary and Proper Clause, 34, 37–38
New England. *See also specific states*
Anglicans in, 18
anti-Baptist restrictions during colonial
era in, 24
anti-Catholic restrictions in, 23
established state churches' civil
functions in, 24
land grants to established state churches
in, 21–22
public financial support for established
state churches in, 22
Puritanism as established church in
colonies of, 2, 11–12, 15–16, 17–18, 22,
26, 28–29, 38, 46–47, 56, 67, 76–77
religious taxes in, 67
New Hampshire, 11–12, 56–57, 63–64,
67, 174–75
New Jersey, 49–51, 66–67, 129–31
New Mexico, 127
New York City, 19, 21–22, 122
New York State
anti-Catholic restrictions in, 23, 52
church incorporation law in, 59
disestablishment of state religion in,
49–50, 52
government funding for religious schools
in, 119, 134–35

legislature's general encouragement of
religion (1784) in, 66–67
school district created for Hasidic
community by, 107–8
textbook lending system in, 132–33
Nineteenth Amendment, 57
Ninth Circuit Court of Appeals, 162
North Carolina, 17, 23, 43, 49–51, 179–80
North Dakota, 127
Northwest Ordinance, 66–67, 120–21
Nyquist case *(Committee on Public Education
v. Nyquist)*, 134–39

O'Connor, Sandra Day, 102, 164–66,
167–68
Oregon, 127–28

Parliament of Great Britain
American colonies and, 19
Church of England and, 11–13, 29
House of Lords and, 26–27
Test Acts and religious restrictions
regarding, 25
Parsons, Theophilus, 69–70
Pawtucket (Rhode Island), 163, 164–66
Pell Grants, 136–37
Penal Acts (Great Britain), 14
Pennsylvania, 23, 49–50, 51
Philadelphia anti-Catholic riots
(1844), 123–24
Philips, Jonas, 33–34
Pierce v. Society of Sisters, 127–28
Pittsburgh (Pennsylvania), 165–66
prayer at public events, 4, 151–53
prayer in public schools
coercion and, 145, 147–51, 153, 155–56
Establishment Clause and, 88, 144–45,
147–49, 154, 155
Free Exercise Clause and, 147–48, 149–
50, 155–56
government funding for public schools
and, 125
Lemon v. Kurtzman and, 92–93
origins of, 146
private prayer and, 154–56
public opinion regarding, 144
right to leave the room during, 145
school events and, 92–93, 153, 155–56
School Prayer Cases (1960s) and, 93, 117–18,
149, 155–56
students with minority religious beliefs
and, 145

Presbyterians
  decentralized leadership structure
    and, 183–84
  schools run by, 119, 124–25
  Scotland and, 14
  state funding for clerical education and,
    71, 118–19
  Toleration Act (1688) and, 13
  in Virginia, 32, 58–60, 65–66
Princeton College, 70–71
Privileges or Immunities Clause (Fourteenth
    Amendment), 78–79, 81
public schools. *See also* common schools;
    prayer in public schools
  compulsory attendance and, 145
  Establishment Clause and, 118
  government funding for, 128
  origins of, 146
  release time for religious instruction
    and, 114–15
  religious music performance at, 158
Puritans. *See also* Congregationalists
  American Revolution and, 22, 31,
    42–43, 67
  compulsory church attendance laws
    and, 20–21
  in England, 13–14
  as established church in New England
    colonies, 2, 11–12, 15–16, 17–18, 22, 26,
    28–29, 38, 46–47, 56, 67, 76–77
  local church control as tenet among,
    17–18, 19, 42–43
  ministerial selection among, 19
  Reformed Protestantism and, 11–12
  religious austerity of, 157–58
  republicanism and, 30

Quakers
  American colonial restrictions against,
    17, 23, 27
  decentralized leadership structure
    and, 183–84
  in England, 13, 14
  military conscription and, 34, 95
  in Pennsylvania, 23
  schools run by, 119

Rakove, Jack, 49
Ray, Domineque, 108
reasonable observer test, 164–65, 169
Reconstruction, 124–25

Reformed Protestants
  Dutch Reformed Church and, 21–22,
    52, 119
  Puritans and, 11–12
  republicanism and, 31
  rights of conscience and, 47–48
Rehnquist, William, 39–40, 136–37
Religion Clauses (First Amendment), 3–6,
    82–83, 175–77. *See also* Establishment
    Clause; Free Exercise Clause
religious clothing, 100, 106–7, 155–56
Religious Freedom Restoration Act
    (RFRA), 100–1
Religious Land Use and Institutionalized
    Persons Act (RLUIPA), 100–1, 105
religious schools
  Blaine Amendment and, 82–84, 125–27
  Catholic schools and, 81–82, 83–84, 122–
    25, 127–28, 129, 132, 133
  colleges run by religious denominations
    and, 126, 131, 136–38
  Establishment Clause and, 4, 127–28,
    130–31, 134–35, 137–38, 139–40, 169
  Freedman's Bureau and, 124–25
  Free Exercise Clause and, 139–40, 149–50
  government-funded college scholarships
    and, 137–38, 139–40
  government funding for specific purposes
    at, 128–37, 138–39, 141–42
  government funding for unrestricted
    purposes at, 4, 81–84, 91, 119–28,
    141–43, 169
  legal status of, 5–6, 127–28
  Lemon v. Kurtzman and, 88, 91, 133–
    37, 138–39
  missionary schools in United States
    and, 120–21
  neutrality principle and, 137–43
  public school teachers' leading of remedial
    classes at, 135, 138–39
  state constitutions and, 127, 139–40, 141
  tax credits for tuition at, 134–37, 141,
    142–43, 149–50
  teacher salaries at, 133–34, 135
  textbooks at, 89, 132–34, 136–37
  voucher programs for tuition at, 138–39
religious symbols in public spaces
  Confederate symbols in public spaces
    compared to, 161–62
  crosses and, 155–56, 157–58, 162, 168–
    69, 170–71

endorsement test and, 92–93, 164–
66, 167–70
Establishment Clause and, 158, 159,
161–64, 166, 169, 187–88
Free Exercise Clause and, 5–6
government seals and, 159–60
justiciability of, 159, 161–62, 163
Lemon v. Kurtzman and, 92–93, 163–64,
167, 170–71
menorahs and, 157–58, 165–66
nativity scenes and, 157–58, 163–66
"passage of time" standard, 171–72
reasonable observer test and, 164–65
Ten Commandments displays and, 158,
166, 168–69
religious taxes. *See also* tithes
church autonomy arguments
against, 72–73
clerical education funding and, 71
in colonial era, 21–22, 24–25, 38
disestablishment of state churches and,
52–57, 64–73
in Massachusetts, 56–57, 68–70
public virtue arguments in favor of, 69–70
rights of conscience arguments
regarding, 69–70
social services supported by, 70
in Virginia, 64–66
Revolutionary War. *See* American Revolution
Rhode Island, 38, 43, 49–50
Roberts, John, 92–93, 171
Roe v. Wade, 92–93
Roosevelt, Franklin, 152–53
Rush, Benjamin, 118–19
Ryan, James, 122–23

Salazar v. Buono, 162
same-sex marriage, 94–95, 109, 180–81
Scalia, Antonin, 92–93
Schempp case *(Abington Township v.
Schempp)*, 145
school prayer. *See* prayer in public schools
School Prayer Cases (1960s), 93, 117–18,
149, 155–56
Seabury, Samuel, 30–31
Second Amendment, 41, 77–78, 97–98
Second Great Awakening, 49, 63–64, 174
separation of church and state
Everson v. Board of Education, 2, 87–
88, 129
Grant on, 125

Jefferson on, 2, 87–88
Lemon v. Kurtzman and, 2, 88–89, 90
no-aid separationism and, 130–31,
139, 142–43
public funding for religious schools
and, 123–25
Silvester, Peter, 36
Sixth Amendment, 77–78
slavery, 17, 23–24, 77
Society for the Propagation of the Gospel in
Foreign Parts, 19
Sotomayor, Sonia, 140–41
South Carolina
anti-Catholic restrictions in, 23
church incorporation law in, 59
Church of England as established church
in, 17, 20
disestablishment of Episcopal Church in,
52–53, 174–75
religious tax prohibition in, 66
religious test for public office in, 26
Spain, 23
Stamp Act (1765), 30–31
Stewart, Potter, 79–80
Storslee, Mark, 70, 118–19
Story, Joseph, 61–62

tax exemptions
Free Exercise Clause and, 106–7
legal concerns about endorsement of
religion via, 106–7
Lemon v. Kurtzman and, 88
Texas Monthly, Inc. v. Bullock and,
106, 110
Ten Commandments displays, 158,
166, 168–69
Test Acts (England, 1670s), 13–14, 25
Texas Monthly, Inc. v. Bullock, 106, 110
Thanksgiving Day prayer proclamations,
152–53, 160–61
Thirty-nine Articles of Faith (England),
12–13, 148–49
Thomas, Clarence, 75, 78–79, 171
tithes. *See also* religious taxes
in American colonies, 21–22
in England, 21–22, 73
opponents of state enforcement of, 45,
68–69, 70
state constitutions and, 50–51
in states of the early American republic,
22, 56, 68–69

Title VII (Civil Rights Act of 1964), 100–1, 102–3, 104, 175–78
Tocqueville, Alexis de, 30, 43–44
Toleration Act (England, 1688), 13, 23–24
transgender rights, 94–95
Trinity Church (New York City), 21–22, 52
Trinity Lutheran v. Comer, 140–41
Trumbull, Lyman, 77
Trustees of Dartmouth College v. Woodward, 62–64

Uniformity Acts (England, 1549, 1559, and 1662), 10–11, 13, 15–16, 19
Unitarians, 13, 56–57, 61–62
University of Pennsylvania, 62–63, 118–19
University of Virginia, 71, 138, 153
US government seal, 159–60

Vermont, 11–12, 50, 56, 61–62, 72
vested rights doctrine, 62
Vietnam War, 106–7, 111–12
Virginia
    anti-Baptist restrictions during colonial era in, 23–24
    Assessment Bill (1785) in, 10, 32, 46–47, 65–66, 72
    Bill for Establishing Religion Freedom (1786) in, 3, 10, 46–47, 54–55, 65–66, 129, 149
    Church of England as established church during colonial era in, 16–17, 19–20, 24–25, 64–65
    compulsory church attendance law in, 21, 54, 64–65
    Declaration of Rights in, 33–34, 54–55
    Diocesan Canons of 1661 in, 16–17
    disestablishment of Episcopal state church in, 33, 45–47, 54, 58–60, 61–62, 118–19
    Episcopal Church during early republic era in, 58–59, 64–65
    ordination of ministers in, 19
    public financial support for established state church in, 22
    religious taxes in, 64–66
    subsidies for denominational schools in, 118–19
    University of Virginia and, 71, 138, 153

Warburton, William, 29
Warren, Earl, 109
Washington, George, 43–44, 97, 120–21, 151–52, 160–61, 186–87
Washington College, 71
Washington Ethical Society, 106–7
Washington Monument, 160
Washington State, 127, 139–40
Watson v. Jones, 182–83
Webster, Daniel, 63–64, 120
West Virginia Board of Education v. Barnette, 191
William & Mary College, 62–63, 70–71
Williams, Elisha, 19–20
Wilson, Henry, 77
Witters v. Department of Services for the Blind, 137–40
Wood, Gordon, 43–44

Yale College, 19–20, 70–71

Zelman v. Simmons-Harris, 138–40
Zorach v. Clauson, vii, 114–15